To MARC

D1548615

Peacebuilding: A Personal Journey

10/21/21

PEACEBUILDING

A Personal Journey

DAVID L. PHILLIPS

Westphalia Press

An Imprint of the Policy Studies Organization

Washington, DC

2020

Peacebuilding: A Personal Journey

All Rights Reserved © 2020 by Policy Studies Organization

Westphalia Press
An imprint of Policy Studies Organization
1527 New Hampshire Ave., NW
Washington, D.C. 20036
info@ipsonet.org

ISBN: 978-1-941755-51-8

Cover and interior design by Jeffrey Barnes
jbarnesbook.design

Daniel Gutierrez-Sandoval, Executive Director
PSO and Westphalia Press

Updated material and comments on this edition
can be found at the Westphalia Press website:
www.westphaliapress.org

To my daughters, Tara and Maya, young humanitarians and human rights activists.

ACKNOWLEDGEMENTS

I am grateful to many people with whom I partnered over the years.

Bonnie Miller made an invaluable contribution editing this book. Tom Miller provided policy analysis. Prusha Hasan was my research assistant.

Other persons contributed to this work: Bob Thurman, Betty Sue Flowers, Wegger Strommen, Chai Ling, Sven Alkalaj, Lulzim Peci, Zoran Illievski, Dogu Ergil, Najmaldin Karim, Van Krikorian, Huseyin Tunc, Suraiya IT, Visaka Dharmadasa, Rudrakumaran, Zo Tum Hmung, Ana Gomes, Sharon Gelman, and Hassan Eltigani. They are friends and colleagues.

TABLE OF CONTENTS

THE DALAI LAMA

FOREWORD

A number of public figures and scholars, moved by the plight of the Tibetan people, have contributes to our efforts to find a solution to the Tibetan issue, and David Phillips is one among them. Growing up in a refugee family himself clearly predisposed him to have empathy for communities like the Tibetans.

He came to India in the early 1980s and worked on community development in our Tibetan settlements. His interests grew from humanitarian activities among groups of refugees to a concern for human rights and extended to the promotion of democracy, conflict resolution, and the advancement of peace. In addition to the help he has provided Tibetan refugees, he has gone on to work in the Middle East, the Balkans, and Southeast Asia. He tells the story of his journey in this book.

I admire the way he has tried to promote peace in regions disturbed by conflict. We have also benefited from his counsel in our efforts to reach out to the Chinese people and government. I hope that before long we can reach a mutually acceptable, peaceful resolution to the Tibetan issue.

Considering the wide range of David Phillips's experiences, I am confident readers will find his memoir of interest for the light it sheds on his efforts to improve international relations.

14 July 2020

PREFACE

I learned the value of helping others by working in war zones and through close contact with victims who face suffering and death on a daily basis. I had not been an armchair activist, until now.

Like everyone in 2020, the prevalence of the coronavirus (COVID-19) has dramatically changed my life and work patterns. I am "social distancing" to preserve my health and the well-being of my spouse and teenage daughters. Columbia University, where I serve as Director of the Program on Peace-building and Human Rights, is locked down. Students have been told to vacate the campus, and all research officers are furloughed until public officials allow the university to open up.

In normal times, my activities concerning peace and conflict are highly interactive, including participating in media and frequent public speaking. I've always believed that effective human rights work rests on human relations. Coalition-building requires interaction with allies and adversaries. I rely on a network of partners around the world with whom I have cooperated over many years. With travel suspended and in-person meetings banned, I have time on my hands. This book is enabled by COVID-19. It is an accounting of my life-long effort to help heal the world.

.   .   .   .   .

My great-great-great-grandfather, Moses Phillips, immigrated to the United States fleeing pogroms in 1898. His wife sewed shirts, which he sold off the back of a pushcart on Mott Street in Lower Manhattan. As sales increased, the Phillips family became an American success story. The family business, Phillips-Van Heusen (PVH), grew to become the largest shirt manufacturer in America with annual sales exceeding one billion dollars.

His son, Isaac Phillips, founded Beth-Israel Hospital (BIH). He laid the cornerstone in a ceremony that launched a generational commitment by the Phillips family to BIH. My grandfather, Seymour, founded the Phillips School of Nursing.

My father, Larry Phillips, followed in the footsteps of his father by supporting BIH and running PVH. The business provided wealth but kept him from doing what he really wanted: to study at Princeton University's Woodrow Wilson School and join the Peace Corps. My father was a romantic who made helping others a priority. He sponsored the Phillips Ambulatory Care Center, a branch of BIH at Union Square. He also founded the American Jewish World Service, a development agency raising funds from Jewish-Americans to benefit disadvantaged non-Jewish communities around the world. Humanitarian work was a family tradition. My mother, Ann, was an activist in her own right.

From my early childhood, I was discouraged from working in the *shmata* trade (Yiddish for "rag" or "piece of cloth"). Though my father was a wealthy man, he lacked a sense of self-worth. Other people working at PVH knew that regardless of merit, he was destined to leapfrog them and become the Chief Executive Officer. He questioned himself and felt he was in the job because it was his birthright. He did not want his son to feel the same way, so he raised me to pursue a different career path.

Part of me appreciated my father's instinct to bar me from the family business. Another part resented being kept out of an enterprise that had been run by my family for four generations. It took a while, but I have come to appreciate the opportunity to blaze my own trail in life. Coming from a good family was empowering. I was emboldened to endeavor great things because I felt financially secure coming from a family that was wealthy and accomplished.

Being self-reliant was ingrained in me at an early age. I had my first swimming lesson during a family vacation in France's Cape d'Antibes. The instructor picked me up and threw me into the pool. "Sink or swim!" he exclaimed. Through lessons like these, I learned to take care of myself. It was not until the last years of my father's life that I learned he had squandered his fortune.

My first charitable act was in 1965. My parents hosted a fundraising event for the Student Non-Violent Coordinating Committee (SNCC), which was attended by the activist Stokely Carmichael. Wearing my pajamas, I joined the adults in the living room. I brought my piggy bank and gave it to Stokely as a contribution to the civil rights movement. SNCC was later radicalized by the Black Panthers. All this happened decades before the Black Lives Matter Movement.

From an early age, I was also active in protesting the Vietnam War. Whenever there was a moratorium to demonstrate against the war, my family would pack a picnic basket and take the Eastern Airlines shuttle from New York to Washington. I enjoyed marching for peace and hoped some right-wing hardhats would throw eggs at us. On one visit, I watched a group of hippies throw bubble bath into Washington's reflecting pool at the foot of Capitol Hill, take off their clothes, and frolic in the fountain. I asked my father, "Pop, when will I be old enough to do that?"

. . . . .

I cultivated spiritual values as an antidote to my family's material world. In a class called the "Poetry of Enlightenment" during my second semester at Amherst College, I dozed off to be awakened by the booming voice of Professor Robert A.F. Thurman, my teacher who was a well-known expert on Tibetan Buddhism and a close colleague of His Holiness the Dalai Lama. "It's working," he proclaimed. Drifting off in Thurman's class was beyond daydreaming. It was one of my first out-of-body experiences.

Like many young people in the 1970s, I was struggling with my spiritual identity. Thurman introduced me to the concept of *samsara*—illusion. Initially, I thought I was the first person to wrestle with the difference between reality and illusion. Reading ancient Taoist poets like Lao Tzu and Chuang Tzu, I was surprised to learn that others had grappled with these thoughts before me. A verse by Chuang Tzu encapsulated my search for understanding:

> Once upon a time, I dreamt I was a butterfly, fluttering hither and thither, to all intents and purposes a butterfly. I was conscious only of my happiness as a butterfly, unaware that I was myself. Soon I awaked, and there I was, veritably myself again. Now I do not know whether I was then a man dreaming I was a butterfly, or whether I am now a butterfly, dreaming I am a man.

Thurman also introduced me to the teachings of the Dalai Lama, which inspired my interest in Tibetan culture. In 1986, after my graduation from college, he facilitated my contact with the Dalai Lama's Private Office, which I contacted about arranging a fact-finding trip to India. I met the

Dalai Lama in India, where I was working as a volunteer to help Tibetan refugees. Meeting him nurtured my humanitarian heart.

During one audience with the Dalai Lama, I asked for a mantra that I could use in meditation. He laughed and embraced me, extending his arms from burgundy and saffron robes. He had a newly shaved head, and the stubbles were growing back short and soft. I remember the velvet feel of his head on my neck. He declared in a deep, husky voice, "David, your mantra is 'go go go!'"

I've been going ever since. I went from the Himalayas to Capitol Hill and then worked as a US official in the Clinton, Bush, and Obama administrations. Because the Dalai Lama set me on the path of service, I tried to maintain a spiritual identity but soon discovered the difficulties of being a bodhisattva in Washington's cutthroat environment. *Bodhisattva* refers to anyone who has made a resolution to become a Buddha but has deferred their own liberation until all other sentient beings have achieved enlightenment. Altruism puts others first.

Though I had top secret security clearances, I was never embedded in the US government and never had a full-time paying job. During my assignments at the State Department, I also worked at the Council on Foreign Relations and Columbia University. I specialized in "track-two" activities, which harness cooperation between government and civil society to shape and inform policy. I was too independent to abide by the strict rules of government, and I ultimately resigned from all three of my assignments with the Clinton, Bush, and Obama administrations.

US officials carry out instructions in service of national interests. They typically work government to government. Peace-making is usually the result of official diplomacy. However, sustainable peace is more possible when civil society lays the groundwork. Peace-building encompasses the entire spectrum, including conflict prevention, facilitating dialogue, and working with civil society to consolidate peace agreements. People-to-people interaction is often overlooked by official diplomacy. Therefore, it is essential both before negotiations and after an agreement to make sure there will be no backsliding. Without buy-in from those directly affected, official diplomacy rarely succeeds.

Three interconnecting themes guide my life. First, I am passionate about helping the underdog. Second, I am more maverick than bureaucrat. I don't function well in an environment that is bound by rules and procedures. And third, I work best in the track-two space with civil society members who are affected by government action. Of course, I am not the only person doing track-two work. Over time, however, I have honed my track-two skills for maximum impact by considering the policy context in which collaboration with civil society occurs and designing activities to complement official diplomacy.

I never had a formal mentor. However, I was fortunate to work with great men like Ambassador Richard C. Holbrooke, Congressman Tom Lantos, and Norway's Ambassador Wegger Strommen, as well as humanitarian luminaries like Elie Wiesel. Any good I have accomplished in the world was inspired by the Dalai Lama. I am also deeply appreciative of Professor Thurman and my father. Although I resented Pop's decision to exclude me from the family business, I recognize in retrospect that he liberated me from a mercantile life to do meaningful work that has an impact on many others.

Each chapter of this book is a personal vignette, not a comprehensive account, explaining my involvement in various conflict situations throughout the world. These personal stories describe my modest contribution to peace-building, tracing the evolution of my activities from humanitarian work to human rights and to democracy promotion, conflict resolution, and political transition from authoritarianism to more progressive forms of government. Over more than three decades, I have been dedicated to helping the oppressed. I have always done so with the advice of my lawyers and fully in conformance with the need to obey existing US laws and regulations, particularly the Foreign Agents Registration Act.

The world's problems are so enormous, complex, and all-encompassing that it would be easy to despair and not even attempt to address them. I learned from personal experience that nine out of ten initiatives do not succeed. Sometimes the impact of one's efforts is unknowable, negligible, or so incremental that it is difficult to quantify; sometimes the impact doesn't materialize until years or even decades later. Signing a peace treaty is an event that occurs on a specific date. Peace-building is a long-term process with milestones that are hard to measure. Discretion and modesty are qualities to which I aspire; I have not always succeeded. It takes a certain amount of ego just to get into the arena. While my overall contribution may have been negligible in the grand scheme of things, my caring and effort were always genuine.

Victims are usually isolated and alone. They need support and solidarity. Through my work, I have tried to give voice to the voiceless and to help in practical and meaningful ways. I have been fortunate to be able to spend my life serving those less fortunate, which has been immensely gratifying to me personally. Given a choice between making peace and making shirts, I would choose peace.

At the end of each semester, I ask my students which of them will do something to change the course of human history, to bend the arc of history towards justice. I hope that my children, students, foreign policy practitioners, and others who read this book will do their part to advance the noble goal of building a better world.

David L. Phillips

New York City
July 2020

SECTION I

ASIA-PACIFIC

CHAPTER 1

TIBET AND THE DALAI LAMA

I mailed corporate qualifications to "His Holiness the Dalai Lama, Dharamsala, India." My business, Energy Resources International, helped California companies export renewable energy technologies to developing countries in the Pacific Rim. I was pleasantly surprised to receive a reply some months later from Tempa Tsering, an adviser to the Dalai Lama. If I wanted to help Tibetan refugees, he suggested that I visit India to research conditions in the Tibetan settlements.

Tibet had been invaded by the Chinese People's Liberation Army (PLA) in 1950.[1] Conquering Tibet gave China access to rich natural resources and control of the strategically important border with India. The *Khampa*, warriors from eastern Tibet, were overwhelmed by battle-hardened Chinese soldiers who had just vanquished the Kuomintang in China's civil war. The PLA imposed martial law in Tibet, rounding up young monks and torturing and killing many of them. Thousands of monasteries were destroyed and their bricks used to build barracks for the PLA. Over one million Tibetans—one sixth of the population—lost their lives, and at least as many were jailed for their religious beliefs.[2]

The Dalai Lama, still a teenager, went to Beijing to discuss a power-sharing agreement with Mao Tse-tung and Zhou Enlai. The Seventeen Point Agreement for the Peaceful Liberation of Tibet was signed in 1951. The deal affirmed Chinese sovereignty over Tibet in exchange for religious and cultural autonomy.[3] Before the ink was dry, China betrayed the agreement and took steps to strengthen its control over Tibet.

Tibetans revere the Dalai Lama. They rebelled against Chinese occupation on March 10, 1959, surrounding the Norbulingka Palace to protect the Dalai Lama. In the middle of the night, the Dalai Lama fled Lhasa with eighty Tibetans in his entourage, family members, close associates, and members of the cabinet (the *Kashag*). When the Chinese discovered his escape, they followed in hot pursuit. Hit teams were sent to kill or capture the Dalai Lama before he could cross the rugged mountains from Tibet into India.[4]

Tibetans knew the terrain but barely escaped their pursuers. When the Dalai Lama entered the Indian State of Assam on March 31, he was welcomed by Prime Minister Jawaharlal Nehru and granted political asylum. About 150,000 Tibetans set off on the harrowing journey to join him. The majority ended up in India, where they established settlement communities, built monasteries, and worked to preserve their culture. The Dalai Lama set up a government-in-exile in the picturesque community of Dharamsala, a British hill station in Himachal Pradesh, nestled on the Indian side of the Himalayas. Eventually his followers established thirty-nine settlements and communities across India on mostly barren and unforgiving lands.[5]

. . . . .

When I wrote the Dalai Lama offering assistance, I was in the middle of preparing a bid to the California Energy Commission (CEC). The State of California had allocated funds for an Energy Czar to help California businesses export their renewable energy technologies, and my company was well placed to win the award. Just as the CEC was about to decide, I received the letter from Tempa. His invitation upended my personal and professional plans.

It is every parent's worry to receive a call from their son with news that he was resigning from his business and moving to India. Becoming the Energy Czar had been my dream. However, I realized in the nick of time that the contract could be golden handcuffs. Peddling solar energy technology was not too different from my father's business, except he was selling shirts, not solar panels. Going to India was jumping off a cliff, not knowing where I would land.

When I arrived at the train station near Dharamsala, Tempa was patiently waiting, puffing on a cigarette. He showed me around McLeod Ganj, a town terraced below the Dalai Lama's palace and the home of the Tibetan government-in-exile. Its streets were lined with tea stalls and guest cottages and crowded with Tibetan and western pilgrims who were devotees of Tibetan Buddhism.

After a short orientation, we set off to South India, where 40,000 Tibetans lived in settlements across Karnataka State.[6] We spent most of our time assessing the Hunsur settlement outside Mysore. Hunsur was a difficult place to live. Without mechanized agriculture, a few backyard kitchen gardens provided families with produce. Communal lands where Tibetans grew cotton were plowed by oxen. A small carpet factory was the only source of earned income. Otherwise, subsistence farming was the norm. I hoped to find a Tibetan thanka at the Hunsur crafts and carpet center. A thanka is a painting framed in silk, depicting a Buddhist deity or mandala. It is an exotic artwork of minute detail, often painted with natural pigments and gold. The Hunsur craft center was so primitive that no thankas were available.

We spent hours with the Hunsur settlement staff, discussing the details of our project, which we named the Farm Assistance, Investment and Development Program (Farm AID). With Yeshe, the project coordinator, we agreed to buy a tractor for the settlement, watering cans for each family, and mango tree seedlings. We also devised an incentives program to encourage farmers to rotate their crops annually from cotton to sunflowers. Without crop rotation, the organic value of the soil would become depleted, and the whole settlement could become a dustbowl. We selected sites for five bore wells and made plans for an irrigation system. Trees were to be planted in public spaces and for shade along the road from the settlement to the adjoining Indian village.

Upon our return to Dharamsala, Tempa and I dined with Jetsun Pema, the Dalai Lama's sister and Tempa's wife. Tempa told me that the next day I'd have an audience with the Dalai Lama. Tempa was modest but well-connected. I was so excited to learn that he had succeeded in scheduling the meeting. Someone from the Private Office met us in the reception area, and we climbed up a hill through a rose garden to the Dalai Lama's residence. I was breathless, partly from the altitude but mostly with excitement. I discovered that the Dalai Lama was very human, warm, and personable with an irrepressible laugh. We discussed my impressions of Hunsur and strategies to improve the lives of Tibetans. We agreed that I'd return to the US and raise funds for the project.

At the end of our meeting, the Dalai Lama spoke a few words in Tibetan to his attendants, and one returned with an armful of thankas, rolled and tied with a silk string. The Dalai Lama selected one as a gift to me. It was an image of the Medicine Buddha, a blue-faced healer who relieves suffering (*dukkha*) through Buddhist teachings. Dukkha is translated as the "suffering," "pain," or "unsatisfactoriness" associated with mundane life and attachment. It is the first of the Four Noble Truths, the core teaching of Buddhism. I was so thrilled by the gift and amazed when the Dalai Lama pulled out a pen and wrote in Tibetan, "To David: An object for your prayers and worship." He placed a ceremonial white silk scarf around my neck called a *Khata*. We hugged and rubbed foreheads. Meeting the Dalai Lama was the happiest moment of my young life.

· · · · ·

Back in the United States, I raised more than $100,000 for projects in Hunsur. After some tedious paperwork, we transferred funds from the American Jewish World Service to the settlement's bank account in India. Some months later, I returned to assess the project in Hunsur. The mango trees were planted, wells were dug, and watering cans were distributed. Kitchen gardens were blooming in neat rows. Everything was in order, except the tractor was missing. Though it had been paid for, the Indian tractor dealer hadn't delivered it. I went into town and spoke with the dealer, paying him a small bribe to make the delivery immediately. A few hours later, Yeshe rolled through the settlement gates seated on a brand-new red tractor. Tibetans lined the main road with newly planted trees and cheered his arrival.

The project faced another difficulty. Farmers refused to rotate their crops. We met with the agricultural extension officer and some farmers to discuss the problem. At first, we focused on technical aspects of the incentives scheme. During the course of our conversation, I learned that the problem was not technical, but rather political. Farmers were reluctant to change their agricultural practices because they believed that the next year they would accompany the Dalai Lama back to Tibet.

After visiting Hunsur, I met with the Dalai Lama to brief him on the project, which covered a range of activities from Farm AID, to upgrading the carpet factory, to supporting the Tibetan Children's Village in Byllakupe. I asked where I should concentrate my efforts, hoping for some strokes as reward for my endeavors. I was disappointed when he replied, "You should go to Washington, DC, and work on human rights." I was anticipating some kudos for what was accomplished. Instead he refocused me in a completely different direction.

The Dalai Lama must have foreseen the course of events that dramatically affected my career path. He urged me to make an appointment with Congressman Tom Lantos, a Democrat from California and champion of human rights, to tell him about my work with refugees. I went to Washington and slept on the couch of a friend who worked at Greenpeace. The next day, I showed up at the Lantos office, at 1707 Longworth House Office Building. The receptionist greeted me; I asked to see the congressman and told her that the Dalai Lama had sent me.

I thought she reached under the desk for a security buzzer. Rather than the Capitol Police, I was greeted by Kay King, Lantos's legislative assistant. She interviewed me, and we discussed the Tibetan issue. She called Annette Lantos, Tom's wife, to join the discussion, and finally the congressman himself sat down to learn about my work with Tibetan refugees in India.

I suggested that we organize a fundraising event at Fort Mason in San Francisco on Losar, the Tibetan new year. Contributions would go to the American Jewish World Service to support Farm AID. The Bay Area is a ripe environment for Tibetan activism because it is a progressive and spiritual community. Hundreds of people gathered on the day of the event. My father flew out from New York, and my sister came from Los Angeles. Congresswoman Nancy Pelosi (D-CA) was there, since the event was in her district.

When Tom and Annette entered the hall, they were flabbergasted by the large crowd and buzz of enthusiasm. The room was reverberating with recorded chants of the Gyuto monks, ceremonial gongs, and people talking about the project. After Tom's speech, he pulled me aside. "Annette and I feel you're a gift from heaven, and we want you to come to Washington and run the Congressional Human Rights Foundation." He explained that the Foundation worked alongside the Congressional Human Rights Caucus, which included hundreds of congressmen and congresswomen from both parties. I went to Washington and met Bob King, Tom's chief of staff, who provided background on the Foundation and outlined the job's responsibilities.

I told Bob that I was honored by the offer but needed advice from the Dalai Lama, so I returned to India and briefed him on developments since we had last met. He smiled knowingly. With his blessing, I returned to the

Lantos office and assumed my duties as Executive Director of the Congressional Human Rights Foundation.

·   ·   ·   ·   ·

The Dalai Lama was invited by the Congressional Human Rights Caucus to address Members of the US Congress on September 21, 1987. He presented a five-point plan for protecting Tibetan human rights, preserving Tibetan culture, and undertaking negotiations with the Chinese government.

> The world is increasingly interdependent, so that lasting peace—national, regional and global—can only be achieved if we think in terms of broader interest rather than parochial needs. At this time, it is crucial that all of us, the strong and the weak, contribute in our own way. I speak to you today as the leader of the Tibetan people and as a Buddhist monk devoted to the principles of a religion based on love and compassion. Above all, I am here as a human being who is destined to share this planet with you and all others as brothers and sisters. As the world grows smaller, we need each other more than in the past."[7]

He continued:

> Tibetans are a peace loving and non-violent people. Since Buddhism was introduced to Tibet over one thousand years ago, Tibetans have practiced non-violence with respect to all forms of life. This attitude has also been extended to our country's international relations. Tibet's highly strategic position in the heart of Asia, separating the continent's great powers—India, China and the USSR—has throughout history endowed it with an essential role in the maintenance of peace and stability."

He lamented China's illegal occupation of Tibet and accused the Chinese authorities of wrongly claiming that Tibet had always been a part of China. The Dalai Lama explained that Tibet was a fully independent state when the PLA invaded. Tibetans are a distinct people with their own culture, language, religion and history.

He presented a five-point plan for Tibet:[8]

1. *Create a Zone of Peace:* The whole of Tibet, including the eastern provinces of Kham and Amdo, would be transformed into a zone of *Ahimsa*, a Hindi term meaning a state of peace and non-violence.

2. *Discontinue Population Transfers:* 7.5 million ethnic Han Chinese settlers were sent to Tibet as of 1987, where they came to outnumber the Tibetan population of six million. The Dalai Lama warned: "Tibetans will soon be no more than a tourist attraction and relic of a noble past."

3. *Respect Human Rights and Democratic Freedoms:* Discrimination is practiced in Tibet under a policy of apartheid. Thousands of Tibetans suffer in prisons and labor camps, punished for their religious or political convictions.

4. *Restore Tibet's Natural Environment and Stop Dumping Nuclear Waste:* The wildlife and the forests of Tibet have been decimated by China, which uses Tibet for the production of nuclear weapons and dumping nuclear waste.

5. *Negotiate Tibet-China Relations:* The Dalai Lama emphasized that he was not seeking independence. Negotiations should focus on autonomy for Tibetans living in western China, U-Tsang, Kham, and Amdo.

The Dalai Lama called for talks with China and sent a delegation to Beijing for negotiations with Chinese officials about a *modus vivendi* in 1982 Instead of a constructive dialogue about the broad concerns of Tibetans, Chinese officials reduced the Tibetan question to a discussion about the Dalai Lama's personal status.[9] After Nixon's trip to China in 1972, the US merely paid lip service to the Dalai Lama's concerns. Without pressure or meaningful engagement by successive US administrations, China continued its policies of apartheid, population transfer, and wholesale abuse of human rights and democratic freedoms.

· · · · ·

Working in Washington, DC from 1988 to 1995 changed my perspective. Shifting from the Himalayas to Capitol Hill politicized me. In my previous audience, I asked the Dalai Lama how I could most effectively advance the interests of Tibetans. When we met again in 1999, I focused on negotiations between the Dalai Lama's representatives and the Chinese authorities.

Beijing rejected outside mediation, insisting that relations with Tibetans were a domestic affair. I proposed a track two dialogue project to the Dalai Lama. Track two is an unofficial exercise in problem-solving. It brings opposing groups together to discuss their differences and, undertaken in consultation with concerned officials, adds value to official diplomatic efforts. It serves as a laboratory for developing ideas and experimenting with solutions. Through track two, non-state actors are able to creatively explore the underlying conditions that give rise to conflict and develop joint strategies for addressing problems through reciprocal efforts. The goal is to foster collaboration so that conflict comes to be seen as a shared problem requiring cooperation and ownership by both sides.

After my presentation, the Dalai Lama summoned members of his negotiating team, led by the Venerable Rimpoche Lodi Gyari, who was also the Tibetan representative in Washington, DC. I offered some ideas about the track two project. After some discussion, we agreed that the way forward should be based on a clear understanding of China's existing rules and regulations governing autonomy in the Tibetan-populated provinces of western China.

Getting the Chinese to the table was the starting point. I contacted Theodore C. Sorensen, President Kennedy's former speechwriter who was now "of counsel" at Paul, Weiss, Rifkind, Wharton & Garrison, a major law firm with offices in China. Sorensen and I were members of the Council on Foreign Relations. I arranged a small travel and research grant from the Norwegian government and went to China. The purpose of my trip was twofold: 1) to engage the lawyers at Paul Weiss in a discussion about the work plan and 2) to make contact with the Tibetology Research Center, a branch of the Chinese Communist Party (CPC) that served as a think-tank on Tibetan issues.

Before my meeting with the lawyers, Sorensen had already explained to them that we wanted to conduct research on Chinese autonomy provisions in China's constitution and at the central government level. The project sought to develop a database of existing decentralization arrangements in the western provinces of Yunnan, Gansu, Qinghai, Sichuan, and the Tibet Autonomous Region. The research would focus on local government, economy, environment, and culture. Harvard University's Belfer Center for Science in International Affairs, where Sorensen was well-known, agreed to publish our report.

Bi Hua was at the helm of China's Tibetology Research Center. She was a cadre and propagandist who had risen up the ranks of the United Front and the CPC to become a senior official working on Tibetan issues.[10] The Center's tasks involved coordinating research with foreigners, managing their access to information, and addressing political sensitivities of scholarly work. Founded in 1986, the Center had nearly two hundred scholars covering history, economy, traditional medicine, and other fields. It managed more than fifty research institutes focused on Tibetology in China. The Center coordinated with overseas counterparts to develop more "fruitful academic results and train experts in other countries."[11]

The Paul Weiss team of twelve Chinese language-speaking lawyers was invaluable. They uncovered reams of information on China's decentralization arrangements. Without them, we could barely scratch the surface of data for the project. Bi Hua welcomed cooperation with Harvard University. I was silent on the role of lawyers from Paul Weiss; I did not want the project to affect clients of the firm.

Sorensen and I returned to China together. Sorensen had suffered a stroke, which affected his balance and eyesight. After a meeting at his law offices, we went to the China Tibetology Research Center to see Bi Hua. With assistance from J. Cobb Mixter, my researcher at the Council on Foreign Relations, we had prepared a detailed report summarizing our research and making the case for a full and final settlement for the Dalai Lama. At the core of the deal, he would fully and finally renounce independence in exchange for meaningful autonomy and his return to Lhasa as a religious leader. In addition to the report, which was produced in both English and Chinese, I brought a large box containing copies of our primary research. These materials documented the CPC's extensive efforts to address the Tibetan question through regional and cultural autonomy. I told Bi Hua that if China would only implement its own laws on autonomy, the situation in Tibet would stabilize and international criticism of China's policies would cease.

She politely thanked us for the materials. "Of course, we are aware of China's rules and regulations on autonomy," she admonished. "We are grateful that you've organized the information for us." Sorensen had jetlag and was snoozing intermittently through the meeting. Midway through the conversation, he perked up and asked Bi Hua, "Why don't you just let the Dalai Lama go back to Tibet and be done with this whole story?" She was inscrutable but was apparently surprised by Ted's proposal. The Chinese do not communicate so directly.

At the end of our meeting, we agreed that she would organize a seminar where I would present the report and research. A few months later, in early 2002, I returned to Beijing to meet a veritable who's who of scholars and policymakers working on the Tibet issue. In my opening remarks, I called Bi Hua a good friend (*Hǎopéngyǒu*). She gently corrected me, saying I was just a friend. The tone of the discussion was different from our previous meetings. Participants were more interested in the role of the Tibetan government-in-exile in the project. They wanted to know if I had briefed the Dalai Lama and, if so, his reaction. They were less interested in the substance of the report than in how the report could be used to manipulate the Dalai Lama to the advantage of the CPC, supporting its claim that the Tibet issue had already been addressed.

I sought meetings with some of Bi Hua's superiors at the United Front in the hope of working my way up the chain of command and arranging meetings with China's more senior policymakers. My request was neither declined nor accommodated. Bi Hua arranged for me to see mid-level researchers and scholars. It was clear that my effort to penetrate the inner sanctum of the United Front had failed. Bi Hua cooperated at first, but then withdrew her support. I never knew why she got cold feet.

Bi Hua and Chinese intelligence agencies must have conducted background research on me. Chinese spies are all over Dharamsala, gathering information on international contacts of the Dalai Lama and cultivating Tibetan officials. I was a board member of Tibet House. My name was listed on a plaque at the entrance, identifying my gift as a founding member. I was also an outspoken advocate for Tibetan rights who had worked on Capitol Hill. We had a series of planning meetings at Harvard that Sorensen chaired and in which Bob Thurman, my professor and an American Buddhist scholar, participated. Lobsang Sangay, a smart young

Tibetan who had received a Fulbright scholarship to study law at Harvard Law School, also attended.

I suspected that Chinese agents infiltrated our meeting. Chinese agents were thorough, monitoring any potentially dissident activity that could be used to question China's authority. A Chinese journalism student employed by CCTV, China's state broadcasting company, approached me. She explained that the Chinese knew about the project because one of the meeting's participants kept them informed. When I asked the participant to confirm this information, he readily admitted that he was in touch with Chinese officials and had shared our research and details about the project. I had told him that we were trying to establish a back channel through Bi Hua. He maintained that making the Chinese aware of our efforts was necessary in order to influence policy.

On March 10, 2011—the anniversary of the Tibetan uprising in 1959—the Dalai Lama shocked the Tibetan community by announcing that he was giving up his political role in the Tibetan government-in-exile and shifting power to an elected representative. The Dalai Lama indicated that he would remain the spiritual leader of Tibetans but had recognized his mortality and was stepping down from politics. The Chinese government dismissed the announcement as subterfuge to mask the Dalai Lama's ploy to advance his separatist agenda. China's Foreign Ministry spokesperson rejected the shift, claiming it was intended to deceive the international community.[12]

Lobsang Sangay returned to Harvard to pursue a Doctor of Juridical Science degree in 2004. Later, he went back to Dharamsala and ran for the post of prime minister (*kalontripa*) in the Tibetan government-in-exile.[13] He conducted a savvy campaign that relied on social media. He defeated more senior Tibetans with a proven history of serving the Dalai Lama. He was both the first non-monk to hold the position, and coming from the Tibetan refugee settlement of Darjeeling in India, he was also the first person born outside Tibet to be elected to the post of prime minister. He was well-connected in China and the Tibetan Central administration, having organized several meetings at Harvard with the Dalai Lama and Chinese dissidents.[14] When Lobsang and I met at Lumi's Restaurant in New York before his presentation around the corner at the Asia Society in July 2011, he was already showing leadership with the Central administration and by working cooperatively with the Dalai Lama.

When the Dalai Lama and I first met, I asked how to best help the Tibetan people. At the time, I was focused on rotating cotton and sunflower crops, and restoring the Hunsur carpet factory. As my political interests evolved, I focused on promoting reforms within China, which would help both the Chinese and Tibetan people. Wise and strategic, Ted Sorensen reminded me: a rising tide lifts all boats.

Notes

1   Richard Cavendish, "The Chinese Invade Tibet," *History Today*, October 2000, https://www.historytoday.com/archive/chinese-invade-tibet.

2   Dalai Lama, "Five Point Peace Plan," Address to the U.S. Congressional Human Right's Caucus, September 21, 1987, https://www.dalailama.com/messages/tibet/five-point-peace-plan.

3   "Facts about the 17-Point Agreement," *Diir Publications*, https://tibet.net/wp-content/uploads/2014/10/FACTS-ABOUT-17-POINT-AGREEMENT.pdf.

4   Sanchari Pal, "Remembering an Epic Journey: How Dalai Lama Escaped Tibet in 1959," *The Better India*, March 17, 2018, https://www.thebetterindia.com/134644/dalai-lama-escape-lhasa-tibet-tawang-india/.

5   Kunal Purohit, "After 60 Years in India, Why are Tibetans Leaving?" *Al Jazeera*, March 21, 2019, https://www.aljazeera.com/indepth/features/60-years-india-tibetans-leaving-190319231424509.html.

6   Amy Lee, "Tibetans Find Freedom in Exile," *Wall Street Journal*, October 8, 2010, https://www.wsj.com/articles/SB10001424052748703843804575534372072487894.

7   Dalai Lama, "Five Point Peace Plan."

8   Ibid.

9   "Chronology of Tibetan-Chinese Relations," *Save Tibet*, https://savetibet.org/advocacy/chronology-of-tibetan-chinese-relations-1979-to-2013/ (accessed May 10, 2020).

10 Tan Yingzi, "Delegation Brings Tibetan Culture to US," *China Daily*, October 21, 2011, http://www.chinadaily.com.cn/china/2011-10-21/content_13947706.htm.

11 Wang Kaihao, "Scholars Come to China so They can Research Tibet," *China

Daily, March 24, 2017, https://www.chinadaily.com.cn/china/2017-03/24/content_28660543.htm.

12 Rob Gifford, "Dalai Lama to Give up Political Role," *National Public Radio,* March 10, 2011, https://www.npr.org/2011/03/10/134432801/Dalai-Lama-To-Give-Up-Political-Role-In-Tibet.

13 Olga Khazan, "The Accidental Prime Minister of Tibet," *The Atlantic,* May 15, 2013, https://www.theatlantic.com/china/archive/2013/05/the-accidental-prime-minister-of-tibet/275860/.

14 Encyclopedia Britannica, https://www.britannica.com/biography/Lobsang-Sangay (accessed April 3, 2020).

CHAPTER 2

CHINA AND THE
PRO-DEMOCRACY MOVEMENT

Hu Yaobang, the former Secretary General of the Chinese Communist Party who attempted to open the Party toward greater liberalization, died in April 1989. His passing triggered a popular movement against China's one-party political system, which was corrupt and ill-prepared to meet economic challenges. The pro-democracy movement was led by students and workers who insisted on accountability and due process. They demanded greater political participation and basic human rights— freedom of expression, freedom of press, and freedom of assembly.[1]

Hardliners accused Hu of being bourgeois and forced his resignation on January 16, 1987.[2] He was replaced by Zhao Ziyang as Secretary General. Like Hu, Zhao was a change agent.

Zhao gave the eulogy for Hu at his funeral on April 22, 1989. He associated himself with concerns about corruption, heralding patriotism of the protesters.[3] People spontaneously gathered at the Monument to the People's Heroes in Tiananmen Square. Students at Tsinghua and Beijing University built shrines to Hu's memory and demanded political liberalization. They issued a petition with "Seven Demands":[4]

1. Affirm Hu Yaobang's views on democracy and freedom as correct.

2. Admit that the campaigns against spiritual pollution and bourgeois liberalization had been wrong.

3. Publish information on the income and assets of state leaders and their family members.

4. Stop press censorship and allow privately run independent media.

5. Increase funding for education and raise the salaries for scholars and professors.

6. End restrictions on demonstrations in Beijing.

7. Provide objective coverage of students in official media.

Some 100,000 students gathered in Tiananmen Square when Hu passed away. Dissidents defied the authorities, assembling at the Great Hall of the People in the heart of Tiananmen. Others congregated at Xinhua Gate, which led to Zhongnanhai, home of the CPC leadership. Protests were organized by the newly-established Beijing Workers' Autonomous Federation and the Beijing Students' Autonomous Federation. Beyond Beijing, demonstrations occurred in four hundred cities across the country.

The number of protesters grew to more than one million. Student leaders demanded implementation of the Seven Demands. In his last public appearance before being placed under house arrest, Zhao addressed the students using a bullhorn. He implored them to think about their futures and asked them to disband and abandon their hunger strike. During a meeting with student leaders, one of them, Wuer Kaixi, confronted Zhao. Many objected to his rude treatment of a senior statesman who was sympathetic to reform. Disrespecting elders is taboo in Chinese culture.

Deng Xiaoping, paramount leader of the People's Republic of China from 1978 until his retirement in 1992, ordered Tiananmen Square cleared of protesters for Russian President Mikhail Gorbachev's visit to Beijing on May 15, 1989. The CPC leadership was divided. Instead of condoning the crackdown, Zhao reached out to the students and offered negotiations. Deng and Premier Li Peng criticized Zhao and rejected negotiations.

On May 20, 1989, the State Council declared martial law and mobilized at least 250,000 troops from remote regions across China. Protesters pleaded with the soldiers, but their exhortations fell on deaf ears, as the soldiers spoke a different dialect of Mandarin. Troops approached Tiananmen Square along Chang'an Avenue in the early morning hours of June 4. Demonstrators and bystanders were killed as the troops and armored columns advanced. Amnesty International reported that at least one thousand people died.[5]

The Tiananmen Square protests produced several iconic images. Students erected a statue of the Goddess of Democracy holding the torch of freedom aloft. Chai Ling, the Supreme Commander of the Chinese Student Democracy Movement, pointed out the difference between the Statue of Liberty and the Goddess of Democracy. The Goddess holds the flame of freedom aloft using two hands, while the Statue of Liberty uses one hand to hoist the torch, with the book of law tucked under the other arm. The rule of law is a foreign concept to many Chinese.

On June 5, a man stood in front of a column of tanks on Chang'an Avenue, carrying bags of groceries. As the tanks moved to avoid him, he pivoted to block their path. The man climbed on the turret of the lead tank to speak to the soldiers inside. The Chinese government boasted about its restraint in dealing with demonstrators because he was not crushed. *Time Magazine* named him one of the one hundred most influential people of the twentieth century.[6]

. . . . .

The Chinese authorities published a list of twenty-one traitors they wanted to capture and prosecute for treason. Chai Ling, Wuer Kaixi, and Li Lu were among the most famous and most sought by the authorities. An underground railroad helped pro-democracy leaders escape. It was called Operation Yellow Bird after a Chinese proverb: "The mantis stalks the cicada, unaware of the yellow bird behind." Ordinary Chinese citizens, sympathetic Communist officials, Hong Kong activists, western intelligence agencies, diplomats, and Hong Kong gangsters helped student leaders escape to the West. They were given false identities, passports, and disguises. All told, eight hundred dissidents escaped to Hong Kong. Many went from there to Paris and later surfaced in the United States.

The Congressional Human Rights Foundation, where I served as director, was tracking the whereabouts of dissidents and had offered to facilitate arrangements upon their arrival in the US. We received a grant from the National Endowment for Democracy to help the Chinese students organize themselves into a cohesive advocacy group. Leading this dialogue project put me in regular and close contact with students who had escaped Tiananmen Square.

Wuer Kaixi, an ethnic Uighur from Xinjang Province, was one of the first dissidents to arrive in North America. He was notorious in Chinese circles for confronting Zhao Ziyang when he tried to reason with the student leaders. His escape from China failed twice, but Wuer was determined and kept trying. Whereas the average cost of escape was about $13,000, Wuer was notorious, which raised the cost of his extraction to $80,000. British Intelligence allegedly paid the bill. Wuer lost many friends during the crackdown. "I am the survivor of a massacre. I have to live with the guilt."[7]

Soon after Wuer arrived in New York, I accompanied him to a speaking engagement at Lincoln Center for the overseas Chinese community. After his remarks, we snuck out a stage door and rushed to a waiting car. We were followed by admiring Chinese youth, enthralled by Wuer's charisma and human rights message. He was like a rock star.

A small, old Chinese woman came running up to Wuer as he was closing the car door. She shoved an envelope in his hand. Inside was a stack of hundred-dollar bills. It was probably her life savings. We didn't even know her name.

I gave Wuer a gold coin that had been my grandfather's. I explained that it was a good luck token. I later learned later that he lost the coin, but I didn't really mind. The gesture was more important than the gift itself.

I did, however, get something in return. I gave a party for Wuer at my home in Georgetown. He brought a soldier's cap that was taken off the head of a Chinese People's Liberation Army (PLA) member in Tiananmen Square on June 4. The cap was obviously too large for the soldier, who had stuffed the inside of the brim with newspaper so it would fit more snugly. Wuer was told that whoever possessed the hat would lead the movement. He forgot it at my home that evening. The cap is still in my possession, the Chinese newspaper yellowing over the years.

Wuer married a pop star from the Republic of China and moved to Taiwan. He remained active in the Uighur human rights movement when it was revealed that China had placed more than one million Uighur in re-education camps. The ongoing re-education and internment of Uighur is a stain on China's reputation. Wuer paid a dear price for his activism. He lamented, "I haven't been able to see my parents for the last 30 years. I cannot go back to China and they denied them traveling abroad. I'm heartbroken for that."[8]

Li Lu, a resilient survivor of Tiananmen, was a deputy commander of the Chinese Students Democracy Movement. His parents and grandparents were imprisoned during the Cultural Revolution for being intellectuals. As a small boy, he was shuttled between foster families. His adopted family died in 1976 during the devastating Tangshan earthquake, which killed more than 240,000 people.

After studying physics and economics at Nanjing University, Li Lu went to Beijing and got involved in the student movement. He was placed on the most wanted list after the crackdown and went into hiding. According to Li Lu, "There were a lot of courageous people who really took it upon themselves to rescue us. It was through that underground railroad that I escaped to Hong Kong, and from there to France, and from France eventually made my way to New York City."[9] He was twenty-three years old.

He enrolled in the American Language Program at Columbia University and subsequently studied at Columbia College, Columbia Law School, and Columbia Business School simultaneously. In 1996, he was one of the few people ever to graduate with three Columbia degrees. I invited Li Lu to the annual gala of the International Rescue Committee, and I seated him next to another of my guests who was a wealthy investment banker. During the dinner, Li Lu shared his amazing life story. The banker was so impressed that he took out his checkbook and wrote a check for $10,000. He called it a loan and had Li Lu sign an IOU on the back of the dinner program. In reality, it was a gift to help Li Lu with his new life in America.

Li Lu lived a charmed life in the United States. He attended a talk by Warren Buffet, the billionaire investor. Inspired by Buffet, Li Lu started trading stocks and setup an investment fund. Charles Munger, vice-chairman of Warren Buffett's Berkshire Hathaway, was so impressed with his "ferocious" intelligence that he invested in Li Lu's fund.[10] "I don't think that leading businessmen of any other country would trust their money with immigrants from a different country," Li Lu reflected. "Your ability, your energy, your integrity, and nothing else—that is uniquely American. That's what makes America so successful in terms of business; everybody has an equal opportunity."[11] Li Lu found Himalayan Capital, a successful investment fund, in 1998.

On the five-year anniversary of the Tiananmen massacre, Li Lu declared a hunger strike. He unfolded a lawn chair in a small public park on Washington, DC's Wisconsin Avenue across the street from the Chinese Embassy. We spent hours together, reflecting on the movement and discussing strategies for human rights in China.

．　．　．　．　．

Of all the dissidents, I was closest to Chai Ling. Ling was strong like a tiger, yet soft like a blossom. She was initially involved in the pro-democracy movement because of her husband, Feng Congde. However, she emerged as a leader in her own right, inspiring protesters by leading the hunger strike in May 1989. Using a bullhorn to amplify her voice, she pronounced:

> For several years, we have had student movement after student movement, but we got nothing. Why? We ask for democracy and freedom from the government. But why could we never get it? We chant "Long Live the People" all the time. But why do people always run away when the police come? We chant "Police Love People" all the time. But why do police always beat us up? Why should we go on a hunger strike? Because we want to use this method, the only freedom we have left, to see the true face of our country and the true face of our people. I want to see if this country is worth our sacrifice and contribution. We are fortunate to have parents who raised us to become college students. But it is time for us to stop eating. The government has time and again lied to us, ignored us. We only want the government to talk with us and to say that we are not traitors. We, the children, are ready to die. We, the children, are ready to use our lives to pursue the truth. We, the children, are ready to sacrifice ourselves. We want to fight to live. We want to fight to live with the resolve of death.[12]

I was glued to my television watching reports from Tiananmen Square, enamored by Chai Ling. When the tanks rolled in, the students scattered and disappeared. Many were unaccounted for. I wondered what happened to her. Had she perished on June 4?

Chai Ling was able to escape Tiananmen and make her way through the underground railroad to Hong Kong, hiding in a shipping crate of rotting fish. From there, she traveled to Paris and then Washington, DC. We were introduced by Charles and Mary Tanenbaum, Chinese art collectors who lived on Park Avenue in New York City. Mary asked to meet me for an "important discussion." She asked if I could help Chai Ling tell her story when she came to the United States. According to Mary, Ling needed a trusted interlocutor to make arrangements and advise her advocacy.

I took Ling to meet senior officials in the administration of President George H.W. Bush. With Vice President Dan Quayle, she batted her eyelashes and flirted, "Mr. Vice President, I didn't realize you were so handsome." She flattered National Security Adviser Brent Scowcroft saying, "You are such an expert on China." She did not mention Scowcroft's secret mission to China after Tiananmen when he kowtowed to Premier Li Peng and other hardliners. Even Acting Assistant Undersecretary Secretary of State Lawrence Eagleburger, a hard-nosed Foreign Service Officer, was charmed by Chai Ling.

Washington was debating conditions for China's Most Favored Nation Trading Status (MFN). MFN is an economic arrangement whereby a country enjoys preferential trade terms. Countries with MFN receive the lowest tariffs, the fewest trade barriers, and the highest import quotas. Congress adopted the Jackson-Vanik Amendment to the Trade Act in 1974, which curtailed permanent normal trading relations to non-market economies that restricted emigration rights. Jackson-Vanik targeted the Soviet Union.

On May 24, 1990, President Bush recommended extending MFN status to China without conditions. China had been awarded MFN in 1980 and each year thereafter. The renewal recommendation was subject to Congressional review.

The Finance Committee of the US Senate met on June 20, 1990. Senators made statements, followed by testimony from Chinese dissidents who had escaped Tiananmen Square. Finance Committee Chairman Senator Lloyd Bentsen (D-TX) opened the hearing by asking if extending MFN would encourage reform or be seen by the Chinese government as an endorsement of its heavy-handed repression of the Chinese people. Senators were far from unanimous in supporting MFN conditionality. Senator Bob Dole (R-KS) supported the Bush Administration's mild sanctions, even though they failed to get China to change its approach to human rights. Senator Max Baucus (D-MT), who would later become US ambassador to China, said, "Last year we were all shocked and appalled at the brutal steps taken by the Chinese government to repress the student pro-democracy movement. I, like you, will never forget the image of a

Chinese student singlehandedly blocking a column of tanks. I will never forget the shock and horror we felt learning of the slaughter in Tiananmen Square." However, he warned against a "shallow show of outrage" that would affect American business. Senator Daniel Patrick Moynihan (Democrat, New York) offered legislation conditioning MFN for China on its human rights record, not merely emigration. He lamented China's invasion of Tibet, which had killed one sixth of Tibet's population and drove more than 100,000 into exile.[13]

In the US House of Representatives, Ling had one-on-one meetings with influential members of Congress, including my co-chairman, Congressman Tom Lantos (Democrat, California), a vocal supporter of sanctions. Chai Ling also testified before the Congressional Human Rights Caucus, describing the assault on Tiananmen Square and her harrowing escape. Ling was good at making an emotional appeal (in broken English), but lacked substance on issues affecting US policy. Overall, her testimony was well received. Congressman Gary Ackerman (D-NY) concluded: "You're living proof that good things come in small packages."[14]

After her testimony, I sat with Ling to reflect on her trip to Washington and her future role. Ling shared her distress about being away from family and uncertainty about her life. I told her, "You're a political refugee in my country. As long as you're here, you have a place to be." I gave her a key to my flat at 3518 T Street and assured her, "My home is your home." She appreciated the gesture of hospitality.

For her birthday on April 15, the date when Hu Yaobang passed away, I brought a gift to her residence in Princeton. The gift was a fluffy white Eskimo puppy that I named Tara. I chose the name because Tara is the patron saint of Tibet. Chai Ling had a theory that China would change if everyone learned to care for a puppy. No time like the present to test her theory.

Chai Ling and I stayed in close contact as she pursued studies at Princeton and Harvard. She married Bob Maginn, a former senior partner, board member, and director of Bain & Company, who was chairman of the Massachusetts Republican Party from 2011 to 2013. Maginn and Chai Ling founded Jenzabar, an internet company providing educational services. After all she had been through, Chai Ling craved normalcy and security.

Ling founded an organization aimed at ending "China's brutal one-child policy that killed over four hundred million babies."[15] She discovered Jesus and became a born-again Christian. When we met some years later at the Harvard Faculty Club, she explained the special role that Jesus had assumed in her life. She wanted to share Him with me and invited me to join her Church. I expressed respect but reminded Ling that I was Jewish. I proposed a deal: if she could enable the Dalai Lama's return to Tibet, I would convert to Christianity and join her Church. She gave me a perplexed cross-eyed look. The bar was set very high.

Notes

1   Verna Yu, "Tiananmen Square Anniversary: What Sparked the Protests in China in 1989?" *The Guardian,* May 30, 2019, https://www.theguardian.com/world/2019/may/31/tiananmen-square-anniversary-what-sparked-the-protests-in-china-in-1989.

2   Edward A. Gargan, "Leader of Party in China is Ousted for His Mistakes," *New York Times,* January 17, 1987, https://www.nytimes.com/1987/01/17/world/leader-of-party-in-china-is-ousted-for-his-mistakes.html.

3   Kathy Long, "Zhao Ziyang: A Reformer China's Communist Party Wants to Forget," *BBC News,* January 17, 2019, https://www.bbc.com/news/blogs-china-blog-46901248.

4   Michael Martina, "Thirty Years after Tiananmen, Protesters' Goals Further away than Ever," *Reuters,* June 1, 2019, https://www.reuters.com/article/us-china-tiananmen/thirty-years-after-tiananmen-protesters-goals-further-away-than-ever-idUSKCN1T3001.

5   Amnesty International, https://www.amnesty.org.uk/china-1989-tiananmen-square-protests-demonstration-massacre (accessed May 10, 2020).

6   Patrick Witty, "Tank Man Revisited: More Details Emerge about the Iconic Image," *Time Magazine,* June 5, 2012, https://time.com/3788986/tianamen/.

7   "Tiananmen Square Survivor Reflects 30 Years Later: I'm Heartbroken," *CBS News,* June 4, 2019, https://www.cbsnews.com/news/tiananmen-square-survivor-wuer-kaixi-reflects-on-30-year-anniversary-im-heartbroken/.

8   Ibid.

9   National Museum of American History, https://americanhistory.si.edu/family-voices/individuals/li-lu (accessed March 18, 2020).

10 Li Peng, "Tiananmen Square: The Long Shadow," *Financial Times*, June 14, 2014, https://www.ft.com/content/4f970144-e658-11e3-9a20-00144feabdc0.

11 Ibid.

12 Eddie Cheng, "Standoff at Tiananmen," http://www.standoffattiananmen.com/2009/05/book-excerpt-hunger-strike-decision.html (accessed March 18, 2020).

13 US Senate, "Hearing Before the Committee On Finance," June 20, 1990, https://books.google.com/books?id=8m61J6aLWKEC&pg=PA52&lpg=PA52&dq=chai+ling+estified+before+congress+in+1990&source=bl&ots=wpURj231sc&sig=ACfU3U1NTJsK46ZioDS5sL9l5w2_Qv8R9A&hl=en&sa=X&ved=2ahUKEwih_aLj2KboAhUxUt8KHUmTCU8Q6AEwBnoECAoQAQ#v=onepage&q=chai%20ling%20estified%20before%20congress%20in%201990&f=false.

14 House International Affairs Committee, June 8, 1990.

15 Email from Chai Ling to the author, March 19, 2020.

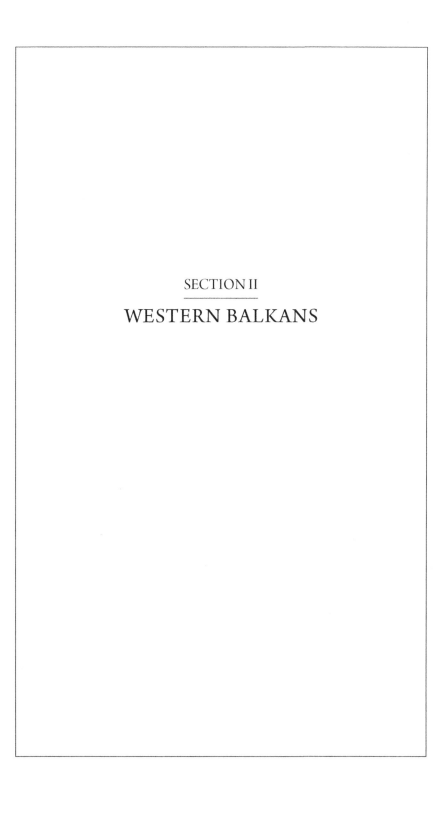

SECTION II

WESTERN BALKANS

CHAPTER 3

THE DEMISE OF YUGOSLAVIA

State television announced the death of Yugoslavia's President, Josip Broz Tito, on May 4, 1980: "Comrade Tito has died. His great heart stopped beating at 15:05 local time."[1] As head of the Partisans, the most effective resistance movement in Europe during World War II, Tito led a guerrilla uprising against Nazi occupation. He resisted Soviet domination during the Cold War and survived Stalin's attempt to depose him in 1948. Tito forged Yugoslavia into a "federal republic of equal nations and nationalities, freely united on the principle of brotherhood and unity." It was comprised of six republics—Serbia, Croatia, Slovenia, Macedonia, Montenegro, and Bosnia and Herzegovina—and two autonomous provinces —Kosovo and Vojvodina. Each republic was allowed the right to self-determination and secession if conducted in accordance with Yugoslavia's 1974 constitution.[2]

While Tito's authoritarian rule maintained coherence among Yugoslavia's disparate ethnic and religious groups, the cherished principle of brotherhood and national unity began to unravel soon after Tito's death. I happened to be in Yugoslavia in June 1980, soon after Tito's passing. I was backpacking with my Croatian-American girlfriend to her family's ancestral village in Herzegovina, an ethnic Croatian region in Bosnia. We traveled by train from Zagreb and then on a bus from Mostar to Medjugorje, close to the border of Croatia in the Čitluk municipality. In 1981, Medjugorje became famous when six teenagers reportedly saw a vision of the Virgin Mary. Medjugorje is still visited by thousands of pilgrims every year.

Tito was a strongman who effectively kept the country together, balancing power between Yugoslavia's ethnic and religious groups. We met soldiers riding the train from Belgrade to Zagreb on our way to Medjugorje who described Tito's power-sharing role. I knew nothing about Yugoslavia's history, but wondered what would become of the delicate balance after his death. Without Tito, Yugoslavia's republics asserted their right to self-determination, which led to civil war and mass killings, which Bosnian Serb leader Radovan Karadžić called "ethnic cleansing."

My girlfriend's grandmother had a sister named Sima. The girls separated in their teens, with Sima staying in Medjugorje and the sister's family migrating to Los Angeles. The sisters had no contact for generations until we showed up in Medjugorje with an old, yellowing photo of the two girls, their names written on the back. We arrived by bus and showed the photo to some old men in a café. They excitedly took us to Sima's house. The ensuing family reunion went on for a week. We drank grappa, a traditional grape brandy, and ate *Croatian pastry with* Strukli cheese for breakfast. The family was warm and welcoming, good people with many stories of how their lives were affected by World War II.

Pavo and his brother Pero, who lost a leg during the war, regaled us with stories of fratricide during the war. Hundreds of thousands of ethnic *Serbs* had been subjected to the genocidal policies of the fascist Ustashe, a puppet state created by Axis Powers on German-occupied territory of Croatia and Bosnia. During this time, between 300,000 and 340,000 Serbs had been killed in massacres and in concentration camps such as Jasenovac. Slaughter was not one-sided; Serbian militias, led by Orthodox Chetniks, slaughtered Muslims and Catholic Croats.

Pero fondly reminisced about the massacre of twenty-six Serbs by Ustashe in Čitluk on August 22, 1941. They were lined up on the edge of a ravine and executed, their bodies tumbling into the crevice below. Pero showed no remorse. He explained that fratricide was necessary to protect Croats from Chetnik Serb gangs.

. . . . .

Slobodan Milošević became Serbia's President on May 8, 1989. He was a Serbian nationalist who aspired to establish a "Greater Serbia" that would unify Serbs across Yugoslavia. US policy supported the unity of Yugoslavia; however, Senator Bob Dole (R-KS) and Congressman Tom Lantos (D-CA) prioritized the democratic rights of Yugoslavia's republics and autonomous regions as a check against Serbian nationalism.[3]

Mira Ricardel, Dole's legislative assistant, was a Croatian-American and a strong proponent of democracy for Yugoslavia. Ricardel was one the smartest, toughest, and most principled people I knew on Capitol Hill. She introduced me to Yugoslav issues and was a constant collaborator on democracy and human rights promotion.

Dole led a Senate delegation to Yugoslavia in August 1990. Upon arrival, he showed US Ambassador Warren Zimmerman a draft press release indicating that the purpose of his visit was to promote human rights and democracy. Zimmerman added "and the unity of Yugoslavia." Serbia was the largest and most powerful of Yugoslavia's republics. Serbian nationalism would polarize the country and cause its fragmentation. The rise of nationalism in other republics was a response to Serbian nationalism and fear of dominance by Belgrade. The US endorsed a stopgap measure proposed by the pro-Western government of Prime Minister Ante Marković, which called for a loose confederation of former Yugoslav republics. His decentralization plan included privatization and investment in a free market economy, pegging the Yugoslav dinar to the German mark.[4]

Ricardel and I met with Curtis Kamman, the Principal Deputy Assistant Secretary of State for European Affairs, to discuss US policy toward Yugoslavia. We were concerned that a Belgrade-centric approach would serve as an endorsement of Milošević's "Greater Serbia" and result in the marginalization of the other republics in Yugoslavia and consequent violent conflict. Milošević was an unabashed nationalist who embraced the "historic chance" to right the wrongs of history. He declared, "It is the strong who dictate the borders. We consider the legitimate right of the Serbian people to live in one state. That is our bottom line. And if it should prove necessary to fight, we shall fight, I swear."[5] Ricardel was strongly opposed to the US policy of keeping Yugoslavia whole under any conditions. When Kamman defended Washington's Belgrade-centric approach, Mira tore into him. Kamman was practically trembling by the end of the meeting. Although I always tried to be diplomatic when interacting with US officials, I learned from Ricardel the value of robust advocacy on behalf of a principled position. This lesson would be underscored later through my work with Ambassador Richard C. Holbrooke.

Secretary of State James A. Baker met the collective presidency of Yugoslavia in Belgrade on June 21, 1991. He warned that "secession would have tragic consequences. The United States wants to see this problem solved through dialogue and negotiations, and not through preemptive unilateral action." Baker was emphatic: the leaders of pro-independence republics should not expect recognition from the United States. He famously told them, "We don't have a dog in this fight." Even as Yugoslavia veered toward civil war, the State Department affirmed, "The US continues to support the territorial integrity of Yugoslavia, including the borders of its member republics."[6]

Slovenia's President Milan Kučan rejected the Marković plan, as the plan's fixed exchange rate with the German mark would undervalue the export of Slovenia's agricultural products. Kučan also rejected the Brioni Agreement proposed by the European Community (EC) on July 7, 1991, which called for a ceasefire and a cooling off period.[7]

Slovenia adopted a new constitution and held elections on April 7, 1991, with Kučan's Demos coalition winning 55 percent of the vote. Slovenia's secession marked the beginning of Yugoslavia's dissolution. A ten-day war ensued between the Slovenian National Guard and the troops in the Yugoslav People's Army (JNA), barracked in Ljubljana, Slovenia's capital.

I was deeply involved with events leading to the demise of Yugoslavia. The Congressional Human Rights Foundation was the first US-based organization to call for the recognition of Slovenia and Croatia. For my assistance, Milan Kučan made me an honorary citizen of Slovenia.

Milošević was prepared to lose Slovenia but was determined to "protect 600,000 Serbs who lived in Croatia, where they represented 12 percent of the population." In the spring of 1990, the Congressional Human Rights Foundation hosted Croatia's President Franjo Tudjman on Capitol Hill. Tudjman was the founder of the Croatian Democratic Union, which adopted the insignia of the Ustashe, the red and white checkered flag. To Serbs, the flag was a symbol of Nazi irredentism.

I met Tudjman's ostentatious, long white limousine in front the Longworth House Office Building. He had come to testify before the Helsinki Commission about the looming conflict in Yugoslavia. He described Croatia as a pro-Western, pro-democratic vanguard and asked for Washington's help, warning that the West's failure to support Croatia would result in war that would spread to Bosnia and Herzegovina, where ethnic cleansing would have even greater consequences. As he spoke, I recalled Pero's tale about fratricide between Serbs and Croats during World War II.

Croatia adopted its constitution on June 22, 1990, which caused the Croatian Serbs to declare independence. Paramilitaries erected roadblocks on the road to Knin, capital of the so-called Krajina Serb Republic. During my visit to Croatia in the spring of 1991, I requested a meeting with Milan

Babić, a dentist from Knin, who led the Krajina Serb Republic. He agreed to meet me, but I didn't make it to our meeting. Croatian Serbs had set up checkpoints on the administrative boundaries of Krajina. When I got to the checkpoint, the Serb paramilitaries instructed me to get out of my Croatian government vehicle and get into one of their cars. I refused, explaining that I was a guest of the government. By the time I returned to Zagreb, the press corps had gotten wind of my aborted trip to Knin, and a spray of journalists was waiting. I explained why I refused to travel in a vehicle provided by the Krajina authorities, which would insult Croats with whom I was working. My refusal was an affirmation of Croatia's right to self-determination and a rejection of separatism pursued by Croatian Serbs. Soon after, Croatia declared independence on June 25, 1991; Slovenia also declared independence on that day.

I still believed that dialogue could resolve communal differences. During my trip, I convened Serb and Croat members of the Pakrac town council. Pakrac was an ethnically mixed community in a volatile part of Croatia called Western Slavonia, a tinderbox of ethnic tensions. Serbs sat at one end of the table and Croats at the other in a smoke-filled room. They argued about personnel for local security, school curriculum, the script of educational texts, street names, and signposts in the town. Instead of reducing communal tensions, our discussion exacerbated hostilities. An hour after we adjourned, a bomb exploded near the town hall.

In October 1991, Congressman James Sensenbrenner (R-WI) and I went to Vukovar in eastern Croatia, which was besieged by the JNA.[8] The JNA was joined by various paramilitary forces from Serbia during the siege, which lasted eighty-seven days from August to November 1991. We interviewed Croatian fighters and civilians in the Vukovar Hospital and issued reports to international media from the front line. We escaped Vukovar during Serbia's shelling of the city, dodging mortar fire on our way out of town.

On November 20, 1991, the JNA overwhelmed the Croatian National Guard and occupied Vukovar. Although the European Community Monitoring Mission and the International Committee of the Red Cross (ICRC) negotiated the evacuation of Vukovar, about three hundred civilians and defenders were detained by Serb forces at the Vukovar Hospital. In violation of the agreement with the ICRC, monitors were denied access to the hospital. Detainees were evacuated to the Ovčara farm south of the city, where they were beaten before the JNA withdrew, leaving Serbian paramilitaries in charge. Later, the prisoners were transported to a site with large, prepared trenches, where they were executed and buried in a mass grave. I was horrified to learn what had happened.

. . . . .

Yugoslavia was unraveling. Instead of a managed deconstruction, the process grew increasingly violent. The Arbitration Commission of the Conference on Yugoslavia was endorsed by the European Community Council of Ministers and chaired by Robert Badinter, the President of France's Constitutional Council. It developed criteria for independence of Yugoslavia's six republics that were seeking to exercise their right to self-determination. In February 1992, Haris Silajdžić, Bosnia's foreign minister, called me from a phone booth at the Mayflower Hotel in Washington, DC; Ricardel had given him my number. I met Haris right away and listened carefully to his dire warning. "Milošević's project was to create a greater Serbia from the ashes of the former Yugoslavia," he warned. "[Serbia's] ethnic nationalism would destroy Bosnia's tradition of multiethnic tolerance and interreligious understanding."[9]

In downtown Sarajevo, Orthodox and Catholic churches, a mosque, and a synagogue had stood in close proximity for centuries. These symbols of tolerance and diversity were targeted by Serbian artillery and snipers bombing these religious institutions and shooting innocent civilians from the hills above the city. With violence flaring, the EC recognized "Bosnia and Herzegovina" as an independent country on April 6, 1992, followed the next day by the United States. Bosnian Serbs responded by declaring an independent Republika Srpska with Pale as its capital. The ensuing conflict was not a civil war. Milošević instructed the JNA to consolidate control over Serb-populated regions in Bosnia and Croatia, connecting them through a corridor to Serbian lands across the Drina River in Serbia.

Radovan Karadžić, a demented Serbian psychiatrist who headed the self-declared Republika Srpska, coined the term "ethnic cleansing" as a brand for his brutality and social engineering.[10] Ratko Mladić, a former general in the JNA, commanded forces that implemented Karadžić's plan through displacement, mass murder, rape, torture, and widespread atrocities. News surfaced of Serb-run concentration camps in Trnopolje,

Omarska, and Manjača. "Their stares burn, they speak only with their ter-rified silence, and eyes inflamed with the articulation of stark, undiluted, desolate fear, without hope."[11]

As a Jew, I was stunned and appalled to see images of emaciated Bosniak prisoners, their ribs protruding, detained behind the barbed wire in con-centration camps in the heart of Europe. Not only Jews, but also many Americans were shocked at Serbia's death camps and campaign of ethnic cleansing. Elie Wiesel, an Auschwitz survivor, spoke for many of us when, at the opening of the US Holocaust Memorial Museum in Washington, DC on April 22, 1993, he declared, "For the dead and the living, we must bear witness. For not only are we responsible for the memories of the dead, we are also responsible for what we are doing with those memo-ries." Then he turned and addressed President Bill Clinton directly: "And, Mr. President, I cannot not tell you something. I have been in the former Yugoslavia last fall. I cannot sleep since for what I have seen. As a Jew I am saying that we must do something to stop the bloodshed in that coun-try! People fight each other and children die. Why? Something, anything must be done."[12]

Wiesel's call to action was inspirational. His lofty rhetoric and down-to-earth humanity set him apart from other Nobel laureates and humanitar-ian luminaries. When Wiesel spoke, he touched lives, including mine. I was honored when he asked me to serve as Executive Director of the Elie Wiesel Foundation for Humanity, where I worked from 2001 to 2004.

My involvement in Bosnia deepened as the situation worsened. The Bos-nian Foreign Minister introduced me to President Alija Izetbegović, who was accompanied by Bosnia's Permanent Representative to the United Nations (UN), Mohamed Sacirbey, with whom I collaborated on a num-ber of political and humanitarian initiatives. I held a fundraising event at my home for War Child, an organization providing music therapy to trau-matized youth in the former Yugoslavia. Opera star, Luciano Pavarotti, was the guest of honor. I introduced Sacirbey as "Mo Sacirbey" and told the audience that my great-grandfather was also called Mo, but it was short for Moses not Mohamed. We are all God's children.

The UN Human Rights Commission (UNHRC) convened a special ses-sion in Geneva. Bosnia and Herzegovina was a new country; its officials were learning on the job. After making sure I was in compliance with the

Foreign Agents Registration Act, I organized a series of tutorials for Sacir-bey about the UN's human rights mechanisms. Frankly, I was no expert, but had experience that was useful to the Bosnian government.

Sacirbey asked if I would go to Geneva as a member of the Bosnian del-egation. Eager to play a constructive role, I showed up at the Palais des Nations and took credentials as a pro-bono member of the Bosnian dele-gation. Bosnia's Vice President Ejup Ganić asked me to draft his remarks, and he gave a powerful presentation to the plenary. The ambassador from Belgrade responded to Ganić by denying Serbia's crimes against humani-ty. John Bolton, the US Assistant Secretary of State for International Or-ganizations heading the US delegation, was incensed and held up a copy of *Newsweek* with a front-page photo of shirtless and emaciated Bosnians in Serb-controlled concentration camps. He shouted, "This is genocide."[13]

Beyond helping to draft Ganić's remarks, I coordinated meetings and messages with Bolton and J. Kenneth Blackwell, a friend who was the US Ambassador to the UN Human Rights Commission. Ganić, Silaj-džić, and Sacirbey viewed the Special Session as a success. The UNHRC overwhelmingly passed a resolution condemning events in Bosnia and appointing a Special Rapporteur to investigate human rights abuses on the territory of the former Yugoslavia. The stage was set for the next phase of international diplomacy.

· · · · ·

As the spiral of deadly violence worsened, the UN and EC convened a summit of world leaders at the Queen Elizabeth Conference Center in London. UN Secretary General Boutros Boutros-Ghali and British Prime Minister John Major co-chaired the London Conference on behalf of the UN and the EC, which was held on August 26-27, 1992. Similar to my role in Geneva, I joined the Bosnian delegation as an unpaid adviser.

Fifty heads of state attended the London Conference. They made speech-es on the first day, while the Bosnian delegation engaged in bilateral meet-ings to discuss strategy and developments on the ground. I coordinated the scheduling and attended many of these meetings. On the 26th, we met Acting Secretary of State Lawrence Eagleburger for breakfast at the Churchill Hotel where the US delegation was staying. Earlier in his career, Eagleburger had been posted in Belgrade as the US Ambassador to Yugoslavia. As we entered the private dining room, Eagleburger was fastening his tie. "Sorry," he told the Bosnians. "I'm still getting dressed. Silajdžić responded, "As long as you're not getting undressed," lightening the mood.

We met John Major the next day before his remarks to open the conference. Major warned Serbia's President Milošević and Yugoslavia's Prime Minister Milan Panić: "If we do not get cooperation, the pressure will inexorably increase. Condemnation. Isolation. Parties who stand in the way of agreement can expect even tougher sanctions, even more rigorously policed. No trade. No aid. No international recognition. Economic, cultural, political and diplomatic isolation."[14]

At midday, Eagleburger and Major asked the Bosnians to meet them in a caucus room adjoining the plenary hall. Eagleburger started by heralding the "special relationship" between the US and the UK. He promised they would work together to sanction Serbia, stop the artillery shelling of Sarajevo, and provide emergency humanitarian assistance via corridors to besieged civilians. From the outset, they made it clear that military action was not on the table.

Silajdžić was incensed at their proposal. "These are just words. We have no guarantees," he protested. "My people are being killed every day."[15] Major leaned forward and said in an earnest tone, "You have my word of honor. If the shelling of Sarajevo does not stop in thirty days, the Royal Air Force will be overhead."[16] Other than the Bosnians, I was the only witness to his false promise.

We emerged from the meeting and headed to the coffee bar where I found myself standing shoulder to shoulder with Radovan Karadžić, Europe's most wanted criminal. I asked, "Are you Dr. Radovan Karadžić?" "I am," he replied. I introduced myself and said, "It is my understanding that you are responsible for the worst genocide in Europe since the Nazis. If you are behind this ethnic cleansing, then you should stand trial before an international tribunal and spend the rest of your life in prison." He was flabbergasted; no one dared speak to him like this. "Who are you?" he asked. "What gives you the right?"

Then Karadžić threatened to kill me. "One night you'll wake up with cold steel on your throat," he warned. "I'll kill you and your children too." He had dull, lifeless eyes like a shark sizing up its prey. Cursing in Serbian, he summoned one of his henchmen. Unshaved and stinking of alcohol, the obese bodyguard got in my face and pushed me up against the wall. I was terrified. I had gratuitously confronted the world's most notorious war criminal. I had to control my fear and maintain a calm demeanor although my heart was pumping wildly. Karadžić's power came from terrorizing people. Smiling and looking him directly in the eye, I said coolly, "You know, Radovan, there is nothing you can do to hurt me, and if you try, you'd only hurt yourself." My confrontation with Karadžić occurred in plain sight. Ibrahim Rugova, the President of Kosovo, saw everything. There were many other witnesses. I contacted Scotland Yard to report the incident.

Jeremy Greenstock, a deputy to British Foreign Secretary Douglas Hurd, approached Izetbegović with bad news. The Serbs had threatened to walk out of the London Conference unless a paragraph identifying them as the aggressor and enumerating their crimes was removed from the draft final statement of the London Conference. Izetbegović insisted that the text of the conference resolution include condemnation of the Serbs. In response, Greenstock suggested that the paragraph be removed from the text and Major read it instead. I pulled Izetbegović aside and reminded him that the conference was not about placating the Serbs. I pointed out that in its current form it did not go far enough. It failed to threaten military action and lacked an enforcement mechanism. Furthermore, the resolution was silent on the arms embargo, which barred Bosnia from acquiring weapons to defend itself. When the arms embargo was imposed by the international community on September 26, 1991, the JNA gave huge stockpiles of weapons to Serbian paramilitaries, locking in their military advantage. Much of our advocacy on Capitol Hill focused on lifting the arms embargo so the Bosnians could exercise their right to self-defense. If the world would not defend Bosnia, then at least Bosnia should have the tools to defend itself.

Izetbegović and his team had withdrawn to a caucus room to discuss the threatened Serb walkout. UN Secretary General Boutros-Ghali and his deputy, former US Secretary of State Cyrus Vance, came to brief Izetbegović on the text. Their draft dropped language accusing the Serbs. It did, however, call for the establishment of a no-fly zone and the sequestering of heavy weapons around Sarajevo and other municipalities. Sanctions on Serbia would be tightened and monitors positioned along the Danube

River. Humanitarian corridors manned by thousands of UN peacekeepers would ensure the delivery of food and humanitarian supplies. The UN would consider establishing a special tribunal for prosecuting war crimes in the former Yugoslavia. A framework for peace talks would be established in Geneva, addressing technical issues arising in the negotiations.

Boutros-Ghali leaned toward Izetbegović and implored, "Mr. President, this is your best and last chance for peace. What is your decision?" Izetbegović objected, "There is no timetable—no guarantee." He asked for time to consider their proposal.[17] The Bosnians debated the offer. Silajdžić and Sacirbey opposed it. Overcome with the stress of the situation, Sabina Izetbegović, the president's daughter, was crying in a corner of the room.

I went to Eagleburger and told him the Bosnians were prepared to walk out unless the resolution clearly identified Serbs as the aggressor. He summoned John Major to hear what I had to say. Shuttle diplomacy went on for some time as I liaised between Izetbegović and the world's most powerful personalities. I told Eagleburger that the Bosnians were about to go downstairs to the press center and blast the conference co-chairmen for betrayal. I did not act on instructions from Izetbegović; I was acting on my own in what I thought was Bosnia's best interest.

Boutros-Ghali and Vance came to the room and tried to enter. I literally put my foot in the door, barring their entry and told them that the Bosnians needed more time. When Boutros-Ghali was finally allowed to enter, he asked: "What is your decision, Mr. President?" After a long silence, Izetbegović agreed to the deal, which became the Vance-Owen Plan. It was named after Cyrus Vance and David Owen, who later became the British Foreign Secretary.[18] The US disappeared during negotiations, ceding leadership to others.

The Serbian delegation celebrated the outcome, which did not threaten the use of force. The Serbs had achieved their primary goal: to prevent a military response. Measures in the Vance-Owen plan proved ineffective at ending the war, which lasted three more bloody, violent, and horrific years. With hindsight, I criticized myself for supporting the deal. I was star-struck being the center of attention with so many prominent members of the international community. I trusted Eagleburger and wanted US diplomacy to succeed. I misunderstood his motivation. Eagleburger and Major wanted to manage the conflict, not end it.

UN Security Council Resolution 819 was adopted on April 16, 1993. It established "safe areas" in Srebrenica. A short time later, Resolution 824 extended the safe areas to other besieged communities: Sarajevo, Tuzla, Žepa, Goražde, and Bihać. UN claims of protection were merely rhetorical. The UN Protection Force (UNPROFOR) lacked the capacity and the political will to protect the safe zones.

I remained in close contact with Bosnian leaders, especially Silajdžić, who later became prime minister. I coordinated outreach and advocacy with Bosnia's ambassador to the United States, Sven Alkalaj, a Sephardic Jew with whom I grew close over the years. In February 1994, I visited Sarajevo at Silajdžić's invitation. Sarajevo was under siege and was being shelled regularly; I flew to Sarajevo on an old Russian Tupelov plane contracted by the UN to bring people in and out. UN flights were called "Maybe Airlines" because their schedule was so unpredictable.

In addition to seeing Izetbegović, Ganić, and other old friends, I met Jakob Finci, President of the Jewish Community of Sarajevo. He asked me to convey a message to Alkalaj. "Tell him he hasn't paid his dues [to the synagogue]." Finci was a hero. His charity, La Benevolencija, helped deliver medical supplies to the Bosnian population. It was the only local organization delivering humanitarian relief on a non-sectarian basis. La Benevolencija managed to get people through the Bosnian Serb checkpoints by organizing mixed convoys of Bosnian Muslim, Croat, and Serb families. Finci also led an effort to rebuild the Jewish cemetery on the hill above Sarajevo. With its sightlines of the city, the cemetery was occupied by Bosnian Serbs during the war as a strategic post for snipers targeting civilians.[19]

Peter Jennings of ABC News happened to be in Sarajevo when the main market in Sarajevo was bombed, killing sixty people and injuring two hundred. His passionate reporting underscored the desperate situation in Bosnia, and the need to "do something."

I had planned to leave Sarajevo two days later, but Maybe Airlines was shut down due to Serbian military activity. The only way out of Sarajevo was via a winding road over Mt. Igman, which ran close to Serbian lines. I arranged a ride with Victor Jakovich, the US Ambassador to Bosnia. We set off in a convoy of three vehicles, armed guards in front and behind us. Mt. Igman was a treacherous route in the best of times.

We made it to Croatia on that trip, but others were less fortunate. On August 20, 1995, a vehicle slipped off the mountain road, plunged down a steep ravine and burst into flames, killing Deputy Assistant Secretary of State Robert Frasure, Deputy Assistant Secretary of Defense for European Affairs and NATO Policy Joseph Kruzel, Nelson Drew from the National Security Council, and a French soldier; two other US officials and two French UN soldiers were injured. President Clinton described the wreck as a "tragic accident."[20]

Richard Holbrooke, who had been traveling in a vehicle just ahead of the one that plummeted down the mountain, was profoundly affected by the loss of his close colleagues. He had been appointed Assistant Secretary of State for European Affairs and the point man for Bosnian negotiations. Deeply perturbed, he redoubled diplomatic efforts to resolve the war.[21]

By July 1995, the situation in the UN safe areas was deteriorating. The resolution establishing safe areas mandated "all necessary means, including the use of force." Mladić was determined to teach Western powers a lesson and brutally attacked Srebrenica, capturing and executing more than eight thousand Bosniak men and teenage boys in only three days. He also attacked the Muslim enclaves of Žepa and Goražde. Mladić wanted to break the back of Bosnian resistance, humiliate the international community, seize Sarajevo, and create facts on the ground that would end the war in Serbia's favor.

I was clamoring for US intervention, partly out of guilt for the role I had played at the London Conference. I understood that Izetbegović had made the decision to agree to the Vance-Owen Plan, yet I wondered if he would have done so without my urging. I supported efforts by Ricardel and others, calling for military action. UN and European officials resisted, using the rationale that intervention would undermine the UN's claim of neutrality. Pinprick air strikes in late May 1995 by the Serb military underscored the limitations of the UN, resulting in nearly four hundred peacekeepers being taken hostage. The United Nations Protection Force (UNPROFOR) had become an obstacle to concerted action. Dutch peacekeepers helped evacuate Muslims from Srebrenica, participating in ethnic cleansing.

The US did not have troops on the ground, which limited its leverage. Going into an election year, Clinton was reluctant to insist on the withdrawal of UN peacekeepers, which would require more troops to safeguard their departure. Srebrenica changed Clinton's calculus. After dithering for years while looking to Europe for leadership, the US finally adopted an "endgame strategy" after the massacre. It would recognize Bosnia's sovereignty and territorial integrity within its existing borders. It would divide Bosnia and Herzegovina into two entities—a Bosnian Serb entity and a Muslim-Croat federation, with federation territory accounting for at least 51 percent of the total. If the Serbs rejected an agreement, then the United States would insist on lifting the arms embargo, providing weapons and training to the Bosnians and launching air strikes against Serb forces. If the Bosnian government rejected it, the US would adopt a policy of "lift and leave"—lifting the arms embargo and leaving the federation to fight it out.[22]

After Srebrenica, US war planes flying under a NATO banner supported Bosnian ground troops to push Serbian forces out of territory they had conquered. The US turned a blind eye as weapons from the Middle East were smuggled to Bosnian fighters via Croatia, turning the tide of battle. The Clinton administration would no longer tolerate further vacillating, negotiating with European officials, or navigating the UN bureaucracy. The US would lead negotiations at Wright-Patterson Air Force Base near Dayton, Ohio. Holbrooke brought together the leaders of Bosnia, Serbia, and Croatia for one last-ditch mediation.

Silajdžić flew in for the negotiations. We met in a holding room on the tarmac at Kennedy Airport before he was whisked away to a US Air Force plane and flown to Dayton. Negotiations were long and arduous. I was regularly on the phone with Silajdžić to discuss developments. Of course, his calls were being monitored. US officials correctly concluded that we had a close relationship, and I was contacted by US Ambassador to the UN Madeleine Albright and Holbrooke asking me to influence Silajdžić. I did weigh in with Silajdžić when doing so was advantageous to the Bosnians. I was not a US official and acted in accordance with my conscience.

The General Framework Agreement for Peace in Bosnia and Herzegovina, also known as the Dayton Peace Agreement (DPA) or the Dayton Accords, was finalized on November 21, 1995.[23] It granted Bosnia and Herzegovina the independence for which it had fought so hard and spilled so much blood. I was attending a dinner for the International Rescue Committee when Holbrooke flew from Dayton to New York. He entered the room to a boisterous standing ovation, announcing that the war was over . The DPA ending Bosnia's war was signed in Paris on December 14, 1995.

I urged Holbrooke to include Kosovo in his negotiations. Rallied by Congressman Eliot Engel (Democrat, New York), Albanian-Americans gathered at the gates of Wright-Patterson demanding that the Dayton Accords address Kosovo's status. However, Holbrooke wanted to deal with one conflict at a time and refused to expand negotiations. The Dayton Agreement was a huge victory for Bosnia and Holbrooke, ending three and half years of slaughter. Resolving the Kosovo issue would have to wait.

Notes

1   Michael Dobbs, "President Tito Dies," *Washington Post,* May 15, 1980, https:// www.washingtonpost.com/archive/politics/1980/05/05/president-tito-dies/0df00f64-f525-4783-8a0c-2af1b92b2f9a/.

2   *The 1974 Constitution,* Socialist Federal Republic of Yugoslavia, https://www.worldstatesmen.org/Yugoslavia-Constitution1974.pdf (accessed May 10, 2020).

3   R.W. Apple Jr., "Conflict in the Balkans, Few Choices, Fewer Hopes, Bush, under Pressure, Now Talks about Guns," *New York Times,* August 7, 1992, https:// www.nytimes.com/1992/08/07/world/conflict-balkans-few-choices-fewer-hopes-bush-under-pressure-now-talks-about.html?n=Top/Reference/Times%20Topics/Subjects/P/Presidential%20Elections%20(US)&pagewanted=print.

4   Interview by the author with Mira Radielović (Ricardel), November 23, 2010.

5   Sonja Biserko, ed., "Kosovo: A Chain of Causes," Report of the Helsinki Committee for Human Rights in Serbia, Belgrade, Serbia, October 2004.

6   Information provided by Vehbi Bajrami, Editor-in-chief of *Illyria,* June 28, 1991.

7   Blaine Harden, "Yugoslav Crisis Pact Sets EC Involvement in Country's Future," *Washington Post,* July 9, 1991, https://www.washingtonpost.com/archive/politics/1991/07/09/yugoslav-crisis-pact-sets-ec-involvement-in-countrys-future/1eb28564-5ff3-4499-a3fe-15e8d64082a0/.

8   "Croatia Remembers Vukovar Victims on 28th Anniversary," *Croatia Week,* November 17, 2019, https://www.croatiaweek.com/croatia-remembers-vukovar-victims-on-28th-anniversary/.

9   Interview with Haris Silajdžić by the author, August 27, 1992.

10 Encyclopedia Britannica, https://www.britannica.com/biography/Radovan-Karadzic (accessed March 22, 2020).

11 Ed Vulliamy, *Seasons in Hell: Understanding Bosnia's War* (New York: St. Martin's Press, 1994).

12 https://www.ushmm.org/information/about-the-museum/mission-and-history/wiesel (accessed April 4, 2020).

13 *The Washington Post,* August 14, 2005, https://www.washingtonpost.com/archive/entertainment/books/2005/08/14/on-april-22-1993-elie-wiesel/c3d51b35-9e4b-456d-8321-bf117d83fb4d/.

14 Allan Little and Laura Silber, *Yugoslavia: Death of a Nation* (New York: Penguin, 1997), 260.

15 Interview by the author with Haris Silajdžić, September 22, 2010.

16 Conversation between Alija Izetbegović and John Major on August 26, 1992. Confirmed by the author during a discussion with Haris Silajdžić, September 22, 2010.

17 David L. Phillips, "Looking Evil in the Eye," *Dani Magazine,* January 1, 2010.

18 *Encyclopedia Britannica,* https://www.britannica.com/topic/Vance-Owen-plan (accessed March 22, 2020).

19 Jakob Finci, "The Savior of Sarajevo Barred from Office for Being a Jew," *Jewish Wikipedia,* http://www.jewishwikipedia.info/finci.html (accessed April 4, 2020).

20 "U.S. Officials Robert Frasure and Joseph Kruzel Die," *Washington Post,* https://www.washingtonpost.com/archive/local/1995/08/21/us-officials-robert-frasure-and-joseph-kruzel-die/e1e670ad-e6b0-482c-ae1f-86abdaa32821/ (accessed May 10, 2020).

21 Tracy Wilkinson, "Accident in Bosnia Kills 3 U.S. Envoys: Balkans: Vehicle Carrying Diplomats Plunges from Mountain. Fatalities Include Washington's Point Man in Effort to Resolve Conflict. Clinton Vows to Press Ahead," *Los Angeles Times,* August 20, 1995, https://www.latimes.com/archives/la-xpm-1995-08-20-mn-37150-story.html.

22 Ivo H. Daalder, "Decision to Intervene: How the War in Bosnia Ended," *Brookings,* December 1, 1988, https://www.brookings.edu/articles/decision-to-intervene-how-the-war-in-bosnia-ended/.

23 *Encyclopedia Britannica,* https://www.britannica.com/event/Dayton-Accords (accessed March 22, 2020).

CHAPTER 4

LIBERATING KOSOVO

Slobodan Milošević was riding high after the Dayton Peace Agreement. The Bosnian Serb delegation in Dayton was a coalition of personalities without the authority to make a deal or implement an agreement. Ambassador Richard C. Holbrooke, the principal negotiator, told me that he knew peace was possible when the Bosnian Serbs designated Milošević as their representative. Milošević, the original sponsor of the Serb ethnic cleansing campaign, was seated alongside Alija Izetbegović and Franjo Tudjman at the signing ceremony in Paris on December 14, 1995.[1]

On behalf of the Council on Foreign Relations (CFR), I visited Belgrade and the Western Balkans in early December of 1995. CFR created a task force on the Western Balkans, which was chaired by Seymour Topping, former managing editor of *The New York Times*. I was hired as project director. During the task force's meeting with Milošević in the presidential palace, Milošević made his case regarding Kosovo, an overwhelmingly ethnic Albanian region that had been integrated into the Federal Republic of Yugoslavia (FRY) and neglected by the international community during the dissolution of Yugoslavia. Milošević asserted, "Kosovo is the heart of Serbia. For every Serb, Kosovo is a holy thing. The chair of our Patriarch is in Kosovo." He disparaged the Kosovo Liberation Army (KLA). "Separatists are killing people, raping children, burning monasteries, digging up graves. There is no retaliation. We recognize these are acts of extremists." He called them "classic criminals, murderers, and crooks." Milošević cynically asserted that the KLA was sponsored by doormen in New York.[2]

I asked Milošević if the United States could set up a liaison office of the US Information Agency (USIA) in Prishtina, Kosovo. He sneered contemptuously, "You Americans can build your library wherever you want."[3] I reported the discussion to Rudolph Perina, the Principal Deputy Assistant Secretary of State working on the Balkans, and then to Holbrooke, who immediately grasped the significance of Milošević's concession. A US flag flying in downtown Prishtina was a big deal. Although Dayton did not address the situation in Kosovo, sustainable peace in southeast Europe would require resolution of the Kosovo question.

Professor Sami Repishti, an Albanian-American scholar, invoked Winston Churchill: "The Balkans produce more history than it can consume." Serbs cite the Battle of Kosovo on June 28, 1389, as the root cause of conflict. That day, Prince Lazar and his forces were defeated by a much stronger Ottoman Army at the Field of Blackbirds in Kosovo Polje. More than a fight for territory, it was a battle between two civilizations: one Christian and European and the other Islamic and Asiatic. Serbs believe in the divine origin of Serbian rule. Artemije, the former Serbian archbishop of Raska and Prizren, called Kosovo our "Jerusalem." He explained, "It is the holiest and most important part of Serbia, the cradle of our spirituality, our culture and our statehood. Kosovo is our inalienable identity."[4]

After World War II, Kosovo was inundated with Slav colonizers who expelled tens of thousands of Kosovo Albanians. Yugoslavia's President Tito would later reverse anti-Albanian policies, not out of love for Albanians, but to keep Serbian power in check. The 1974 constitution gave the provinces of Kosovo and Vojvodina many of the same prerogatives as the six republics, except the right to secede. With Tito's death in 1980, Yugoslavia became a loose-knit coalition of communist parties and rival security structures.[5]

Kosovo Albanians, numbering about 1.5 million, rejected Kosovo's status as a minority province within Serbia. Milošević's rise to power accentuated and manipulated historic grievances, drawing on Serbian nationalism. When ethnic Albanian police used force to disperse a riotous Serbian crowd, Milošević delivered an incendiary speech to Kosovo Serbs on April 24, 1987. "They will never do this to you again. No one will ever have the right to beat you."[6]

A cult of personality arose around Milošević. At his direction, the Serbian Assembly prepared amendments to Serbia's constitution, repealing Kosovo's autonomy within Serbia. He also launched a cultural war against Albanians: place names were changed to Serbian using the Serbian alphabet. The Kosovo Academy of Sciences, the Kosovo Ballet Company, and the Kosovo Theater Group were closed. Mandatory family planning was introduced for ethnic Albanians to restrict their large families. Radio-TV Prishtina and the Albanian language newspaper, *Rjlindija*, were banned. Quotas were implemented to limit the number of Albanians who could receive higher education.[7]

Milošević threw down the gauntlet on the six-hundred-year anniversary of the Battle of Kosovo, addressing a seething crowd of Serbs in Kosovo Polje: "The Kosovo heroism does not allow us to forget that at one time we were the brave and dignified who went into battle undefeated. Six centuries later, again we are in battles and quarrels. They are not armed battles, though such things should not be excluded."[8]

Battle lines were drawn, but Ibrahim Rugova, President of the Democratic League of Kosovo (LDK), did not take the bait. Rugova was a Gandhian-like figure who guided Kosovo's non-violent resistance against Serbian rule. He turned the other cheek when Serbia adopted a new constitution declaring that Kosovo was an inalienable part of Serbia, revoking Kosovo's autonomy, and expanding the powers of the Serbian president.

I first met Rugova at an LDK rally in Slovenia in the fall of 1988 and we were in regular contact until his death from cancer ten years later. Rugova and I became fast friends through the struggle for Kosovo rights and independence. We met as many as forty times in Prishtina and Washington. I often visited Kosovo, sometimes flying to Belgrade and driving south, other times walking across the border from Macedonia. We also met frequently in Washington, where I helped organize his visits and appointments with US officials. Rugova always wore a signature silk scarf with paisley designs. He was a chain smoker, and his fingers were a burnt orange from holding a cigarette. He spoke halting English, so we communicated in French. Beginning in 1988, Kosovo was a major activity of mine; Albanian-Americans generously supportedthe Congressional Human Rights Foundation.

Kosovo did not have an embassy in Washington, DC. Instead, it planned to establish "Kosovo House" as a cultural and political liaison office. However, in-fighting among Albanians prevented this plan from being realized. I did much of the work that Kosovo's ambassador would have done, if they had diplomatic representation. Dr. Alush Gashi, a senior LDK official and close adviser to Rugova, was my point of contact. Whenever I crossed the border from Macedonia, he was always there. Whenever I needed to coordinate activities, Alush was reliable.

One of the first big events I helped organize in Washington was a Congressional briefing on human rights in Yugoslavia. Congressman Tom Lantos (D-CA) invited Rugova to address the Congressional Human Rights

Caucus on April 29, 1990. Sami Repishti also testified. In addition, Do-brica Ćosić, representing the Serbian Academy of Sciences, and Bishop Artemije attended. Congressional events are open to the public. Senator Bob Dole (R-KS) told the Albanian-Americans, whom Holbrooke called the "AAs," "to show up with a lot of people and you'll get respect." Bruno Selimaj, a restaurateur from New York, rented fifty-six buses to transport the AAs to Washington. Jim Xhema, a builder from Connecticut who comes from Preshevo, an ethnic Albanian region in Serbia, was close to Dole. Xhema gleefully recalled, "There was a line of Albanians a mile long waiting to get in the hearing room." In addition to Dole, Senators D'Amato, Pressler, and Kennedy came over from the Senate side.[9] The hearing room was packed and so tense that I feared a riot. Capitol Police escorted witnesses to and from the hearing room.

I was Lantos's point person with the Albanian-American community. Xhema was the ringleader; Repishti was the public intellectual. Other prominent Albanian-Americans included Harry Bajraktari and Ekrem Bardha. Mira Ricardel, Dole's staff member, worked the issue and we interacted extensively on all matters concerning Yugoslavia. She made Kosovo a bipartisan cause, involving Democratic Senators Claiborne Pell (D-RI), Joe Lieberman (D-CT), and Dennis DeConcini (D-AZ). Bajraktari worked with Representative Eliot Engel, who established the Albanian Issues Caucus. Ekrem Bardha, a hairdresser from Detroit who purchased a Mc-Donald's franchise and ended up owning more than twenty McDonald's restaurants, delivered Bill Broomfield (R-Mich.) and Ben Gilman (R-NY), chairman of House International Relations Committee. Bajraktari and other Albanian-Americans invested in members of Congress by raising money for their campaigns. In 2004, Holbrooke and I met Bajraktari and about twenty AAs at my home to plan a fundraising event for John Kerry's presidential campaign. General Wesley Clark and Eliot Engel attended. The event was a huge success and raised more than $500,000.

In addition to his political interests, Bajraktari was also a humanitarian. After NATO's intervention in Kosovo in 1999, I arranged for the American Jewish World Service to give one hundred computers to the school in Peja. We went together to deliver the computers to the excited Kosovo students.

· · · · ·

Rugova and his delegation attended the London Conference on Former Yugoslavia in August 1992.[10] I scheduled a meeting between Rugova and Ambassador Larry Eagleburger, the Acting Secretary of State, who had previously served as US ambassador to Yugoslavia. Eagleburger made it clear that the US was concerned about conflict escalation in Kosovo but was presently focused on the war in Bosnia. To placate Rugova, Eagleburger reaffirmed US support for the "outer wall of sanctions" on Serbia. The outer wall was part of the strategy to isolate Serbia by prohibiting membership in international organizations such as the United Nations (UN), the Organization for Security and Cooperation in Europe, and international financial institutions, such as the World Bank, the International Monetary Fund, and the European Bank for Reconstruction and Development. Rugova, Gashi, and the entire Kosovo delegation had witnessed my previous confrontation with Radovan Karadžić. Going toe-to-toe with Europe's worst war criminal and Milošević's genocidal proxy enhanced my standing with Kosovo Albanians.

Kosovo simmered during the Bosnian war. Albanians sought an invitation to Dayton but were excluded. Engel went to Dayton for a public demonstration organized by Bajraktari and the AAs. Ambassador Morton I. Abramowitz, founder of the Bosnia Action Council, explained: "We're addicted to solving one problem at a time. Leaving Kosovo off the agenda was a very practical decision. People are very practical in democracies. In the end, we had to fight again because we didn't solve Kosovo [at Dayton]."[11] After Dayton, European Union Member States tried to ignore the outer wall of sanctions. Many recognized FRY in accordance with their respective national procedures. Only US insistence prevented total normalization.

Kosovo Albanians increasingly questioned Rugova's strategy of non-violence. Discredited by his exclusion from Dayton, Rugova lost influence. Radicalized Kosovo Albanians founded the KLA in 1996. According to Jakup Krasniqi, a founder of the KLA, "Leaving Kosovo in Yugoslavia was a compromise to get Serbia's cooperation on Bosnia. Relying on Milošević to implement the Dayton Accords was a mistake."[12] Failure to address conditions in Kosovo not only exacerbated problems on the ground, but also diminished America's influence.

Opening the US Information Agency (USIA) Office in Prishtina was a visible sign of US support and confirmation of the LDK's internationalization strategy, but it was not enough. According to Albin Kurti, a student activist who had been jailed by the Serbian authorities for on-campus activism and would become prime minister in 2020, "Defeat of the Yugoslav Armed Forces (VJ) in Croatia and Bosnia showed that [Serbs] could be beaten. The myth of the Yugoslav Army was burst." He continued, "Even Montenegro was talking about fighting Serbia. Every Slavic Republic had challenged Milošević, but the Albanians had not."[13] Submission was prohibited by the Code of Lek, which requires Albanians to resist their oppressor.

Chiefs from the Drenica Valley organized self-defense groups and vowed to fight for Kosovo's freedom. Beginning in February 1996, they targeted police stations across Kosovo. The KLA rejected the LDK's "internal regime" and announced a guerilla campaign to liberate Kosovo. Rugova denied the KLA's existence, insisting it was a hoax designed by Serb security forces to discredit him and justify a crackdown.[14] After the USIA Office was opened, we focused on developing confidence-building measures to calm the situation.

I went to Rome and met Monsignor Vincenzo Paglia of the Community of Sant'Egidio. Paglia was mediating a dialogue between the LDK and the government of Serbia on normalizing Kosovo's education system. The education agreement was announced on September 1, 1996. It provided for the unconditional return of Albanians to their schools and resumption of classes at the University of Prishtina. The LDK heralded the education agreement, as "the first step towards a comprehensive solution to the Kosovo issue."[15] With US officials, I explored ways that Washington could provide expertise, materials, or financing to help implement the agreement. My cooperation with Holbrooke put me in a position to more fully involve US officials.

The education agreement languished, resulting in a confrontation between 20,000 students and Serbian riot police. As people lost faith in Rugova's leadership, Holbrooke brokered a face-to-face meeting between Rugova and Milošević at the home of Richard C. Miles, the chargé d'affaires at the US Embassy in Belgrade in May 1998. According to Miles, "We were pleased the meeting took place, but it just didn't work. The split was so clear and both sides were too far apart."[16] Serbian media portrayed Rugova as weak and submissive, worsening Rugova's standing with Kosovo Albanians and fueling the KLA's rise.

Kosovo Albanians were shocked when Ambassador Robert S. Gelbard, Special Representative of the President and Secretary of State for Implementation of the Dayton Peace Agreement, called the KLA a terrorist organization during a press conference in Belgrade.[17] Breaking with US policy, Gelbard was reacting to the KLA's attack on Serbian villages in Kosovo and roadblocks the KLA set up across Kosovo. Gelbard was a highly accomplished US diplomat, experienced in dealing with unsavory characters and international criminals. He had previously headed the State Department's Bureau of International Narcotics and Law Enforcement, nicknamed the Bureau of "Drugs and Thugs." According to Gelbard, "I know a terrorist when I see one and these men are terrorists." He called the KLA an Islamic terror group after the US embassies in Kenya and Tanzania were bombed.

Hashim Thaçi, the KLA spokesman who would become Kosovo's President, said the terrorist label was "coordinated with Rugova and Milošević to discredit the KLA."[18] During a meeting between Milošević and Gelbard in mid-March 1998, Gelbard showed Milošević photos of mutilated Albanian women and children. He also provided Milošević with an unflattering article in the *Financial Times* comparing him to Saddam Hussein.

Gelbard's relations soured with Belgrade. The KLA and LDK also lost faith in Gelbard. I asked Rugova to write Secretary of State Madeleine Albright to request that Holbrooke replace Gelbard as special envoy. Execution of the letter was coordinated by Sami Repishti, who provided my draft to Rugova. Rugova sent the letter to Albright's fax number on March 16, 1998, which read, "I am writing to inform you that I am ready to meet President Slobodan Milošević without any preconditions, under the mediation of the United States. I urge you to appoint Mr. Richard Holbrooke as the mediator." Holbrooke had returned to Wall Street after brokering the Dayton Accords. Rugova sent a copy of the letter to Holbrooke with a cover note: "I look forward to working closely with you for the benefit of peace and stability in the region."[19]

Gelbard was furious when the letter arrived and hunted for its source. Gelbard was a formidable and intimidating character. He learned that Repishti was involved, and when confronted, Repishti told Gelbard about my role. Although Gelbard never discussed it with me directly, our relationship was profoundly affected. Albright acted on Rugova's request, shifting responsibility from Gelbard to Holbrooke.

Holbrooke often said that Milošević would deal with a problem by creating a bigger one. Serbia launched an extensive counter-insurgency operation in the spring of 1998. On March 5, 1998, KLA members were massacred in the village of Prekaz. Adem Jashari, a KLA founder, militant maverick, and symbol of the revolution, was killed along with fifty-one members of the Jashari clan, including women and children.[20]

· · · · ·

Holbrooke and I met every month with the AAs at Bruno's Ristorante, an elegant place on 58th Street in New York with a private dining room on the second floor. US policy focused on the KLA, but no US official knew the KLA's commanders or how to reach them. Since AAs were raising money for the KLA, Holbrooke asked point blank who knew the KLA and how a meeting could be arranged. No one responded; Dino Asanaj approached me after the meal. When we shook hands, he slipped me a piece of paper with three names and cell phone numbers. I provided the information to Holbrooke who shared it with his trusted adviser, Chris Hill. That is how the US government identified and made contact with the KLA.

Holbrooke travelled to Kosovo and met KLA members on June 23, 1998. He expected senior KLA commanders, but the KLA downgraded the level of his meeting to mid-level representatives, Lum Haxhiu and Gani Shenu. Holbrooke was photographed with the KLA, sitting on a farmhouse floor in Dukagjini drinking tea. The meeting was supposed to be off the record. However, the image went viral, fueling speculation that the US was behind the uprising.[21]

Holbrooke focused on securing the release of Serbian hostages. At my own initiative, I contacted Bujar Bukoshi, who was prime minister of the Kosovo government in exile and controlled the KLA's purse strings. Bukoshi and I had known each other for many years, and I spoke frankly, asking what the KLA required to release the hostages and lift its roadblocks. I told Bukoshi that I was in close contact with Holbrooke and would share our conversation with him. Bukoshi asked for US air strikes, targeting specific Serb military positions.

It turned out that Bukoshi, who lived in Germany, was on a German list of suspected terrorists. According to German law, the communications of suspected terrorists can be monitored without a warrant. A transcript of my conversation with Bukoshi was provided to US intelligence, which reported it to Holbrooke. I was never formally reprimanded, but I knew that US officials were annoyed by my unauthorized efforts. I came to understand why the US was concerned about my renegade diplomacy as NATO considered air strikes.

Serbia's counter-insurgency campaign was in full swing by September 1998, resulting in the displacement of 300,000 people. Some Kosovo Albanians found refuge with extended family; many camped in the mountains without shelter or escaped to the neighboring countries of Macedonia and Albania. When it started to snow in October, Internally Displaced Persons (IDPs) faced a humanitarian catastrophe. Holbrooke visited Belgrade and Prishtina October 5-6, 1998. On October 13, the North Atlantic Council issued an Activation Warning Order, a stage in force-generation, one step short of authorization for combat operations. The threat was meant to support diplomatic efforts, make the Milošević regime withdraw forces from Kosovo, and compel cooperation with the return of refugees to their homes.

With backing from NATO's Secretary General Javier Solana and the Supreme Allied Commander Europe, General Wesley Clark, Holbrooke used a credible threat of force to leverage concessions from Milošević. He convinced Milošević to allow NATO access to Serbian air space, the return of IDPs to their homes, and access to Kosovo by humanitarian agencies. I kept the AAs informed of diplomatic developments. Endorsed by UN Security Council Resolution 1203 (October 24, 1998), Milošević agreed to the deployment of the Kosovo Verification Mission (KVM), comprised of two thousand unarmed "verifiers," aimed at monitoring Serbia's compliance.[22] Staffing the KVM was a challenge; its members were unarmed.

I contacted Howard Safir, commissioner of the New York Police Department, to recruit volunteers for the KVM. Safir was sensitized to the issue. His son was married to Ava Repishti, Sami Repishti's daughter. Safir encouraged members of the NYPD to volunteer, offering them a fully paid six-month administrative leave. The NYPD database does not identify the ethnicity of police officers. It does, however, identify languages that they speak. A search identified about fifty Albanian language-speaking police officers, whom Safir invited for lunch at Bruno's. Almost every invitee attended. It was unusual for the NYPD commissioner to invite rank-and-file to a social occasion.

New York was hit by a huge snowstorm the day we were scheduled to meet the NYPD. Ambassador James Pardew, who served as the Department of Defense representative in Dayton and a member of Holbrooke's team, was supposed to pitch participation to the NYPD. However, he was grounded in DC, so I led the discussion at Bruno's, with Pardew joining on the phone. Some of the police who showed up were administrators, some worked on homicide and narcotics, and others were undercover agents. It was a rough bunch. Not only were they New York cops, they were ethnic Albanians.

We explained that KVM verifiers would be unarmed. By way of assurance, NATO would establish a rapid reaction force nearby in Macedonia in case the situation turned violent. The cops were reluctant to go to Kosovo without a side-arm, although some would later join an international police force after Serbia's forces withdrew.

The prospect of violent conflict increased when six Serbian youth were killed at the Marco Polo Club in Peja, Kosovo in January 1999. A week later, forty-five Kosovo Albanians were massacred in Račak. The victims, elderly men, women, and three children, each had been executed with a single shot to the head. One corpse was beheaded; the body of a pregnant woman had been mutilated. US Ambassador William Walker, who chaired KVM, called the Račak massacre an "unspeakable atrocity [and a] crime very much against humanity."[23] When Pardew met Milošević on January 21, 1999, Milošević denied the massacre of civilians, calling them terrorists. Pardew tried to get agreement from Milošević to pull his forces out of Kosovo and move toward meaningful autonomy for Kosovo. Račak made it clear that the KVM was not working.

Following failed negotiations at Rambouillet, France, Holbrooke visited Belgrade in March 1999 for one final attempt to negotiate the withdrawal of Serbian forces and the transition to autonomy for Kosovo. Holbrooke called Deputy Secretary of State Strobe Talbott, affirming that the US would start bombing unless Milošević withdrew his forces. Holbrooke knew the call was being monitored and was sending a message to Milošević. I, too, was involved in the disinformation effort.

On March 23, my phone rang as I was leading a seminar at Columbia University on post-conflict reconstruction in East Timor. At this point, I was employed as Director of Columbia's Conflict Resolution Program. The caller ID indicated "Richard C. Holbrooke." That's odd, I thought; Holbrooke was supposed to be in Belgrade negotiating with Milošević. Jim O'Brien, an Albright protégé and trusted adviser to Holbrooke, was on the line. O'Brien said he was with Holbrooke on the Air Force plane, calling from the tarmac in Belgrade. Negotiations with Milošević had broken down, he told me, and NATO would start bombing the following day. Holbrooke asked that I call the AAs so they could alert their families to seek safety.

My heart pounded. The US was about to go to war and I was the only one who knew it, or so I thought. Holbrooke expected that Serbian intelligence agency would monitor the calls. Instead of returning to the United States, he flew to Budapest and called Milošević the next morning. Milošević rejected Holbrooke's entreaties. Air strikes against targets in Serbia and Kosovo started on March 24, 1999, and lasted seventy-eight days.[24] Holbrooke told me, "I knew that war was inevitable when Milošević started believing his own propaganda."[25]

. . . . .

In May, after Serbian forces withdrew and Kosovo was rid of occupation, I met US Representative Eliot Engel and a group of Albanian-Americans in Macedonia, and we drove across the border to Kosovo. The group was jubilant entering newly liberated Kosovo. I recalled walking from Macedonia to Kosovo during the years of Serbian rule. I also thought about Ibrahim Rugova who, stricken with cancer, had died the previous year in 1998.

During my last appointment with Rugova at his home, Rugova was wearing a baseball hat to cover his hair loss from chemotherapy. We talked about his illness and what lay ahead. He was determined to finish his life's work and realize Kosovo's independence. Sadly, Rugova died before NATO's intervention.

Kosovo was a very different country without him. Hashim Thaçi became president, and the KLA crowd took over Kosovo's government. SHIK, the National Intelligence Service of Thaçi's Democratic Party of Kosovo

(PDK), generated huge sums through bribery, extortion, and racketeering. Close ties between Thaçi and organized crime were confirmed by US intelligence. Thaçi launched a smear campaign to discredit me when I published an article exposing SHIK's criminality. Its media mouthpiece, *Infopress,* called me a "Serbian spy," a "pseudopatriot," and a "public enemy." It alleged that I was paid €500,000 to write a report that was critical of Thaçi and the PDK.

Thaçi accosted me at a black-tie dinner of the National Albanian American Council in New York. He accused me of being paid to write critical articles, but I told him that was not the case. I had a job at Columbia University; I did not need the income. Moreover, I come from a family with means. I would never allow money to influence my views or loyalties.

Thaçi and I also disagreed over policy matters. Beginning in 2017, Thaçi conducted secret negotiations with Serbia, proposing a land swap. Kosovo would relinquish Serb-populated territories north of the Ibar River. In exchange, Serbia would give Kosovo lands in Serbia's Preshevo Valley where Albanians reside. I strongly oppose border adjustments or land swaps. Many people died for Kosovo's independence, fighting for a multicultural and pluralist country. Only Russia and Serbia would benefit from border adjustments. It was a betrayal of the Albanian nation. I was sure that Holbrooke would have agreed had he been alive. Holbrooke worked himself to death and died of a burst aorta in December 2010, while trying to negotiate an end to the conflict in Afghanistan.

. . . . .

In March 2019, I traveled to Kosovo with my twin daughters, Tara and Maya, who were then fourteen years old. Every year, the girls and I undertake an international humanitarian project. For example, one year we raised funds for girls in Uganda to buy bicycles so they could get to school. Another year, we supported the Malala Fund to purchase book bags for girls in Afghanistan. Yet another year, we sold lemonade for emergency earthquake relief in Nepal. In third grade, they arranged for their classmates to co-sign a letter to China's Premier Xi Jinping asking him to allow the Dalai Lama to return home to Tibet.

In 2019, we decided to sponsor a project renovating a library in Mitrovica where Kosovo Albanians and Kosovo Serbs could meet, study, work, and socialize together. Mitrovica is a divided city in northern Kosovo with Serbs living north of the Ibar River and Albanians to the south. It is a flashpoint for ethnic violence. The Mitrovica Library and Cultural Center is more than a physical facility; it is intended as a safe space to foster reconciliation. In 1998, I walked across the Mitrovica Bridge with Bernard Kouchner, the UN Special Representative for Kosovo, who founded Médecins Sans Frontières (Doctors Without Borders) and later became France's Foreign Minister. He explained the situation in Mitrovica, which he described as the most dangerous place in Kosovo.

Tara and Maya organized a bake sale at their school and solicited friends and family, raising $15,000 for the library's renovation. As a courtesy, I went with my daughters to inform Thaçi about the project. Thaçi had no interest in the project or in reconciliation. In front of my daughters, he asked why I opposed his partition plan. He wanted to know who was paying me, suggesting that I was on the take. He accused Prime Minister Ramush Haradinaj, who opposed partition, of buying my loyalty. I reminded Thaçi that I could not be bought. My opposition to partition was based on principle, not bribes. I was deeply insulted by his rudeness, especially in front of my children.

On that same trip, my daughters and I were invited to lunch with Haradinaj. We showed up at his office, greeted by the media. Haradinaj awarded me with the "Skenderbeg National Medal" for my service to the Albanian people over more than three decades. Gjergj Kastrioti, known as Skenderbeg, was an Albanian nobleman and military commander who led a rebellion against the Ottoman Empire in the early fifteenth century. Haradinaj spoke glowingly of my contribution to liberating Kosovo and peace-building. I was so touched by the award and the prime minister's words of commendation. The fact that my daughters were there to participate in the ceremony and hear Haradinaj's remarks made it even more special.[26]

I did not allow Thaçi's rudeness and disrespect to tarnish my relations with Kosovo. Rugova is no longer with us, but I have enduring friendships with Kosovo Albanians, forged over years of shared struggle. Albin Kurti, who briefly served as prime minister in early 2020, Alush Gashi who became foreign policy adviser to Kurti's successor, Ardian Gjini, Lulzim, Peci, and other friends are steadfast. So are the AAs. We struggled together and cooperated during the darkest days of Serbia's occupation. Kosovo faces many challenges to state-building and to endemic corruption. Kosovo Albanians owe a debt of gratitude to the KLA for fighting to free them from oppression. On June 24, 2020, the Kosovo Specialist Chambers and Specialist Prosecutor's Office publicly revealed its indictment of Thaçi on more than one hundred counts of murder. The indictment killed Thaçi's partition plan and signaled a new phase in the consolidation of Kosovo's democracy. It was an indictment of Thaçi, not of the KLA's fight for freedom.

Kosovo was always plagued by rivalries between political factions. When I met Kurti in Prishtina on February 6, 2020, he indicated that his coalition was shaky and might fall. The coalition collapsed sooner than expected. Kurti and Thaçi disagreed over a strategy for dealing with the coronavirus. Egged on by US Special Envoy Richard Grenell, a Trump political appointee who supported Thaçi's partition plan, the Kosovo Assembly passed a no-confidence vote on March 26, 2020. Resolving relations between Kosovo and Serbia would be a diplomatic triumph for President Donald J. Trump. US Ambassador Philip Kosnett tweeted that he was "pleased" by the vote. Just two weeks before, he met the AAs in New York. When I asked him about Kosovo-Serbia dialogue, Kosnett replied: "Just trust me."[27]

Many milestones define my work on Kosovo over thirty years. Independence day, February 17, 2017, was one of the happiest memories. The date was a closely held secret, but I luckily had a reservation to transit through Kosovo to Istanbul that weekend. There were no seats, and many of Kosovo's most stalwart friends like Eliot Engel and Richard Holbrooke were not able to attend. It was a snowy day as I strolled down Mother Theresa Avenue and joined friends for dinner at Tiffany's Restaurant for a joyous celebration. Serbia stubbornly opposed Kosovo's independence and, as of this writing, blocks its international recognition. Nonetheless, the United States and 111 other countries recognize Kosovo as a sovereign and independent state. Its right to independence has been validated by the International Court of Justice. Playing a role to help liberate Kosovo has been a source of enormous personal satisfaction, but Kosovo's sovereignty and state-building are ongoing efforts and concerns of mine.

Notes

1   Encyclopedia Britannica, https://www.brannica.com/event/Dayton-Accords, Bill Clinton, Nov 14, 2019.

2   Meeting notes of David L. Phillips. Goran Milošević, Milošević's chef of the cabinet, joined the meeting as note-taker.

3   Interview by the author with Slobodan Milošević, December 7, 1995.

4   See Serbian History 101, http://babamim.com/kosovo.

5   "The World Today," *Adam Roberts*, 34, no. 4 (Apr. 1978): 136–46.

6   Robert D. Kaplan, *Balkan Ghosts: A Journey Through History* (New York: Picador, 2005), 39.

7   Richard Nelson "How Milosevic Stripped Kosovo's Autonomy—Archive, 1989," *The Guardian*, March 20, 2019, https://www.theguardian.com/world/from-the-archive-blog/2019/mar/20/how-milosevic-stripped-kosovos-autonomy-archive-1989.

8   Remarks by Slobodan Milošević, Kosovo Polje, June 28, 1989.

9   Interview by the author with Jim Xhema, August 13, 2010.

10 "Conference Statement on Bosnia: Text of the Final Declaration of the London Conference Regarding the Conflict in Bosnia-Herzegovina," *The Independent*, August 28, 1992, https://www.independent.co.uk/news/world/europe/conference-statement-on-bosnia-text-of-the-final-declaration-of-the-london-conference-regarding-the-1542891.html.

11 Interview by the author with Morton I. Abramowitz, November 4, 2010.

12 Interview by the author with Jakup Krasniqi, September 10, 2010.

13 Interview by the author with Albin Kurti, September 10, 2010.

14 Eve Gerber, "Who is the Kosovo Liberation Army?" *Slate*, April 23, 1999, https://slate.com/news-and-politics/1999/04/who-is-the-kosovo-liberation-army.html.

15 Kosova Information Center, Kosova Daily Report No. 989, October 15, 1996.

16 Interview by the author with Richard C. Miles, October 2010.

17 Gary Dempsey, "An Accomplice to War in Kosovo?" August 5, 1998, https://www.cato.org/publications/commentary/accomplice-war-kosovo.

18 Interview with Hashim Thaçi, *Frontline PBS*, http://www.pbs.org/wgbh/pages/frontline/shows /kosovo/interviews/thaci.html (accessed May 10, 2020).

19 Correspondence from Ibrahim Rugova, March 16, 1998.

20 Chris Hedges, "On a Garage Floor in Kosovo, A Gruesome Serbian Harvest," *The New York Times,* March 10, 1998, https://www.nytimes.com/1998/03/10/ world/on-a-garage-floor-in-kosovo-a-gruesome-serbian-harvest.html.

21 Marcus Tanner, "Holbrooke Meets Albanian Fighters in War Zone," *The Independent,* June 25, 1998, https://www.independent.co.uk/news/holbrooke-meets-albanian-fighters-in-war-zone-1167376.html.

22 "OSCE Kosovo Verification Mission," OSCE Task Force for Kosovo, https:// www.osce.org/kvm-closed (accessed May 10, 2020).

23 PBS Frontline, Ambassador William Walker, https://www.pbs.org/wgbh/ pages/frontline/shows/kosovo/interviews/walker.html (accessed May 10, 2020).

24 Preben Bonnén, *Towards a Common European Security and Defence Policy: The Ways and Means of Making it a Reality* (2003).

25 Interview by the author with Richard C. Holbrooke, March 1998.

26 *Oculus News,* March 2019, https://www.ocnal.com/2019/03/david-phillips-honored-with-gjergj.html.

27 Notes from the meeting with Ambassador Philip Kosnett, February 28, 2020.

CHAPTER 5

THE NAME ISSUE BETWEEN GREECE AND MACEDONIA

When Yugoslavia disintegrated, the Republic of Macedonia—one of the country's six republics—became independent. It was the only republic to secede without violent repercussions. Macedonia was spared inter-ethnic conflict until 2001, when the troubles in Kosovo spilled over the border and a small civil war erupted.

Macedonia's 1994 census reported that Albanians represented 22.9 percent of the population. However, the actual number was significantly greater. The gap has continued to grow given the high birth rate of ethnic Albanians. Villages along the border with Albania and Kosovo are like autonomous entities, flying the Albanian flag, living apart, and maintaining a distinct identity from ethnic Macedonians, who are Orthodox.[1]

In 1993, I attended a conference on conflict prevention in Macedonia organized by the Fafo Institute for Labour and Social Research, a Norwegian think-tank. The conference considered preventive actions, lest the country go the way of Bosnia and become engulfed by ethnic and sectarian violence. I supported international engagement before the outbreak of hostilities, subscribing to the view that "an ounce of prevention is worth a pound of cure."

The United Nations Security Council (UNSC) adopted Resolution 983 on March 31, 1995, creating the United Nations Preventive Deployment Force (UNPREDEP).[2] UNPREDEP was an innovation. The international community usually gets involved after conflict has broken out, at which point peace-making is harder and humanitarian assistance more expensive. UNPREDEP was mandated to monitor potential flashpoints that could undermine the country's stability and territorial integrity. It was authorized to report potential conflict to international stakeholders and seek remedies before violence worsened.

Complementing UNPREDEP's security role, the Commission for Security and Cooperation in Europe established a Mission in Skopje, Macedonia's capital. The "Spill Over Monitoring Mission" was led by former Ambassador Robert Frowick before he became head of Search for Common Ground in Macedonia. Frowick focused on bi-communal projects with practical benefits, which also helped reduce tensions and institutionalize dialogue between communities. Activities had practical value. He worked with journalists and educators. He organized waste disposal by Albanians in ethnic Macedonian communities. Ethnic Macedonians cooperated with their Albanian counterparts to restore cultural sites and mosques. I served as a board member of Search for Common Ground and strongly supported its work with civil society.

Another highly innovative project involved collaboration between Common Ground Productions and the Sesame Workshop to produce children's television positively impacting society. "Our Neighborhood" (*Nashe Maalo*) was the first children's television created to promote cultural understanding and conflict resolution skills. Its characters were ethnic Macedonian, Albanian, Turkish, and Roma children who lived in the same apartment building. Under one roof, they grappled with the issues of friendship, love, stereotypes, and prejudice.[3]

In February 1994, I lectured at Tetovo University in Macedonia with ethnic Albanian faculty, many of whom came from the University of Pristina just ninety minutes away in Kosovo. As a private initiative, Tetovo University lacked accreditation and credibility. Huddled around an electric space heater with Tetovo University's President, I empathized with the struggle of Albanians for opportunity in a country that was marginalized within Yugoslavia and which, in turn, marginalized its ethnic Albanian minority.

·   ·   ·   ·   ·

The Task Force on the Western Balkans of the Council on Foreign Relations (CFR), which I directed, sent a delegation to Macedonia in December 1995. A huge fog bank rolled in as we slowly drove along the A1 Highway from Albania. It seemed as though we were on another planet with visibility no more than a few feet. Macedonia was isolated; time seemed to have stood still for this former Yugoslav republic rife with ethnic tensions.

The CFR delegation met with UNPREDEP commanders. We were especially impressed by US personnel who were proactive with a "can-do" approach toward conflict prevention. UNPREDEP is widely considered a successful deployment of United Nations (UN) peacekeeping forces aimed at preventing civil strife. Nonetheless, Macedonia remained a volatile tinderbox.

The notion of "Greater Albania" is shared by many Albanians in Southeast Europe who live in Macedonia, Kosovo, Albania, and Serbia. Albanians have large, extended families. About one million Albanians also reside in Greece, many in an area called Chameria in the region of Epirus. Other than in Kosovo and Albania, where ethnic Albanians are the dominant majority, Albanians resent their minority status in countries where Orthodox Christians predominate.

After the 1999 Kosovo war, Albanians in Macedonia looked across the border at what Kosovo Albanians had achieved and aspired to greater cultural, economic, and political rights for themselves. They demanded use of the Albanian language in public institutions, greater access to Albanian-language media, the right to fly the Albanian flag, and new electoral districts to enhance their voting strength. Albanians wanted to change Macedonia's constitution so it would declare Albanians as the country's second nation. They also sought to make Albanian an official language. Albanians aimed for greater representation in the public sector and affirmative action hiring in the police and armed forces.

The CFR issued a policy report with recommendations to mitigate conflict in Macedonia, many of which were incorporated into the Ohrid Framework Agreement (OFA) of August 13, 2001. Earlier in 2001, Macedonian Albanians formed the National Liberation Army (NLA) and launched an armed insurgency.[4] OFA required the disarmament of the NLA, the devolution of power, and greater minority political and cultural rights. It established Albanian as a co-official language and stipulated affirmative action in government hiring. OFA was envisioned as the first step in a reform agenda, which would be consolidated by Macedonia's eventual membership in the North Atlantic Treaty Organization (NATO) and the European Union (EU), which have strict democracy and human rights membership criteria.

However, implementation of OFA languished, as did Macedonia's aspirations to join Euro-Atlantic structures. Some ethnic Macedonians resented the privileges given to the country's Albanian minority. The dominant political party, the Internal Macedonia Revolutionary Organization (VMRO), capitalized on these resentments to build a base of nationalist supporters. Macedonia's democratic development was further compromised by its dispute with Greece over the "name issue."

. . . . .

The United States is an ally of both Greece and Macedonia. With the rise of ISIS, it sought cooperation from both countries to stem the tide of Islamist extremism. Macedonia was the center of radicalization and recruitment for Muslim Albanians who went to Syria and joined the caliphate. Resolving the name issue would facilitate Macedonia's Euro-Atlantic integration and consolidate its democracy, free market reforms, and fight against corruption. It would also improve Greece's relations with creditor nations, as Greece's economy started to collapse in 2010. Greek-Macedonian reconciliation was a win-win, normalizing relations and overcoming old enmities. However, some Greek politicians opposed Macedonia sharing a name with the Greek region of the same name. Opposition was led by Antonis Samaras, who disputed the name "Republic of Macedonia" since 1992 when Macedonia became independent.

Many coffee shops in New York are owned by Greek-Americans. I frequently saw posters reading "Macedonia is Greek." I did not know what was behind this until I became involved in the name issue. Many Greeks objected to the official and constitutional name, the "Republic of Macedonia," which they believed hijacked Greek history and culture. Symbols that were historically Greek, such as the Vergina Sun and images of Alexander the Great, were flashpoints for controversy between the countries. Greece also rejected the newly independent Republic of Macedonia calling its language Macedonian.

Why would Greece be concerned over Macedonia's name? Greece is a NATO and EU member. It has a rich history as the birthplace of democracy. Why would a European country feel its identity threatened and history stolen by a small country like Macedonia? The dispute goes to the heart of identity and sense of security for both peoples.

Greeks feared that Macedonia had territorial ambitions over the northern Greek province of the same name. Greeks feared that Macedonia would embrace the concept of "Greater Macedonia" and make territorial claims in Greece, Bulgaria, Albania, and Serbia. The ancient Greek kingdom was called "Macedon" after Philip of Macedon, the father of Alexander the Great. Modern Greece also has a province named "Macedonia," and more than two million Greeks identify themselves as "Macedonians." The struggle is rooted in the Balkan Wars of 1912 and 1913.[5]

The international community was preoccupied with the demise of Yugoslavia in the 1990s. Since the name dispute could not be resolved at that time, Ambassador Richard Holbrooke mediated the "interim accord," which was finalized under UN auspices on September 13, 1995.[6] Under the accord, Macedonia would bear a provisional reference as "The Former Yugoslav Republic of Macedonia," otherwise known as FYROM. The Republic of Macedonia was not recognized by the UN and other international organizations by its official name. However, 137 countries, including the United States, established bilateral relations with Macedonia, using its provisional name, FYROM.

Newly independent, Macedonia sought membership in the EU and NATO and signed a Stabilization and Association Agreement with the EU in 2001. The Council of Europe identified Macedonia as a potential candidate for EU membership at the Thessaloniki European Council Summit in 2003, and Macedonia was granted candidate status in 2005.[7] Beginning in 2009, EU visa liberalization made it possible for Macedonia's citizens to travel without visas across Europe for periods up to ninety days.[8]

When Macedonia took steps to join NATO, Greece conditioned membership on resolution of the name issue and blocked Macedonia's application at the NATO Bucharest Summit in 2008. The Bucharest Summit Declaration affirmed, "An invitation to the Former Yugoslav Republic of Macedonia would be extended as soon as a mutually acceptable solution to the name issue has been reached."[9] Years later, in 2018 under a left-wing government led by the SYRIZA party, Greek authorities consented to "a compound name with a geographical qualifier for use in relations to everyone."[10] Former Prime Minister Samaras and his party, now in opposition, joined with former Defense Minister Panos Kammenos and other Greek nationalists in stubbornly opposing any mention of "Macedonia."

. . . . .

The name issue should be seen in the context of domestic politics in both countries. As a result of its financial crisis, Greece held early elections in May 2012. Greek voters rejected the Panhellenic Socialist Movement (PASOK) led by George Papandreou and turned to Samaras and New Democracy, which formed a coalition government with the social democratic PASOK party, the Democratic Left, and leftist parties that supported fiscal policies to keep Greece in the Eurozone.

In the 2015 election, New Democracy gave way to SYRIZA as the Greek populace rebelled against the dire economic situation and the traditional two-party system that had ruled Greece for decades. SYRIZA's leader, Alexis Tsipras, was a populist who campaigned against austerity measures imposed by the EU and the International Monetary Fund (IMF).[11] He was a brash and self-assured thirty-seven-year old former communist youth activist, an iconoclast who rode his motorcycle around Athens and broke conventions by refusing to wear a necktie. Tsipras promised to freeze payments to creditors and renegotiate terms of the "Memorandum" with its creditors, which required Greece to make deep budget cuts in exchange for financial assistance.

Tsipras sought both a bailout to keep the Greek government afloat and relief from its €300 billion debt that was strangling Greece's recovery. Debt relief would allow the European Central Bank to include Greece in its bond-buying program, known as quantitative easing, thereby boosting investor confidence. Tsipras tried to convince Germany, Greece's primary creditor, to relax its austerity demands. While Tsipras cultivated a relationship with Chancellor Angela Merkel, Greece's left-leaning press demonized German Finance Minister Wolfgang Schäuble for demanding budget cuts that inflicted pain on Greek pensioners and humiliated the Greek people.

SYRIZA had won elections in 2015 by promising to reverse austerity measures. Despite a referendum confirming popular opposition to the bailout terms, Tsipras reversed course. He recognized that a confrontation with Germany would lead to the collapse of Greece's banking system and its exit from the Eurozone. Tsipras fired Yanis Varoufakis, the celebrity finance minister, and adopted a more practical approach to Greece's fiscal policy. He would later demonstrate a similarly practical approach to the name issue.

The Peace and Reconciliation Unit of Norway's Ministry of Foreign Affairs was the largest and most consistent funder of Columbia University's Program on Peace-building and Human Rights ; it supported Columbia without interruption for more than a decade. When it came time to renew support, the Norwegians requested a list of proposed projects. Dialogue between Greek and Macedonian civil society was not on the list, but Norwegian officials identified it as a priority. I was asked to visit Oslo and meet Ambassador Haakon Blankenborg, Norway's expert on the Balkans. Haakon emphasized that an agreement on the name issue would require concessions from both sides and support from civil society.

I had not been involved in the name issue previously, so I had no baggage that would be seen as bias by one side or the other. Columbia was known in Macedonia for its work on Albanian rights and convening an "OFA Implementation Review" on the ten-year anniversary of the agreement in 2011. The conference brought all the signatories together for the first time since the agreement itself. International mediators, US Ambassador James Pardew and Soren Jessen-Petersen, former UN Deputy High Commissioner for Refugees, also attended. I had good relationships with a broad cross-section of Macedonian society and political elites. I was also in good standing with the Greeks. My working relations with Richard Holbrooke and Ambassador Tom Miller, who was well regarded in Athens, were *bona fides* for our Greek partners. With Norwegian financing, Columbia launched a dialogue between Greeks and Macedonians to identify confidence-building measures (CBMs).

A dialogue project requires dialogue partners. Norway's Ambassador to the United States, Wegger Strommen, introduced me to Macedonia's Ambassador Zoran Jolevski, who helped organize my fact-finding trip to Skopje. He introduced me to Professor Zoran Ilievski, chair of the Political Science Department of the Law Faculty at Saints Cyril and Methodius University in Skopje, and an adviser to President Gjorge Ivanov. Zoran was smart and well-connected; he was eager to engage with Greek counterparts and try innovative strategies aimed at breaking the logjam.

Prime Minister Nikola Gruevski and his VMRO party exacerbated problems by building huge statues of Alexander the Great, whose name and image were plastered on monuments, the highway, the airport, sports halls, and stadiums. Gruevski was pandering to Macedonian nationalists who rejected compromise with Greece. Greece's veto over Macedonia's NATO and EU membership compounded Macedonia's isolation, fueling corruption by Gruevski and his VMRO crowd.

On my assessment trip to Greece and Macedonia, I met scholars from the law, history, and political science faculties at Saints Cyril and Methodius University. Darko Angelov, Macedonia's ambassador in Athens, became an adviser and a friend. US Ambassador Jess Baily, whom I knew from work in Iraqi Kurdistan, was also an invaluable partner. Ambassador Matthew Nimetz had served as the personal envoy of the UN Secretary-General regarding the naming dispute since 1999 and had also been President Clinton's envoy on the name issue. He introduced me to Nikola Dimitrov, who would become foreign minister, and facilitated my contact with Nikos Kotzias, Greece's foreign minister. Nimetz is a skilled and determined diplomat, a gracious gentleman and student of history, who worked for decades as a mediator between Athens and Skopje.

I was warned that Kotzias was a left-leaning anti-American academic. However, Kotzias was always gracious and willing to get together. I found him to be open-minded and flexible. In June 2017, Kotzias stated that Greece would support Macedonia's integration "in every way, once the name issue has been resolved."[12] I also became familiar with the Foreign Ministry's Political Director, Petros Mavroidis, a tough guy and strident negotiator. He was deeply involved in the name issue prior to his assignment in Ankara as Greece's Ambassador to Turkey. During our first meeting, Mavroidis scolded me for convening a seminar about Chameria, the ethnic Albanian area in Epirus, northern Greece.

I also reached out to scholars such as Dimitris Keridis, an international personality and public intellectual based at Panteion University in Athens, who became a great friend, adviser, and project partner. The Hellenic Foundation for European and Foreign Policy (ELIAMEP), a center-right think-tank in Athens, also became an important partner. Its scholars included Thanos Veremis, with whom I had interacted at conferences over the years, and Ioannis Armakolas, a Balkan expert who divided his time between Athens and Thessaloniki.

Some Greeks in Thessaloniki had more progressive attitudes towards Macedonia because of their proximity to Greece's northern neighbor. Thessaloniki's maverick mayor, Ioannis Boutaris, was a likable and colorful personality. He wore an earring and had a tattoo of a salamander on his wrist. He is a member of the Vlach ethnic community and an outspoken advocate for LGBTQ rights and legalization of cannabis. His family business was known for its excellent wine. Jordan Karatzas, the former CEO of Olympic Airways, introduced me to Boutaris, and I am deeply grateful to Jordan for facilitating this relationship, which proved fruitful in many ways.

My initial efforts focused on the business communities in both countries. There was a big disparity between Greek and Macedonian businesses in terms of their capacity and interest in cooperation. While Athens-based businesses had little interest in working with counterparts in Macedonia, businesses in northern Greece stood to benefit. I met Kyriakos Loufakis, President of SEVE, the Chambers of Commerce of Northern Greece, and proposed a meeting between SEVE and the Macedonia Chambers of Commerce (MCC), chaired by Daniela Arsovska. However, "Macedonia" in the title was a deal breaker. Loufakis warned that many Greek businesses would not participate, and his board would disapprove. We found a creative work around by using acronyms. The first meeting was hosted by Columbia, SEVE and MCC in Thessaloniki on October 16 and 17, 2015.

To follow up, SEVE visited Skopje on November 20, 2015. We sponsored a research report on "Trade and Investment Opportunities between Greece and the Former Yugoslav Republic of Macedonia," which was widely covered by Macedonia's media and the Greek press. Loufakis and Arsovska signed a Memorandum of Understanding "for the purpose of expanding trade and investment opportunities through the exchange of information on commercial opportunities and institutionalizing cooperation beneficial to their members."

Mayor Boutaris attended the SEVE/MCC signing ceremony and briefed journalists from both countries. He also held discussions with President Ivanov and Foreign Minister Nikola Poposki. He met Skopje Mayor Koce Trajanovski and eleven mayors on the board of ZELS (The Association of the Units of the Local Self-Government) to discuss practical issues such as garbage collection, recycling, energy production from waste, student and school exchanges, protection of Byzantine churches, cultural and sports cooperation, and local administration. During his briefing to journalists, Boutaris used the term "Macedonia," which shocked the Greek media.

In response to Macedonia's floods in August 2016, Boutaris wrote Ivanov and Trajanovski to offer assistance. As a result of their growing amity, Ivanov invited Boutaris to lecture on "Diplomacy of Cities" at his Academy in Ohrid where Boutaris discussed regional water and environmental issues with the mayors of Krushevo and Ohrid.

Columbia University sponsored projects on civil society contact, communication, and cooperation with the goal of letting "a thousand flowers bloom." For example, hydrologists and water officials discussed information sharing and flood control. They explored the establishment of a Vardar/Axios River Commission to promote sustainable water and river basin resource management. Interaction was not always constructive. Greek officials from the Ministry of Agriculture walked out of the conference when Macedonians used the country's official name in their slide presentation.

Greek Ombudsman Vassilis Karydis, Deputy Macedonian Ombudsman Vaska Bajramovska-Mustafa, and Thessaloniki Deputy Mayor Spiros Pengas met in Thessaloniki on October 19, 2015. They organized a joint fact-finding trip to assess conditions for refugees on the Greece-Macedonia border and issued a joint report to members of our media group.

Scholars from Panteion University in Athens and Aristotle University of Thessaloniki worked with counterparts from Saints Cyril and Methodius University and Southeast European University, Tetovo to launch joint research projects and faculty and student exchanges. *The Balkan Human Corridor: Essays on the Refugee and Migrant Crisis by Scholars and Opinion Leaders in Southeast Europe* was published on June 21, 2016. Some of the essays were co-authored by Greek and Macedonian contributors. Others wrote parallel papers on the same topic.[13] Boutaris arranged for Macedonian journalists to meet Greek officials from the Interior Ministry, National Police, and humanitarian actors involved in refugee and migrant issues. They reported extensively on the Divata Refugee Camp where Syrian refugees were languishing en route to northern Europe.

In 2017, we tried to organize a roundtable in Athens with ELIAMEP involving journalists from both sides. We also contacted the Foreign Ministry to arrange interviews for the Macedonian journalists. Up to this point, we had been flying below the radar. Seeking official meetings drew unnecessary attention to the project, and the Greek government killed it. At my request, US Ambassador David Pearce, with whom I'd worked on the Future of Iraq Project, contacted the Foreign Ministry to seek its support. Involving the US Government only made matters worse, and we were forced to postpone the meeting.

However, we were persistent and, some months later, Greek and Macedonian journalists finally met at ELIAMEP and explored a mechanism for regular exchange of information. Our media partnerships enabled collaborative reporting and addressed negative stereotypes of "the other," which impacted the climate for bilateral relations.

A shared history project resulted in a co-publication by Panteion University and Saints Cyril and Methodius University, *Balkan Crossroads: Historical Dialogue between Scholars in Southeast Europe.*[14] We explored cooperation with Professor Christina Koulouri, well-known for her textbook on Balkan history that refuted irredentism. Faculty from both countries started to interact regularly, attend conferences together, and develop dynamic scholarly and personal relationships.

The Navarino Network hosted a public panel, "The Former Yugoslav Republic of Macedonia: What Next" on February 17, 2016.[15] Chaired by Dimitris Keridis, the panel was the first time that Macedonian scholars presented in a public forum to Greek counterparts, civil society, and media representatives.

Ilievski and Keridis attended a conference on the "Geopolitics of the European Borderlands: The Western Balkans," organized by the Delphi Economic Forum.[16] Cooperation between Ilievski and Keridis expanded, drawing on their strong personal relations.

Ioannis Armakolas and Vladimir Bozinovski from the Skopje Institute for Political Research conducted sociological surveys on mutual perceptions, including the name issue. They developed parallel questionnaires, coordinated research methods, and adopted a joint plan for dissemination including events in Athens and Skopje.

This impressive collection of collaborative activities was undertaken in spite of huge obstacles. Our efforts were beset by difficulties from the beginning. They occurred in the context of an economic crisis in Greece, a domestic political crisis in Macedonia, and the refugee and migrant crisis that affected both countries.

By the end of 2016, after two years of facilitating dialogue, I was frustrated by the lack of measurable progress and was ready to throw in the towel. I felt that 90 percent of what was possible had been accomplished, and there was not much more that could be done under current conditions.

However, Norway wanted the project to continue and offered funds for a third year. Our partners had developed close personal and professional relations; I did not want them to feel abandoned, so I agreed to keep going. I remembered Madeleine Albright's phrase, "Reconciliation is like riding a bicycle. You fall off the moment you stop peddling."

. . . . .

Macedonia's 2017 EU progress report described dramatic deterioration of democracy standards. Under the VMRO government, Macedonia fell far short of the Copenhagen criteria requiring prospective members to have stable democratic institutions that uphold the rule of law, human rights, and respect for minorities. Macedonian-Greek relations also suffered from VMRO's statue and monument-building, naming edifices after Alexander the Great.[17]

A crisis resulted when illegally intercepted communications revealed plots by VMRO against political opponents, as well as sordid details about corruption. The EU mediated the Przino Agreement, envisioning the transfer of power to the Social Democratic Union of Macedonia (SDSM) led by Zoran Zaev. The agreement required Gruevski to step down and general elections to be organized by a caretaker government. Rather than enhance stability, elections were polarizing. The election scheduled for April 24 was postponed to June 5, and then postponed again to December 11, 2017.[18]

Accountability was also a lightning rod. The Przino Agreement called for a special prosecutor to investigate the wiretapping scandal. However, President Ivanov issued pardons to figures in both parties, effectively undermining the special prosecutor. Popular demonstrations and counter-demonstrations ensued. When elections were finally held, VMRO won fifty-one of 120 seats in Parliament. Since it did not gain an absolute majority, the balance of power rested with parties representing ethnic Albanians.

During this time, I was in regular contact with ethnic Albanian leaders needed to form a government. I was introduced to Zijadin Sela, leader of the Alliance of Albanians, by John Dauti, an Albanian-American from New Jersey. Sela insisted on constitutional reforms as a condition for joining an SDSM-led government. I advised him to wait. Government formation was the first priority. Enshrining Albanian rights would follow.

After Albanian parties came together in Tirana to adopt a common platform, Zaev agreed to expand constitutional rights of Macedonia's ethnic Albanians in exchange for their support. Though SDSM assembled a parliamentary majority to form a government, Ivanov refused to award a mandate to SDSM. He maintained that the consensus among Albanian parties was a foreign construct, negotiated under the auspices of Albania's Prime Minister. Albanians refuted this claim, criticizing Ivanov. Zaev also accused Ivanov of deliberately stalling the political process, helping Gruevski cling to power.

Ivanov's actions undermined his credibility at a time when nonpartisan leadership was needed to guide the country.[19] When Macedonia failed to form a government, the crisis became more acute. The longer it took to resolve the impasse, the greater the risk of political violence. The delay also opened Macedonia to malign influences of external powers. Russia labeled the SDSM a tool of the West and sought to discredit US and EU influence.

On April 27, 2017, VMRO-backed thugs attacked the Parliament while police stood by and watched. Zaev and Sela were beaten and bloodied.[20] I was shocked by the lengths to which VMRO would go to stay in power. Sela and I spoke on April 28. We had grown close, maintaining regular contact, meeting in New York, Skopje, and his hometown of Struga, where we dined on local trout at a fish restaurant on the shores of Lake Ohrid. After lengthy deliberations, SDSM and Albanian political parties came together to form a new government on June 1, 2017. US Ambassador Baily played a pivotal role helping to form a coalition.

VMRO seemed deeply entrenched. As is often the case when there is a dramatic shift, the tipping point that brought SDSM to power was not foreseen. SDSM's rise created new opportunities for resolution of the name issue. Support from civil society would be critical to making a deal, which required parliamentary approval.

Zaev made NATO and EU membership a high priority. While the EU suffered from "enlargement fatigue," it devised new ways to advance relations with candidate countries while withholding actual accession negotiations.[21] The name issue remained a sticking point.

. . . . .

The University Partnership Program was the most productive project of our track two program. The business group was also a dynamic partner. To cap off activities, a Greek business delegation visited Macedonia on September 29 and 30, 2017. The delegation included twenty Greek businesses with commercial activities in the fields of agro-industry, viticulture, and construction materials. The delegation interacted with business counterparts and government officials. There were roundtables for each sector that twinned Greek and Macedonian enterprises, and field visits to business sites outside of Skopje. Ambassador Baily gave an elegant toast at the VIP dinner to open the conference. He was always an understated yet positive influence.

The CEO of a company that exported olives and related products such as olive oil and olive paste spoke with me at the Skopje Trade Fair and later sent a big box of every imaginable olive and olive product to my home in New York. It was a fringe benefit; I might have been obliged to decline the gift had I been employed by the US Government.

To cap off the Southeast Europe Dialogue Project, we convened all of our partners in Thessaloniki for a Civil Society Summit on October 2, 2017. The conference was a complicated administrative challenge, ably managed by Aspa Kyriaki of the Navarino Network with guidance from Dimitri Kerides. As usual, Zoran did the lion's share of work in coordinating the participation of Macedonians. Boutaris opened the conference. Participants discussed how the project had evolved over nearly three years. Panelists from both sides considered work in the fields of (i) municipal/local government, (ii) business/trade promotion, (iii) university partnerships/faculty and student exchanges, (iv) think-tanks/research, (v) environmental, pollution control/water resource management, (vi) and culture. A Greek nationalist attended the conference and was disruptive, accusing the Greek participants of selling out. As the chair, I wanted to evict him but constrained myself. It was better to let him talk until he had nothing more to say. Shutting him down risked an incident that would distract from our productive discussion.

After we adjourned, participants sat on the veranda, mixing and mingling. Relations were well established after three years of working together. The project had reached a critical mass, and partners from both countries were interacting regularly and attending conferences together. They had developed dynamic scholarly and personal relationships. I had successfully worked myself out of a job, which should always be the goal of track two. There was a melancholy moment at the end of the Thessaloniki Summit. We had all been through a lot together, but there was still work to do.

We went into executive session with Ilievski, Bozinovski, Armakolas, and Keridis and made a list of Confidence-Building Measures (CBMs) that were proposed to both capitals. Civil society started a process that was continued by officials. Zaev and Tsipras discussed Macedonia's Euro-Atlantic perspective, the "name issue," and possibilities for development of bilateral relations during a telephone call on June 7, 2017. They also exchanged views on CBMs.[22]

The Prespa Agreement finally resolved the disputed name issue on June 12, 2018 after several decades. Macedonia was renamed "The Republic of North Macedonia." Prespa also addressed the issue of nationality, identifying people as "Macedonian/citizen of the Republic of North Macedonia and confirming use of the 'Macedonian' language."[23] Diplomacy is about compromise. In a successful negotiation, nobody gets their full wish-list of demands. To their credit, Zaev and Tsipras decided it was time to resolve the dispute and acted in their mutual interests. The decision was based on a desire to move on from problems in the past.

Some VMRO-backers and hardline Greek nationalists did not like the new name. Parliamentary ratification and popular support barely passed. Changing the name was intended to trigger action by NATO and the EU on North Macedonia's membership. NATO finally acted on February 6, 2020, but the EU dithered, with France, Denmark, and the Netherlands obstructing a decision. In response to delays, Zaev resigned and scheduled new elections for April 12. These elections, however, were delayed due to the coronavirus.[24]

On March 26, 2020, the EU finally agreed to begin membership talks with North Macedonia.[25] The applications of North Macedonia and Albania were coupled, which delayed North Macedonia's progress. Reforms by Albania lagged behind progress in North Macedonia. Reinvigorating OFA was necessary to consolidate democratic development and institutionalize benefits to Albanians. In my private meetings with Zaev, I urged the government to adopt specific benchmarks and a timetable for measuring progress.

Instead of being rewarded for his statesmanship, Alexis Tsipras was repudiated by Greek voters on July 18, 2019. Voters were simply tired of austerity and wanted a change. The newly elected New Democracy government of Kyriakos Mitsotakis faced huge domestic challenges to stabilize the economy. It ably managed the coronavirus crisis from the outset, resulting in relatively few cases and a low rate of fatalities. It also took practical steps to improve relations with North Macedonia, demonstrating that resolution of the name issue was in Greece's interests.

Zaev and Tsipras were nominated for the Nobel Peace Prize.[26] They surely deserved commendation for navigating difficult negotiations and concluding an agreement that addressed tensions still lingering from the Balkan Wars in the early twentieth century. The Dialogue Project for Southeast Europe demonstrated that civil society can help to shape the political debate, bringing politicians along in its constructive wake. Columbia's Macedonian and Greek partners also deserve a prize for their vision, courage, and effective work. Make no mistake: the tough decisions to agree on a compromise were attributable to Greek and Macedonian political leadership. I do believe, however, that our track two dialogue and practical cooperation projects were instrumental in setting the stage for those difficult political decisions and solidified the base of support in the face of strong nationalist backlash in both countries.

．．．．．

Tetovo University honored me with an Honorary Doctorate on May 31, 2017. Many friends with whom I'd worked over decades attended the ceremony. In my acceptance speech, I recalled my visit to the university in 1994 when we sat in the cold basement. I also reflected on other challenges to Macedonia and my role helping to address them. Macedonia has made great progress since becoming independent. With the name issued finally resolved, the Republic of North Macedonia still faces a myriad of challenges as a small country tucked away in a remote corner of Southeast Europe.

Notes

1 Robert W. Mickey and A.S. Albion, "Success in the Balkans? A Case Study of Ethnic Relations in the Republic of Macedonia," in *Minorities: The New Europe's Old Issue* (Institute for East West Studies, 1993).

2 Deborah Mayersen, "Current and Potential Capacity for the Prevention of Genocide and Mass Atrocities within the United Nations System," Australian Political Science Association Conference 2010: Connected Globe: Conflicting Worlds, University of Melbourne.

3 "Nashe Maalo—Children's Television," *Centre for Common Ground,* http://www.sfcg.org.mk/index.php/en/completed-projects/nashe-maalo (accessed April 17, 2020).

4 "Macedonia's 'Liberation' Army," *Zurich: World Press Review,* June 20, 2001.

5 "The War Between Bulgaria and Turkey 1912–1913," Volume V, Ministry of War.

6 Ian Jeffries, *The Former Yugoslavia at the Turn of the Twenty-First Century: A Guide to the Economies in Transition* (London: Routledge, 2003), 240.

7 "Setting EU priorities, 2014-19: The Ten Points of Jean-Claude Juncker's Political Guidelines," *European Parliament,* October 2014, http://www.europarl.europa.eu/EPRS/EPRS-Briefing-538963-Setting-EU-Priorities-2014-19-FINAL.pdf.

8 European Commission, "Enlargement Strategy and Main Challenges 2012-2013," Communication from Commission to the Council and the European Parliament, Brussels, 2012.

9 "Bucharest Summit Declaration," *NATO,* http://www.nato.int/cps/ua/natohq/official_texts_8443.htm (accessed October 21, 2017).

10 "FYROM Name Issue," http://www.mfa.gr/en/fyrom-name-issue/ (accessed November 1, 2017).

11 Patrick Donahue, "Europe's Anti-Austerity Calls Mount as Elections Near," *Bloomberg,* April 30, 2012, https://www.bloomberg.com/news/articles/2012-04-29/europe-seeks-to-restore-calm-after-spain-downgrade-growth-spat.

12 Karolina Tagaris, "Name in Frame, Macedonia Seeks Greek Support to Join EU, NATO," *Reuters,* June 14, 2017, https://www.reuters.com/article/us-europe-greece-fyrom/name-in-frame-macedonia-seeks-greek-support-to-join-eu-nato-idUSKBN19521N?il=0.

13 "The Balkan Human Corridor: Essays on the Refugee and Migrant Crisis by

Scholars and Opinion Leaders in Southeast Europe," *Columbia University,* June 21, 2016, https://www.researchgate.net/publication/306065245_BAL KAN_HUMAN_CORRIDOR_Essays_on_the_Refugee_and_Migrant_ Crisis_from_Scholars_and_Opinion_Leaders_in_Southeast_Europe.

14 "Balkan Crossroads: Historical Dialogue between Scholars in Southeast Europe," *Columbia University,* March 6, 2017, http://www.humanrightscolum bia.org/publications/balkan-crossroads-historical-dialogue-between-schol ars-southeast-europe.

15 Navarino Network, https://www.navarinonetwork.org/the-former-yugoslav-republic-of-macedonia-what-next/ (accessed April 17, 2020).

16 East West Bridge, http://www.ewb.rs/editone.aspx?id=463 (accessed April 17, 2020).

17 Boris Georgievski, "Ghosts of the Past Endanger Macedonia's Future," *Balkan Insight,* October 27, 2009, https://balkaninsight.com/2009/10/27/ghosts-of-the-past-endanger-macedonia-s-future/.

18 "Prime Minister Resigns in Line with Przino Agreement," *The Economist,* January 22, 2016, http://country.eiu.com/article.aspx?articleid=653869649&Coun try=Macedonia&topic=Politics&subtopic_9.

19 "Macedonia's President Refuses to Give Opposition Leader Mandate for New Government," *RadioFreeEurope Radio Liberty,* March 1, 2017, https://www. rferl.org/a/macedonia-president-refuses-to-give-oppositioon-leader-man date-government/28341718.html.

20 Sinisa Jakov Marusic, "Violence Erupts as Protestors Storm Macedonia Parliament," *BalkanInsight,* April 27, 2017, https://balkaninsight.com/2017/04/27/macedonia-elects-parliament-speaker-amid-ongoing-tension-04-27-2017-1/.

21 Zoran Radosavljevic, "New Macedonia Leaders Vow to Revive EU/Nato Bid," *Eurativ,* June 12, 2017, https://www.euractiv.com/section/global-europe/news/new-macedonia-leaders-vow-to-revive-eunato-bid/.

22 "Zaev, Tsipras Discuss Bilateral Relations, Name Issue," *European Western Balkans,* June 7, 2017, https://europeanwesternbalkans.com/2017/06/07/zaev-tsipiras-discuss-bilateral-relations-name-issue/.

23 Niki Kitsantonis, "Macedonia and Greece Sign Historic Deal on Name Change," *New York Times,* June 17, 2018, https://www.nytimes.com/2018/06/17/world/europe/greece-macedonia-name-dispute.html.

24 Alastair Jamieson, "North Macedonia PM Zoran Zaev Resigns Over Stalled EU Talks," *Euro News,* March 1, 2020, https://www.euronews.com/2020/01/03/north-macedonia-pm-zoran-zaev-resigns-over-stalled-eu-talks.

25 Jorn Fleck, "EU Greenlights North Macedonia and Albania Membership Talks: Breakthrough or Symbolic Gesture?" *Atlantic Council,* March 26, 2020, https://www.atlanticcouncil.org/blogs/new-atlanticist/eu-greenlights-north-macedonia-and-albania-membership-talks-breakthrough-or-symbolic-gesture/.

26 "Members of European Parliament Nominate Tsipras and Zaev for Nobel Peace Prize," *European Western Balkans,* January 1, 2019, https://europeanwesternbalkans.com/2019/01/28/members-european-parliament-nominate-tsipras-zaev-nobel-peace-prize/.

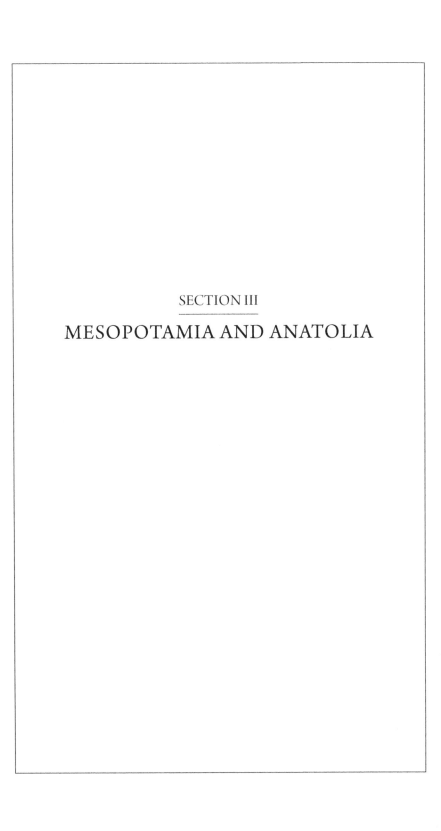

SECTION III

MESOPOTAMIA AND ANATOLIA

CHAPTER 6

NO FRIEND BUT THE MOUNTAINS

In April 1988, Najmaldin Karim, a Kurdish neurosurgeon from Bethesda, Maryland, visited my office in the Rayburn House Office Building in Washington with graphic photos of Kurdish civilians killed in Halabja, a Kurdish city near the Iran-Iraq border. On March 16, 1988, an Iraqi Air Force plane discharged a deadly yellow cloud containing mustard and sarin nerve gasses killing at least five thousand Kurds. The bodies lay in piles, twisted corpses with anguished expressions frozen in death, mouths foaming from exposure to chemical weapons (CW).

Karim and I traveled together to Iraqi Kurdistan right after the First Gulf War in January 1992. We flew to Diyarbakir in southeast Turkey and boarded a minibus to the Habur Gate on the Turkish-Iraqi border. Habur was a major transit point for food and other commodities being smuggled into Iraq. There was a slick surface of oil leaking from canisters strapped to the bottom of trucks crossing the border. When we stopped at a roadside restaurant serving lamb kabobs before crossing over into Iraq, we noticed that everyone had an AK-47 or Kalashnikov at their side. That night we encamped in a private home with three walls collapsed from artillery strikes.

The next day, we had lunch in Dohuk with the brother of Sami Abdul Rahman. Sami founded the Kurdistan Popular Democratic Party, which joined the Kurdistan Democratic Party (KDP), when he became a Politburo member and Deputy Prime Minister. From Dohuk, we journeyed to Kirkuk, which was under the control of Saddam's forces. We snuck into Kirkuk's Kurdish neighborhood where Karim had an emotional reunion with his family. He had not seen his parents or brothers since 1972, when he fled Iraqi forces attacking the Kurdistan Region of Iraq (KRI). The KRI includes Suleimania, Dohuk, and Erbil provinces.

Karim introduced me to Peter W. Galbraith, a senior staff member on the Senate Foreign Relations Committee (SFRC). Galbraith wanted to bring Kurdish leaders to Washington for a conference to review US-Iraq policy. The SFRC could not pay the costs, so the Congressional Human

Rights Foundation became a sponsor. The conference on "The Future of Democracy in Iraq" was held the same day that Saddam surrendered and the Gulf War ended. Jalal Talabani, head of the Patriotic Union of Kurdistan (PUK) and Iraq's future president, attended the conference. Hoshyar Zebari, who later became Iraq's foreign minister and finance minister, also attended, as did Sami Abdul-Rahman.

Because the US supported Iraq in the Iran-Iraq War and Kurds were the enemy of Baghdad, it was taboo at the time for US officials to receive the Kurdish delegation at the State Department. Instead, we met a mid-level official across the street at a coffee shop in Columbia Plaza on 22nd Street in Washington, DC. In contrast, after Saddam's overthrow, Iraqi Kurds assumed prominent positions in the Iraqi Government. Washington rolled out the red carpet for them, and Kurds were received at the highest levels of the US Government.

Dick Cheney, President George H.W. Bush's Secretary of Defense, strongly opposed US troops marching on Baghdad at the end of the Gulf War in 1991. He warned,

> If you're going to go in and try to topple Saddam Hussein, you have to go to Baghdad. Once you've got Baghdad, it's not clear what you do with it. It's not clear what kind of government you would put in place of the one that's currently there now. Is it going to be a Shia regime, a Sunni regime or a Kurdish regime? Or one that tilts toward the Baathists, or one that tilts toward the Islamic fundamentalists? How much credibility is that government going to have if it's set up by the United States military when it's there? How long does the United States military have to stay to protect the people that sign on for that government, and what happens to it once we leave?[1]

National Security Adviser Colin Powell was also cautious. He invoked the Pottery Barn rule: "You break it; you buy it."[2]

. . . . .

The Gulf War started with aerial and naval bombardments on January 17, 1991 and lasted forty-two days. With Saddam's vaunted Republican Guard in chaotic retreat, the US signed a ceasefire agreement that barred

Iraq from flying fixed-wing aircraft but allowed helicopters to transport Iraqi officials. Jubilant Kurds consolidated their control over Iraqi Kurdistan, seizing Kirkuk and emptying the jails of political prisoners. The celebration was short-lived. Helicopters and Iraqi ground forces launched a counterattack, killing many Kurdish fighters called Peshmerga, "those who face death."[3]

More than one million Kurds feared attacks with CW and fled to the mountains and across the border into Turkey and Iran. The US and Turkey collaborated to provide relief to the Kurds through "Operation Provide Comfort," which started in April 1991. The UN Security Council adopted Resolution 687, mandating "Operation Northern and Southern Watch." A no-fly-zone was established north of the thirty-sixth parallel that stretched from Kirkuk's northern suburbs to Kurdistan's borders with Turkey and Iran. In addition, an aerial embargo was established south of the thirty-second parallel to protect Shi'a in the marshlands and southern provinces. The UN Oil for Food Program managed Iraq's oil sales, pledging 13 percent of revenues for humanitarian activities in Iraqi Kurdistan. Kurds referred to the period between 1991 and 2003 as the "golden years." They made the most of international security guarantees and their opportunity for self-rule.[4]

Representing the Congressional Human Rights Foundation, I attended the Congress of the PUK in February 1992. The conference burst into wild applause when I pledged support from the American people for freedom, democracy, and human rights (*Azadi, Demorasi, Buji*). My translator, Barham Salih, a PUK official who would later become president of Iraq, covered the microphone and said with a grin, "You should run for president of Kurdistan."

Next we went to Halabja. The CW attack was part of a broader genocidal campaign by Saddam against the Kurds called the Anfal, a term drawn from the Quran's eighth verse (*Sura*), which describes how the followers of the Prophet Muhammad razed and pillaged the villages of non-believers. The 1988 Anfal Campaign was led by Saddam's cousin, Ali Hasan al-Masjid, nicknamed "Chemical Ali" for his use of weapons of mass destruction (WMD). About 182,000 Kurds perished during the Anfal, thousands of Kurdish villages were destroyed, and hundreds of thousands were displaced.

On my 1992 trip, I interviewed four Shi'a women at a camp for internally displaced persons outside Suleimania. They were dressed in black burqas from head to toe, with only their bright blue eyes showing. Tears cascaded down their cheeks as they described atrocities by Iraqi troops in their hometown of Hilla in southern Iraq. Their fathers, husbands, and brothers were forced to perform sexual acts on one another; glass bottles were inserted in their rectums and shattered. The men of Hilla were systematically murdered. The Shi'a women were not seeking comfort in relating their accounts; they wanted me to share their stories so their suffering would not be forgotten.

The Kurds seized millions of documents from the Iraqi intelligence agency (*Mukhabarat*), which were compulsively detailed and self-incriminating. In addition to written accounts and data, they included audiocassettes and videos of torture and executions. The Kurds gave me a pile of paper, which I brought to Washington. The Defense Intelligence Agency would later transport millions of pages in 857 cartons to be stored in the US National Security Archives.

· · · · ·

I returned to Iraqi Kurdistan in August 1993 to attend the KDP congress. In my remarks, I called for the US to establish a consulate in Erbil. Flying a US flag would be a gesture of solidarity with the Kurds. Some other international participants thought I had gone too far and were concerned that I was raising unrealistic expectations. It took a while, but a US consulate was established in 2003 after the US invaded and occupied Iraq, removed Saddam, and dismantled his Ba'ath Party.

Kurds are their own worst enemies; internal rivalries undermined their national aspirations and self-rule. In 1995, the Central Intelligence Agency (CIA) launched a botched coup attempt against Saddam Hussein that was infiltrated by the Mukhabarat. A civil war broke out between the KDP and PUK, the two largest parties in Iraqi Kurdistan. When Talabani sought assistance from Iran, Barzani responded by inviting the Republican Guard to attack Talabani's stronghold in Suleimania. The Republican Guard overran the headquarters of the Iraqi National Congress (INC), a dissident umbrella group headed by Ahmed Chalabi.

In July 1993, I visited the INC communications bunker in Sallahudin. The CIA had provided state-of-the art equipment that was piled from floor to ceiling. Scores of dissidents were executed when Sallahudin was occupied by Saddam's Republican Guard, and Chalabi fled to save himself. I did not pick sides in the Kurdish civil war. My interest was solely in helping the Kurdish people, not backing one party against the other.

France's then-First Lady Danielle Mitterrand was the most prominent international personality working on the Kurdish issue. Mme. Mitterrand attended our conference on the Future of Democracy in Iraq. For many years after, I was in close contact with her and Annick Thebia-Melsan, her trusted personal assistant seconded from the Quai d'Orsay to Mitterrand's Fondation France Libertés. Mitterrand played a pivotal role in negotiating an end to the intra-Kurdish conflict, which was formalized with the Washington Agreement in September 1998.[5] In the agreement, the parties concurred to share revenue, share power, and prevent Iraqi troops from entering the Kurdish region. The agreement also barred the Kurdistan Workers Party (PKK), militant Kurds from Turkey who were fighting for an independent Kurdistan.

I learned two important lessons from Karim and Mitterrand: Iraq's problems arose from abuses by the central government and decentralizing power was the best way to harmonize competing claims and keep Iraq from fragmenting. Many Iraqis, especially the Kurds, viewed federalism as the most effective system for power-sharing. If the Kurds could not achieve independence, they would settle for a democratic, federal republic of Iraq.

After the terror attacks on 9/11, President George W. Bush abandoned the Cold War emphasis on deterrence and embraced a Doctrine of Preemption in which the US would take action before it was attacked. President Bush identified Iraq, Iran, and North Korea as the "axis of evil" in his State of Union speech on January 29, 2002.[6]

Vice President Cheney's views had evolved considerably from the First Gulf War. He and neo-conservatives (neo-cons) in the Bush Administration sought to make Iraq a prototype for democratizing the Middle East. The "new Iraq" would undermine the Ba'athists in Syria. Regime change would pressure the mullahs in Iran. It would enhance Israel's interests and transform rogue states into democracies serving US energy and security interests.

The neo-cons relied on Ahmed Chalabi to provide information on Iraq's WMD, which bolstered their case for a US invasion. Chalabi promised that conquering US troops would be welcomed with flowers. He predicted that the US would be in and out in thirty days, with Iraq's hydrocarbons producing revenue to support the country's reconstruction and political transition. Iraqi exiles, led by Chalabi, would then act as America's agents and run the country.

It was clear that Bush wanted to take out Saddam, though there was no evidence linking al-Qaeda to Iraq, as he had claimed. As a peace activist, I reflexively opposed military action. Since attacking Iraq looked increasingly inevitable, I sought guidance from the Kurds. Through Qubad Talabani, Jalal's son, who represented the PUK in Washington, I contacted the Kurdistan Regional Government (KRG) and proposed travel to Iraqi Kurdistan. I reached out to Ambassador Marc Grossman and notified him of my plan. He asked colleagues in the State Department Bureau of Near Eastern Affairs (NEA) to brief me.

. . . . .

Turkey tightened its border with Iraq, blocking passage through Habur. The only way of getting in was via boat from Syria across the Tigris River. Referring to his father, Qubad Talabani informed me that the "big guy" had made arrangements with Syrian intelligence for my transit. I asked for a letter confirming travel arrangements. Instead, I was given a code number—3462—and told to appear at the border on July 5, 2002.

The first leg of my journey was by plane to Damascus. I was told that a man named Mohammed would be there to greet me and facilitate my travel. The Damascus airport was packed. Sure enough, I found Mohammed as the crowd thinned. We went to his apartment and I slept on the couch before we returned to the airport early the next morning. I bought a one-way ticket to Qamishle for $20. There I was met by representatives of KDP in Syria who drove me to a small cinderblock building overlooking the Tigris River. The Syrian official had a book identifying visitors authorized to visit Iraq. I saw my name in the book, next to the number 3462, and prepared for the next leg of my journey.

The Tigris River swept us downstream until the boatman started the outboard engine and we turned into the current and headed upriver, making our way from Syria to Iraqi Kurdistan. Republican Guard military bunkers were visible on the hillside a few miles away; I could make out human figures in the watchtower. I was assured that Iraqi marksmen were drinking tea, not readying their weapons. As we approached the boat landing, a sign came into view: "Welcome to Iraqi Kurdistan."

A convoy of Toyota land cruisers waited in the parking lot. A KDP official, Mustafa Falah Bakir, stepped out of the lead vehicle to greet me. He was accompanied by a Peshmerga security detail. We went directly to the presidential palace to meet Masoud Barzani. Without reservation, Barzani welcomed Bush's plan to overthrow Saddam. I was surprised by Barzani's unqualified support for regime change. Kurds had made the most of their golden years, developing economically and enjoying *de facto* independence. They had a lot to lose.

From Erbil, I drove to Suleimania on a road that skirted Iraqi military lines. A wrong turn would lead me to an Iraqi checkpoint. Barham Salih and I had become close during his time as the PUK representative in DC. He called soon after arriving in DC and told me he did not have a place to work. I took a spare phone from my desk drawer, plugged it into the wall, and told Barham to share my office until he was settled. We were together in a small office of about two hundred square feet for the next three months. Barham genuinely believed that "Iraq's transformation would change the dynamics of Middle East politics." The new Iraq would become a pillar of stability in the Middle East and a catalyst for change in the region's balance of power.[7]

During my visit to Iraqi Kurdistan, I stayed at the KDP guest house in Salahuddin, a picturesque town in the hills above Erbil. Sami Abdul Rahman had been working on a draft constitution. We sat on the porch overlooking the scenic Mesopotamian plain and held in-depth discussions about Iraq's future governance. Abdul-Rahman had vast experience, having served as Minister for Northern Affairs responsible for carrying out the autonomy agreement proposed by Saddam after the Kurdish rebellion in 1970.

Upon my return to Washington, I briefed Marc Grossman and Ryan Crocker, the Principal Deputy Assistant Secretary of State in the NEA, on July 15, 2002. Although the Kurds were staunchly pro-American, both Barzani and Talabani worried about a preemptive strike by the Iraqi military if they conspicuously supported regime change. Religion and ethnicity are important to Iraqis who, as a people, lack a strong sense of national identity. Decentralization was critical to the development of Iraq's democracy. The Kurds prefer federalism because it offers greater assurance than autonomy, which can be more easily revoked by the central government. Federalism is a voluntary association between equal parties who decide it is in their common interest to form a state, whereas autonomy is bestowed by the central government to a lesser party. The Kurds envisioned a federal entity called Iraqi Kurdistan with Kirkuk as its capital. Rather than a center-out approach, democracy-building should start in the regions.

Since I was focused on Iraq, my contract as a Special Government Employee was transferred from the Bureau of European Affairs to the NEA. I was one of the few US officials working on Iraq who had actually set foot in the country. Crocker invited me to join the Future of Iraq Project and assist the Democratic Principles Working Group. The Future of Iraq Project was an effort to engage Iraqis in planning the future of their country. Launched in April 2002, it was led by the State Department and included seventeen federal agencies at a cost of $5 million. About 240 Iraqis from across the political spectrum produced two thousand pages of policy recommendations. According to Grossman, the Future of Iraq Project was established "to begin practical planning for what could be done between now and the aftermath of the transition."

The INC's Ahmed Chalabi opposed the project; he wanted to control decision-making in order to advance his own personal ambitions. There was always tension between the Iraqi Diaspora, led by Chalabi, and Iraqis in the country. Grossman testified on Capitol Hill: "Iraqis on the outside will not control decisions that will, ultimately, have to be made by all Iraqis. The Iraqi diaspora is a great resource but not a substitute for what all Iraqis will need to do to build a free and democratic Iraq."[8]

The Iraqis called the Democratic Principles Working Group "the mother of all working groups." It considered some of the most contentious issues: security and de-Ba'athification, the role of religion in future governments, oil revenue sharing, and the establishment of a transitional authority paving the way for elections and a new constitution. After multiple meetings in the United Kingdom, we produced a report that highlighted challenges. Liberating and stabilizing Iraq was no cakewalk.

The Future of Iraq Project was opposed by the US Office of the Vice President and neo-cons committed to military action. The process of planning necessarily surfaced problems, which could slow America's march to war. It was also opposed by Chalabi and the INC, who feared that decision-making would shift from the exiles to Iraqis in the country.

I supported US military action to overthrow Saddam but preferred that the Iraqis do it themselves. Having been to Halabja, I had seen firsthand the impact of CW. Not only did Saddam use CW to attack the Kurds, CW was used extensively during the Iran-Iraq war from 1980 to 1988. I believed those who concluded that Saddam possessed WMD and would use them against his own people.

The US initiated massive air strikes against Iraq on March 20, 2003. Secretary of Defense Donald H. Rumsfeld called it "shock and awe." When I met Crocker that day in his office at the State Department, he expressed reservations, forewarning, "I fear we have unleashed a Pandora's box of forces that we don't understand and can't control."[9]

After my meeting with Crocker, Qubad Talabani and I had lunch at a restaurant near Dupont Circle in Washington. We ordered a bottle of champagne and jubilantly toasted Bush's decision to take military action. The Kurds had suffered terrible atrocities committed by Saddam; they were glad to get rid of him.

$$\cdot \quad \cdot \quad \cdot \quad \cdot \quad \cdot$$

Saddam's Republican Guard quickly collapsed as US troops moved north towards Baghdad. On May 1, 2003, President Bush boarded the USS Abraham Lincoln and declared victory before a large banner reading "Mission Accomplished." Saddam may have been vanquished, but problems identified by the Democratic Principles Working Group would surface, destabilizing Iraq and exacerbating its ethnic and sectarian tensions.

While I supported regime change, I was deeply critical of the Bush Administration for willfully ignoring our recommendations and giving free reign to Chalabi and the exiles. Zalmay Khalilzad was appointed Special Envoy to "serve as the focal point for contacts and coordination among free Iraqis for the United States Government and for preparations for a post-Saddam Hussein Iraq."[10] The center of gravity on Iraq shifted from the State Department's NEA Bureau to the National Security Council, which diminished my role. The Defense Department airlifted Chalabi and seven hundred of his Free Iraqi Forces to Nasiriyah on April 6, 2003. Chalabi wanted to be sent to Baghdad, but General Tommy Franks feared a backlash by Iraqis and vetoed the idea.

As the Saddam regime collapsed, Iraqis looted government buildings, stealing everything that was not bolted to the floor. Despite 150,000 American and coalition troops on the ground, Iraq descended into chaos and civil war. I resigned my post in a letter to Assistant Secretary of State William J. Burns on September 11, 2003. Chalabi was scheduled to address the UN General Assembly, and I wanted to publish an op-ed in *The New York Times* titled "Talking to the Wrong Iraqi." My article blasted the Bush administration for its shortcomings in post-war stabilization. Soon after, I ran into Chalabi on Madison Avenue while he was taking his grandson out for ice cream. Chalabi was visibly annoyed and resentful. Under criticism for relying on exiles, the US discontinued its monthly payment of $347,000 to the INC.

The Future of Iraq Project morphed into the Office for Reconstruction and Humanitarian Assistance, which became the Coalition Provisional Authority (CPA), headed by Ambassador L. Paul "Jerry" Bremer III. Bremer's initial efforts focused on de-Ba'athification. On May 16, 2003, he issued a decree that "disestablished" the Ba'ath Party. Overnight, 120,000 Iraqis were dismissed from their jobs. On May 23, he issued another edict targeting the Iraqi armed forces, discharging 400,000 Iraqis from their jobs in the security sector. I supported Bremer's edicts at the time. The Ba'ath party and Iraq's armed forces had committed terrible atrocities and should have been dismantled. As an unintended consequence, however, targeting Ba'ath and security structures fueled the insurgency of Sunni Arabs who opposed the US invasion.

Without a credible process to restore self-rule, Iraqis became embittered and turned against Bremer and the CPA. I discussed a series of local conferences so that the voices of Iraqis could be heard with Burns and Crocker. I maintained that it was critical to talk with Iraqis about their country's transition. Distrust by Iraqis toward the United States worsened after the US sponsored UN Security Council Resolution 1511 (October 16, 2003), which identified the US-led coalition as Iraq's "occupying power."[11]

The Transitional Administrative Law (TAL), Iraq's interim constitution, was adopted in March 2004. Bremer relied on the Kurds to support the TAL, and then turned on them. He demanded that the Kurds disband the Peshmerga, abandon claims of oil in Kirkuk, and accede to the new Iraqi state in all matters. However, the Kurds and other Iraqis resisted his instructions.

Again, US officials relied on the Kurds to help negotiate Iraq's current constitution, approved in a referendum on October 15, 2005. While stressing Iraq's unity, the constitution established federal rule. The constitution's bill of rights included significant protection and affirmative duties to promote linguistic, religious, and ethnic minority rights. It enshrined Kurdish cultural symbols such as a flag, anthem, and cultural and national holidays. It acknowledged the Kurdistan Regional Government's control over provinces in the north and northeast, as well as the Kurdish provinces as a "region." Article 110 guaranteed proportional distribution of revenues for existing oil and gas fields. New fields in the KRI would be the sole domain of the KRG. Article 122 assigned the Peshmerga responsibility for security in Iraqi Kurdistan. It also restricted their deployment outside of Iraqi Kurdistan without approval from the Kurdistan Parliament.

Negotiators could not finalize the status of Kirkuk, an oil-rich region contested by Kurds, Arabs, and Turkmen. Article 140 of the constitution envisioned the return of internally displaced persons to Kirkuk, followed by a census and referendum on Kirkuk's status. Kirkuk was my special concern, not only because it was Karim's hometown. I contributed ideas to the creation of a property claims and compensation commission for Kirkukis who had been displaced over several generations.

Other than remote input, I was not directly involved in negotiations on the constitution. Galbraith was physically present, advising the Kurds. At the same time, he cut a deal with DNO, a Norwegian energy company, giving DNO extensive oil development rights in exchange for a personal share of the royalties.[12] The international media contacted me with questions about self-dealing by Galbraith. I told them that potential earnings had no bearing on his advice. He counseled the Kurds based on their best interests, not his own.

Prime Minister Nouri al-Maliki ignored the December 31, 2007 deadline for determining Kirkuk's status. Moreover, he contested Kurdish claims in other disputed territories. Naming himself commander in chief, he refused to share weapons provided to Iraq by the United States. As relations with Baghdad worsened, the Kurds feared that Maliki would use sophisticated US weapons against them. Their concern materialized in August 2014, when Maliki deployed the Dilja Operations Command that confronted the Peshmerga in Kirkuk, Diyala, and Sallahudin governorates.

．．．．．

When ISIS invaded Iraq in June 2014, Kurds faced a disastrous perfect storm. A humanitarian crisis resulted as Iraqis fled to Kurdistan for sanctuary. Iraqi Kurdistan also faced an economic crisis. When the KRG circumvented the State Organization for Marketing Oil (SOMO) and contacted energy consumers directly, Baghdad refused to pay the share of oil revenues it had committed to the KRG. Barzani's term as president expired, but the Kurdistan Parliament kept making exceptions that allowed him to stay in the job.

The 2005 constitution was a compromise. Kurds made a strategic decision to forego their dream of independence in favor of a federal, democratic republic that devolved political, economic, and cultural rights from the central government to Iraq's regions. With Iraq's government increasingly dysfunctional and ISIS advancing, Barzani sought a referendum on independence.

I met Barzani on May 5, 2015, right after his visit to the White House when he made his case to President Barack Obama. He believed that independence could only occur with support from the United States. Barzani was adamant about independence, indicating that Maliki's failure to implement the constitution was pushing Kurdistan to disassociate itself from the central government. Since Kurdistan voluntarily entered into a federal union, Kurdistan, as an equal party, had the right to secede. He maintained that "the people of Kurdistan have the right to self-determination and under this right they are free to determine their own politics and free to achieve their own economic, social, and cultural development from Iraq."[13] I warned Barzani that US officials would be reluctant to support the break-up of Iraq. His maximum leverage would be before the battle for Mosul. If the Pentagon needed the Peshmerga, the US would be more accommodating toward Kurdistan's national aspirations.

Columbia University's Program on Peace-building and Human Rights organized a Task Force on State-Building in Iraqi Kurdistan. Ambassador Nancy Soderberg, President Clinton's former Deputy National Security Adviser, chaired the task force, which included experts such as Galbraith and Brendan O'Leary, a law professor at Penn State and legal adviser to the KRG. I launched the task force to help the Kurds prepare for independence. The report made detailed recommendations to the KRG about getting its house in order and suggested roles for the international community. According to Soderberg:

> Iraqi Kurds have been building a de facto independent state since 1991. In the years since the US-led invasion, the Iraqi Kurds have sought to work with the central government in Baghdad. With Iraq's collapse, they will no longer do so. We do not yet know how and when they will seek de jure independence, but it is not in the interests of the international community to block the legitimate aspirations of the Kurds for self-determination. Rather, the international community should work with the Kurdistan Regional Government, Baghdad, and the concerned countries to ensure that the process is consultative, democratic, responsible, and stable.[14]

The task force report was largely ignored. Barzani left his meeting with President Obama understanding that the US was focused on degrading and destroying ISIS. Until that happened, KRG's independence bid would be a distraction. The Obama Administration welcomed the replacement of Maliki with Heider al-Abadi in September 2014. US officials hoped that Abadi would rule in a more conciliatory fashion, draining support for ISIS in Iraq's Sunni-majority regions.

Barzani was focused on his legacy, knowing his time as president was coming to an end. When Barzani announced plans for independence, Secretary of Defense James Mattis visited Erbil. With ISIS advancing and Kurdistan's economy struggling, Mattis asked for a delay. Ambassador Brett McGurk, the Special Presidential Envoy for the Global Coalition to Defeat ISIS, was a dutiful proponent of the US government's "one-Iraq policy." I spoke to an audience in Dag Hammarskjöld Plaza across from the UN on the day of the referendum. Spirits were high, but the Kurds were wary. The referendum's outcome was certain, but what happened next was unforeseeable.

The referendum asked, "Do you want the Kurdistan Region and Kurdistani areas outside the Kurdistan region to become an independent country?" On September 25, 2017, Kurds voted overwhelmingly for independence—92.7 percent voted yes.[15] In response, the Iraqi Government in Baghdad coordinated recriminations with Iran and Turkey, closed air space, sealed borders, and threatened to block hydrocarbon exports. Independence was stillborn.

Iraqi Kurds faced another disastrous situation on October 17, 2017. Bafel Talabani, Qubad's brother, and his cousin Lahur conspired with General Qassem Soleimani, head of Iran's Quds Force, to betray Kirkuk. Iraqi Shiite militias, backed by the Iranian Revolutionary Guard Corps, attacked Kirkuk and tried to assassinate Governor Najmaldin Karim, who barely escaped as Iraq seized control of Kirkuk's oil fields and the K1 military base. US Ambassador Douglas Silliman encouraged Iraqi forces, including Shiite militias, to take Kirkuk and go all the way to the border with Turkey. He believed that defeating the Kurds would strengthen Abadi's political position.

I desperately tracked Karim's whereabouts, fearful he would be killed. Some Karim family members felt that US officials had conspired with the PUK to betray Karim. When I first met Jalal Talabani thirty years prior, he had called Kirkuk his "Jerusalem." In the span of a few weeks in 2017, independence was thwarted, and Kirkuk betrayed. I was ashamed of the PUK. In the end, I was glad Karim was alive in KRG-controlled territory.

There is a Kurdish adage: "Kurds have no friends but the mountains." Throughout history, they have suffered betrayal and abuse. I supported the Kurdish cause when few others were involved. My steady engagement was appreciated by the Kurds, to whom I was a battle-tested champion of their cause. My access and partnership with Kurds in Iraq, Iran, Syria, and Turkey was a result of *bona fides* dating back to the 1980s and lasting to this day.

Notes

1   Timothy Noah, "Dick Cheney, Dove," *Slate News*, October 16, 2002, https://slate.com/news-and-politics/2002/10/more-on-why-cheney-didn-t-want-to-go-to-baghdad-the-last-time.html.

2   Robert Siegel, "Powell's Caution on Iraq," *National Public Radio*, April 20, 2004, https://www.npr.org/templates/story/story.php?storyId=1844476.

3   "Remembering the Kurdish Uprising of 1991," *BBC News*, April 7, 2016, https://www.bbc.com/news/in-pictures-35967389.

4   Ruth Wedgwood. "The Enforcement of Security Council Resolution 687: The Threat of Force Against Iraq's Weapons of Mass Destruction," *The American Journal of International Law* 92, no. 4 (1998): 724–28.

5   "Iraqi Kurdistan Profile," *BBC News*, October 31, 2017, https://www.bbc.com/news/world-middle-east-15467672.

6   Andrew Glass, "President Bush Cites Axis of Evil," January 1, 2019, *Politico*, https://www.politico.com/story/2019/01/29/bush-axis-of-evil-2002-1127725.

7   Claudia Rosset, "The Real World," *Wall Street Journal*, September 4, 2002.

8   Testimony by Marc Grossman, Senate Foreign Relations Committee, February 11, 2003.

9   Conversation between the author and Ryan Crocker, March 20, 2003.

10 "Iran Contra Figure Named to a Senior Post in the White House," *Washington Post*, December 13, 2002.

11 "Resolution 1511, The Situation between Iraq and Kuwait," *UNSCR*, October 16, 2003, http://unscr.com/en/resolutions/1511.

12 James Glanz, "Ex-Diplomat Who Advised Kurds Gets Millions in Oil Deal," *The New York Times*, October 6, 2010, https://www.nytimes.com/2010/10/07/world/middleeast/07galbraith.html.

13 Cited by David L. Phillips in "The Great Betrayal: How America Abandoned the Kurds and Lost the Middle East," (I.B. Taurus, 2019), 97.

14 *Task Force Report, State-Building in Iraqi Kurdistan*, Columbia University, October 2015.

15 Bethan McKernan, "Kurdistan Referendum Results," *The Independent*, September 27, 2017, www.independent.co.uk/news/world/middle-east/kurdistan-referendum-results-vote-yes-iraqi-kurds-independence-iran-syria-a7970241.html.

CHAPTER 7

TURKEY GOES ROGUE

My work in Turkey spans three decades and has focused on freedom of expression and democratic rights of the country's twenty million Kurds. Turks are a noble and decent people, afflicted by incompetent and sometimes criminal political leaders. The 1991 Gulf War, the 2003 Iraq War, and the rise of the Islamic State in Iraq and Syria in 2014 greatly complicated US-Turkey relations.

Traveling from Suleimania, Iraq to Diyarbakir, Turkey after attending the Patriotic Union of Kurdistan Congress in 1992, I was stopped and questioned no less than ten times by Turkish police. The Kurdistan Workers' Party (PKK) had launched an insurgency against the Turkish authorities and was seeking an independent state on Kurdish-inhabited territories in Turkey, Syria, Iraq, and Iran. Although the PKK would later drop its demand for independence, preferring greater political and cultural rights, Southeast Turkey was heavily militarized in the 1990s. The gendarmerie wanted to know what I was doing there and if I had made contact with the PKK.

Being hassled by the police was my first encounter with human rights violations in Turkey. I started researching the situation by visiting the field and scouring secondary sources from Human Rights Watch and Turkish organizations such as the Diyarbakir Human Rights Association. Understanding Turkey today requires knowledge of Turkey's past. I learned the Kurdish term "Serhildan," which means rising up against oppressors. As I got more deeply involved, I came to understand the term's significance, affirming the constant struggle of Kurds against the Turkish state. For Kurds, the struggle goes beyond basic human rights; it is also about their dignity in the face of a more powerful, repressive and merciless regime.

．　．　．　．　．

The history of Kurds is one of betrayal and abuse. Kurds are the largest stateless people in the world, numbering between thirty-five and forty million. They reside in Turkey (North Kurdistan), Iraq (South Kurdistan), Iran (East Kurdistan), and Syria (West Kurdistan). Far from homogeneous, Kurds are divided by geography, culture, and language. Kurds in Turkey and Syria speak the Kurmanji dialect; Kurds in Iran and Iraq speak the Sorani dialect. Zaza and Gorani are sub-dialects spoken in Iranian Kurdistan and northeastern Iraq. In his youth, Abdullah Öcalan, who founded the PPK, sought to advance the goal of a coherent, unified Kurdish community on all lands where Kurds reside. He learned, however, that Greater Kurdistan is a romantic and unrealistic notion opposed even by the Kurds themselves, as well as by the United States and other Great Powers.

The Sykes-Picot Agreement of 1916 was an informal understanding between Britain and France about the division of Ottoman lands at the end of World War I.[1] It was formalized during the Paris Peace Conference at Versailles and enshrined by the 1920 Treaty of Sèvres. While other nations emerging from the Ottoman and Austro-Hungarian empires gained sovereignty and independence, the national aspirations of Kurds were denied.

Confounded by the Kurdish issue, Great Powers deferred a decision on Kurdistan. The Treaty of Sèvres promised the Kurds an internationally supervised referendum within one year to determine their national status. However, the referendum was never held.[2] Mustafa Kemal Atatürk launched a rebellion, and the Great Powers, weary of fighting, succumbed to Atatürk's demands. The 1923 Lausanne Treaty derogated commitments in Sèvres. Nowhere in the text were the words "Kurd" or "Kurdistan" even mentioned.

President Donald J. Trump said the Kurds were "good fighters."[3] On this point, at least, he is correct. Over the years, Kurds have never accepted their subjugation. Sheikh Said Piran launched the Azadi rebellion in February 1925. When Piran's rebellion was put down, he was hung from the gallows in the central square of Diyarbakir, the largest Kurdish city in southeast Turkey.[4] Subsequently, Atatürk institutionalized a policy of Turkification, which bore his name: "Kemalism."[5]

The Turkish Grand National Assembly passed the Resettlement Law on June 14, 1934, which authorized local authorities to collect taxes, seize land, and resettle Kurds deemed a security risk. Subject to violent assimilation, Kurds launched the Dersim rebellion in 1937, during which up to seventy thousand Kurds were killed.[6] Draconian measures were instituted to suppress Kurdish identity. Turkey banned the Kurdish language, use of Kurdish language for personal and geographic place names was prohibited, and celebrating the Kurdish new year, "Newroz," was outlawed. The very existence of Kurds was denied. They were called "Mountain Turks."[7] On my first visit to Diyarbakir in 1992, a giant banner was unfurled across the main street reading: "Happy is the one who says I am a Turk." Atatürk first used the expression on the tenth anniversary of Republic Day, October 29, 1933. The Ministry of Education added this phrase to the student oath in 1972.

The first wave of Kurds leaving Turkey for Syria occurred after Sheik Said's hanging in 1925. Another wave ensued after the Dersim rebellion was suppressed in 1937. To escape Atatürk's "Turkification" policies, many Kurds resettled in Syria, where they enjoyed considerable rights through an autonomy arrangement provided by the French administration. These rights existed until the French Mandate ended in 1943. A third wave followed the Siverek and Hilvan rebellions, which were launched in Sanliurfa province on the Turkish border with Syria in 1979, during which Kurds targeted feudal landlords who were exploiting the peasants and collaborating with the Turkish state against the Kurdish people. Another wave followed the military coup in 1980 and the adoption of Turkey's constitution two years later, which further institutionalized repression as Kurds tried to escape draconian security measures and Turkey's scorched earth tactics.[8]

The PKK was founded by Abdullah Öcalan in 1978 in the aftermath of the Siverek and Hilvan rebellions. The PKK was a product of the Revolutionary Left. Its ideology was a mix of radical Marxist-Leninism and Kurdish nationalism. The PKK declared itself a "worker- peasant alliance" and the vanguard of the global socialist movement.[9] Violent conflict was strategic: Öcalan viewed armed struggle as a means to bring Turkey to the negotiating table. Over time, he abandoned his goal of a Greater Kurdistan and sought to address the Kurdish question in Turkey through negotiations and democratization. He concluded that "democratic autonomy" could resolve differences between the center and the periphery, between the majority and the minority, and between the powerful and the powerless.[10]

Beginning in 1984, the Turkish state rejected negotiations and sought a security solution to the PKK uprising. It launched military operations against Kurdish civilians in 1989 and 1992, involving up to 150,000 troops. Kurds paid a steep price for their involvement in the movement. Between 1989 and 1996, approximately 1,500 Kurds were victims of unidentified killing, execution by government-backed death squads, disappearances, and death from torture while in police custody. Thousands of Kurdish villages were razed in counter-insurgency operations. To eliminate popular support for the PKK, up to four million Kurds were displaced by Turkey's scorched earth policy.[11] However, instead of breaking the back of the PKK, Turkey's crackdown actually increased its popular support.

Öcalan was under constant pressure and moved the PKK's headquarters from Southeast Turkey to the Syrian-controlled Beqaa Valley in 1989. After the 1991 Gulf War, the PKK took advantage of international security guarantees and relocated again, this time to the Qandil Mountains in Iraqi Kurdistan. Both Iraqi and Turkish troops tried to dislodge the PKK with assistance from the Peshmerga, Iraqi Kurdish fighters whose name means "those who stand before death." According to Kurdish leader Masoud Barzani, many thousands of Peshmerga were martyred fighting the PKK.

Syria's President Hafez al-Assad thought he could use the PKK to destabilize the Turkey-Syria border and reclaim Hatay Province, which was annexed by Turkey in 1939. Assad had no affinity for the PKK. He treated the organization as a pawn in Syria's struggle with Turkey, which he loathed for being pro-Western and a NATO member.

The US State Department listed the PKK as a Foreign Terrorist Organization on August 10, 1997.[12] Western intelligence agencies aligned with Turkey's National Intelligence Agency (MIT), concluding that the PKK was involved in extortion and weapons and narcotics smuggling. They accused Öcalan of ordering the deaths of hundreds of civilians, the kidnapping of Western tourists, and the destruction of public properties. Scores of Öcalan's Kurdish colleagues had allegedly been executed for challenging his policies. Even his ex-wife was imprisoned for disloyalty.

The Turkish General Staff ordered troops to the Turkey-Syria border in September 1998. Turkey demanded that Assad deport Öcalan. Ratcheting up the pressure, Turkey threatened to cut off water supplies from the Euphrates River to Syria. The Adana Agreement was finalized on October 20, 1998. It required Syria to list the PKK as a terror organization, close PKK bases in Syria, and evict Öcalan.[13]

Öcalan was arrested in February 1999 by Turkish Special Forces in Nairobi after a global manhunt with assistance from US intelligence. Drugged and hooded, he was brought to Imrali Prison, an island fortress in the Aegean Sea. Öcalan disappointed militants in Turkey and Syria by abandoning armed struggle. He appeared on Turkish television, contrite for his crimes. "Separation is neither possible nor necessary. We want peace, dialogue and free political action within the framework of a democratic Turkish state. The democratic option is the alternative to solving the Kurdish question."[14]

· · · · ·

Over many years, I worked to foster reform in Turkey using a variety of techniques: dialogue between Turks and Kurds, raising awareness about human rights conditions in Turkey on Capitol Hill and agencies of the US government, and mobilizing the United Nation's (UN's) human rights machinery in defense of the Kurds.

I was in Athens the day Öcalan was captured. On the way to the city from the airport, streets were crowded with protesters. I asked my taxi driver what was happening. "Öcalan, he arrested," the driver replied in halting English. He pointed to a fireball on the steps of the Greek Parliament on Syntagma Square. A Kurd had doused himself in petrol and self-immolated. Kurds protested across Europe for weeks, targeting the embassies of governments that cooperated in Turkey's manhunt. The United States was deeply involved in the search for Öcalan. When US intelligence identified his location in Nairobi, former Foreign Minister Ilter Turkmen told me: "US intelligence delivered Öcalan to us like a pizza."[15]

It is difficult for outsiders to understand the extreme devotion of Kurds to Öcalan. Marc Grossman, who served as the US Ambassador to Turkey from 1994–to 1997, introduced me to Prof. Dr. Dogu Ergil, chair of the Political Science Department at Ankara State University, who was researching Kurdish perceptions of the Turkish state. His surveys found that an overwhelming majority of Kurds rejected political violence and sought a *modus vivendi* as citizens of Turkey. Dogu explained that Öcalan was revered for dignifying Kurds, opposing Turkey's tyranny, and enabling Kurds to feel pride in their armed struggle.

When I visited Dogu at his home in Ankara, we discussed how to operationalize his research. Dogu was at-risk. Academic work casting doubt on the state's claim that Kurds supported terrorism was anathema to the authorities. Although he was always careful in choosing his words, Dogu lived in constant fear of court cases against him. Dogu also risked recriminations from militant Turkish nationalists, called "grey wolves." He kept a small revolver with a mother of pearl handle in his dresser drawer. I almost laughed when he showed it to me. The pistol looked like a toy gun; it was an ornament, useless against potential attackers.

With encouragement from Ambassador Grossman and initial financing from the National Endowment for Democracy, Dogu and I launched a dialogue project involving prominent Turks and Kurds, excluding ultra-nationalists on both sides. Dogu selected and managed relations with participants. With additional funds from the Winston Foundation for World Peace and the Swiss Authorities, we organized a series of meetings at a chateau outside Paris, a conference center on Lake Lugano in Switzerland, and finally a monastery in Belgium. William Ury, whose mediation techniques are chronicled in his book, *Getting to Yes*, joined the meetings as a facilitator. Bill was a great asset, knowledgeable and personable, skillfully helping participants identify mutual interests.

After more than one year of discussions, participants adopted a manifesto summarizing their efforts. "Walking Together in History" identified common ground between the Turks and Kurds. The manifesto rejected violence and endorsed Turkey's democratic development and integration into European structures to address the Kurdish issue.

At the end of the third meeting, we took the project participants to an outdoor fish restaurant in the Beyoglu district of Istanbul. I felt pride, admiration, and sympathy for Dogu: pride because of what we had accomplished, making dialogue a real alternative to political violence, admiration for his personal achievements through hard work and application of his outstanding intellect, and sympathy. Dogu was a maverick with the capacity to achieve in any setting. If he had been born in the West, he would be a public intellectual of great standing. As a Turk, he was limited by the constraints of his society and the shortsightedness of Turkish officials.

Hands-on involvement taught me the nuances of conflict between the Kurds and the Turkish state. I applied this new-found knowledge to raise awareness on Capitol Hill, where the Congressional Human Rights Foundation held briefings on human rights conditions in Turkey. I met

Congressman Stephen Solarz (D, NY) at a hearing of the Commission on Security and Cooperation in Europe, an independent US government organization created by Congress in 1975 to monitor and encourage compliance with the Helsinki Final Act. Before my testimony, Solarz pulled me aside and told me to "go easy on the Turks. They're really not so bad." He was from Brooklyn but known as "the congressman from Istanbul."[16] He and his wife, Nina, had a summer home in Bodrum on the Turkish seaside.

It was difficult to gain Congressional support for the Kurdish cause. Influenced by the American-Israel Public Affairs Committee, Jewish Members of Congress like Solarz and Tom Lantos were reflexively pro-Turkish because of the country's avowed secularism and engagement with Israel. Turkey was the first Muslim majority country to recognize Israel in 1949.[17] Israel's "peripheral pact" focused its diplomacy on non-Arab states of the Middle East, such as Iran and Turkey. Cooperation included intelligence sharing and weapons sales. In addition, Turkey allowed Israeli war planes to use Turkish air space for training its F-16 pilots.

After decades of cooperation, the close Israeli-Turkish relationship collapsed when Turkey sent a flotilla to Gaza to deliver humanitarian supplies in May 2010. In fact, it was not a humanitarian mission but a publicity stunt by Turkish Islamists. Nine activists on board the *Mavi Marmara* were killed by Isreali commandos when the ship's captain refused instructions to turn back and Israeli Defense Forces boarded the ship in international waters of the Mediterranean Sea. Turkey condemned Israel for its "genocide" of Palestinians while denying Turkish involvement in the genocide of Armenians between 1915 and 1923.[18]

Turkey emphasized "hard power" against the PKK. From 1984 to the present, more than 40,000 people have died as a result of the conflict.[19] While pursuing a security solution, the Turkish government also tried soft power to diminish popular support for the PKK, focusing on economic development and expanding educational opportunity and health services. However, no combination of hard and soft power could address the root cause of the problem. Kurds demanded dignity and were prepared to struggle until their political and cultural rights were assured.

. . . . .

In 1996, I visited Diyarbakir to conduct field research and make contact with Turkish civil society representatives. I was accompanied by my board member at the Congressional Human Rights Foundation, J. Kenneth Blackwell. Ken served as the US Ambassador to the UN Human Rights Commission during the administration of George H.W. Bush. We had collaborated during my visits to Geneva with the Bosnian delegation in the early 1990s. After Bill Clinton defeated Bush in 1992, Ken and I traveled together on human rights missions to Turkey, Kosovo, and Kashmir. It was an asset to have a well-respected former US ambassador with human rights experience as an advocacy partner. Sharing visits to these places of hardship strengthened our collegial and fraternal bond.

We invited the board of the Diyarbakir Human Rights Association to dinner at the Hotel Karavanserai, a traditional layover for Silk Road traders, in August 1997. The Silk Road connected the occident and the orient from the second century BC to the eighteenth century. After dinner at the Karavanserai, Blackwell and I escorted our guests to the front door. Waiting on the corner was a large white van. Police jumped out of the vehicle and detained the Kurds. No "Miranda warning" or due process, just intimidation and fear.

Blackwell and I visited the Diyarbakir governor the next morning. The province was under curfew and heavily militarized. Guards gave me a laminated pass to enter the facility, which I was supposed to return after the visit. I deliberately retained the badge and gave it to Kendal Nezan, a Kurd from Turkey who heads the Kurdish Institute of Paris. Kendal attended our conference on "The Future of Democracy in Iraq" and was my liaison with Mme. Danielle Mitterrand. Targeted by Turkish authorities many times in his youth, I knew Kendal would appreciate possessing the badge.

Blackwell and I hired a taxi and headed north from Diyarbakir to the PKK strongholds of Lice and Van. We did not get very far. On the outskirts of Diyarbakir, we were stopped by the gendarmerie. Blackwell protested, "We're with the United Nations!" Local security couldn't care less. After remanding us to our vehicle for more than an hour, we were ordered to turn around and return to Diyarbakir.

We traveled from Turkey to Geneva. I prepared a testimony on "Human Rights Conditions in Turkey," which recounted our recent experiences and drew on credible secondary sources. We had breakfast at the Hilton Hotel near the Palais des Nations with Turkey's Ambassador Gunduz Aktan to share findings from the trip. After our discussion, I gave him a copy of the testimony that was embargoed until the next day. Ken was furious with my rookie mistake. He admonished me for tipping our hand and warned that Aktan would have his legal team scrutinize every word and prepare a rebuttal. Sure enough, Aktan distributed an official reply the next morning in the plenary of the UN Human Rights Commission.

Turkish officials like Aktan worked with an array of "K Street" public relations firms tasked with discrediting the PKK. I conformed to the view that the PKK was a terror group. Over the years, however, Kurdish friends maintained that Turkey was a terror state and that the PKK was merely trying to defend the Kurdish people. I was sympathetic to their entreaties but feared losing credibility by showing sympathy with the PKK.

I also believed it was important to maintain ties with Turkish colleagues in the secular establishment. These included Sarik Tara, the chairman of ENKA Construction, and Ishak Alaton of Alarko Construction and Engineering. Sarik and I got to know one another through Holbrooke's mediation on Cyprus, which included Greeks and Turks. Tara was kind and generous. We shared many experiences, including a "blue voyage" along the Turkish coast in his yacht, the "Sipituba."

Alaton was a leading member of Turkey's Jewish community. I became very friendly with him and his daughter, Leyla. Both Tara and Alaton were sympathetic to victims of the Turkish state, but they dared not question Turkey's demonization of the PKK. Their companies relied on public tenders, and they were reluctant to jeopardize their business interests.

Alaton was my first port of call during many visits to Istanbul. His office had a wrap-around patio overlooking the Yavuz Sultan Selim Bridge, one of the tallest bridges in the world that spanned the Bosphorus. We spent hours sitting on the patio, discussing the situation in Turkey. Alaton was helpful and well-connected. He would just pick up the phone and arrange meetings beneficial to my work. He often loaned me his driver and hardshell armored vehicle to navigate Istanbul's tangled traffic.

I met many prominent Turks, including Ustun Erguder, in Ishak's private dining room. Educated at Manchester and Syracuse universities, Erguder was the President of Boğaziçi University and a board member of the Open Society Foundation. He was a world-class academic and a real gentleman. I appreciated Erguder and many other noble Turks who favored reform and accountability of government institutions. Solarz was right: Turks are good people; it's their government that is to blame for conflict in the country.

· · · · ·

Although Turkey was a NATO member, EU membership was held back by its military and secular political parties. The military conducted coups d'état in 1960, 1980, and 1993, and issued memoranda in 1971 and 1997 aimed at consolidating power. Turkey was never a true democracy; the military was always lurking in the background, ready to suppress any attempts at opening the government and society.

It was a breath of fresh air when the Justice and Development Party (AKP), led by Recep Tayyip Erdoğan and Abdullah Gül, swept elections in November 2002 and established a single-party government early the following year.[20] I met with Ambassador Grossman soon after the election. He and other members of the US foreign policy establishment welcomed Erdoğan's rise.

However, Erdoğan was neither a democrat nor secular. As Mayor of Istanbul in 1996, he proclaimed: "Democracy is like a streetcar. You get off when you have reached your destination."[21] For Erdoğan, elections were a vehicle for seizing power.

In December 1997, he addressed a political rally in Siirt: "The mosques are our barracks, the domes our helmets, the minarets our bayonets and the faithful our soldiers." He was convicted of dividing society using religion, sentenced to ten months in prison, and prevented from holding public office because of his criminal record.[22] Parliament changed the constitution to allow Erdoğan to stand for a bi-election in Siirt, which he won handily in late 2002. He became prime minister in February 2003.[23]

Erdoğan practiced *taqiyah*, an Islamic term for obfuscating the truth to achieve a greater goal. He was driven by domestic political considerations, not principle. He launched the "Democracy Opening" in 2010. It was also known as the Kurdish initiative and the Unity and Fraternity Project.[24] Its stated objective was to improve the human rights of *Turkish* citizens of Kurdish origin in order to end conflict with the PKK. According to Interior Minister Beşir Atalay, the initiative sought to improve democratic standards and end terrorism in Turkey.

To engage civil society, Erdoğan held several meetings with prominent figures of Turkish society at the Dolmabahçe Palace in Istanbul. The meetings were a tool for public diplomacy, broadcast live on television and radio. Erdoğan told participants, "Deep down in my heart I believe that you will shoulder the process and lend your support, contribute and make an effort to solving Turkey's painful problems." The project lost momentum and was soon discontinued.

In 2013, Erdoğan established a group of "Wise Men." It was comprised of sixty-three prominent figures, including celebrities, academics, musicians, journalists, writers, authors, business experts, consultants, and directors of human rights and law organizations, economic foundations, and associations.[25] Dogu was a member. Through him, I tried to influence developments by sharing ideas and information. Unfortunately, the commission was merely window-dressing and was soon disbanded.[26]

Turkey also tried back-channel negotiations.[27] In September 2011, it was revealed that Turkish officials, including Hakan Fidan, who later became the head of MIT, met with members of the European wing of the PKK in Oslo, Norway. I was receiving funds from the Norwegian government for a range of activities, including work in Turkey. Norway's role was so secret that I knew nothing of the Oslo process. The channel collapsed when audio recordings of the meeting leaked. Fethullah Gülen, a close Erdoğan associate at the time, condemned the dialogue and urged the government to prosecute Fidan for treason.

I was in Athens at the Grand Bretagne Hotel when disaffected members of Turkey's Armed Forces allegedly launched a coup on July 15, 2016. The conspirators bungled the operation so badly that some called it a "false-coup," which Erdoğan organized to justify a crackdown against oppositionists. More likely, either the coup was infiltrated by MIT or Russia tipped off the government. Erdoğan allowed the coup to progress just far enough to appear credible so he could justify a crackdown.[28]

In his first public remarks during the early morning of July 16, Erdoğan issued a chilling threat: "This latest action is an act of treason. This attempt, this move, is a great gift from God for us. Why? Because the move will allow us to clean up the armed forces, which needs to be completely cleaned." He vowed to purge all state institutions of "the virus" spread by supporters of Fethullah Gülen,[29] whom he blamed for the coup attempt.

The Turkish government had already prepared lists of oppositionists and moved immediately to arrest them. About 50,000 members of the security services and civil servants were arrested and another 150,000 dismissed from their jobs. Approximately 150 journalists were jailed, more than any other country according to the Committee to Protect Journalists. Members of Parliament, judges, and educators were fired or arrested. Erdoğan also threatened to sign a bill reinstating the death penalty.[30]

My room at the Grand Bretagne in Athens turned into a media hub. I conducted a series of interviews, questioning the coup's credibility. The Turkish military is notoriously efficient. How could it have bungled the operation? Erdoğan was vacationing in Marmaris when mutinous soldiers arrived at his hotel to arrest him. He had checked out and was on his way to the Dalaman Airport. Although mutineers controlled the Air Force, they did not shoot down Erdoğan's plane. The conspirators did not shut down all media outlets, failing to control the flow of information. Nor did they issue a public statement, explaining the events or presenting an alternative. US officials did not respond immediately, gauging the events. Erdoğan accused the US of instigating the coup, which further polarized US-Turkey relations.

After the attempted coup, Erdoğan intensified pressure on the pro-Kurdish Party (HDP) in Turkey, arresting HDP co-leaders Selahattin Demirtaş and Figen Yüksekdağ in November 2016.[31] They were among the thirteen deputies detained on bogus terrorism charges. In addition, some six thousand HDP members and elected officials were jailed for a variety of charges related to terrorism. Erdoğan slandered the HDP, calling them "terror lovers."[32]

Even prior to the attempted coup, Erdoğan had been intensifying his crackdown on the Kurds. In the June 2015 elections, the HDP won eighty seats in Parliament, denying the AKP an absolute majority.[33] When Kurdish youth set up barricades in some cities of Turkey's southeast and declared autonomous areas, the armed forces attacked with overwhelming force, killing more than four thousand people and displacing some 350,000 civilians.

My views about Turkey were evolving in the face of its naked aggression. Breaking with US orthodoxy on the PKK, I published an article in the Brookings Institution's journal, *Lawfare*, in February 2016, titled "The Case for Delisting the PKK as a Foreign Terrorist Organization." I argued that removing the PKK from the State Department's list of Foreign Terrorist Organizations would:

> create conditions for greater security cooperation between the United States and the PKK in the fight against the Islamic State in Iraq and Syria (ISIS). In exchange for delisting, the PKK could be required to reiterate its rejection of ISIS, pledge to further support the campaign to degrade and destroy the terror group, and officially renounce violence aimed at achieving political objectives. Delisting could also catalyze political negotiations between the Turkish government and the PKK, resulting in an arrangement enhancing Turkey's security while enshrining greater political and cultural rights for Kurds.[34]

By this time, I had abandoned hopes of working collaboratively with Turkish officials on reform initiatives. A friend in the Counter-Terrorism Unit of the Istanbul Police warned me not to visit Turkey; I was a marked man and would be arrested. I was advised not even to transit through Atatürk Airport in Istanbul.

Turkey, under Erdoğan's dictatorship, had become anti-democratic and stridently anti-American. When Turks gathered in Gezi Park near Taksim Square in May 2013 to protest plans to build a shopping mall in a green space, they were attacked by riot police.[35] Crowds gathered in sixty cities to protest police brutality. There was scant media coverage; Turkish national television chose to broadcast a documentary about the migration of penguins instead.

In 2016, Erdoğan pushed through constitutional reforms affecting the Kemalist judiciary. Pro-government prosecutors conjured fantastical plots, Ergenekon and Operation Sledgehammer, which were used to crack down on retired and current military officers. Arrests sent shock waves through Turkey's security establishment.[36]

Approved in a referendum on April 16, 2017, Turkey's new constitution transformed Turkey from a parliamentary to a presidential system, consolidating the head of state, head of government, and head of the ruling party all into a single powerful office. It eliminated the prime minister's leading position and drastically curtailed the parliament's oversight of the executive branch.[37]

Turkey suffered a worsening democracy deficit. Article 8 of the Turkish Anti-Terror Act and Article 301 of the Penal Code were used to silence dissent and prevent freedom of expression. US-Turkey relations deteriorated. Secretary of State Mike Pompeo, an evangelical Christian, strongly criticized the detention of US pastor Andrew Brunson, who was jailed for more than two years.[38] Several US citizens and consular officials were also imprisoned on bogus, politically motivated charges.

Erdoğan's Turkey became increasingly Islamist, supporting jihadists fighting the regime in Syria. After Ghouta was attacked with chemical weapons on August 21, 2013, Erdoğan intensified efforts to support the rebels. MIT established the jihadi highway from Sanliurfa to Raqqa. Assistance ranged from military cooperation and weapons transfers to logistical support, financial assistance, and the provision of medical services to wounded warriors. Vice President Joe Biden confirmed Turkey's involvement in a speech at Harvard University on October 3, 2014.

> Our allies in the region were our largest problem in Syria. The Turks ... the Saudis, the Emiratis ... were so determined to take down Assad and essentially have a Sunni-Shia proxy war, they poured hundreds of millions of dollars, thousands of tons of weapons to anyone who would fight against Assad .... The people that were being supplied were Al Nusra and Al Qaeda and the extremist elements of jihadis coming from other parts of the world. We could not convince our colleagues to stop supplying them .... President Erdoğan told me, he's an old friend. "You were right. We let too many people through."[39]

Turkey assisted ISIS in plain sight. On May 29, 2015, the journalist Can Dündar, editor in chief of *Cumhuriyet*, reported on trucks laden with weapons crossing the border. Dündar wrote, "Here are the weapons Erdoğan claims do not exist." *Cumhuriyet* also published a video and photos supporting its report. Dündar was arrested and charged with espionage, divulging state secrets, and membership in a terrorist organization. He was convicted for "disclosing documents concerning the security of the State" and given a five-year sentence.[40]

I recruited a team of researchers in the US, Turkey, and Europe to document Turkey's support for Islamist groups. Columbia's report garnered a lot of media attention, infuriating Turkish officials. At a meeting of the Council on Foreign Relations in New York City, Erdoğan looked my way, criticizing "so-called friends of Turkey who sought to tarnish Turkey's reputation." Instead of cooperating in the fight against ISIS, Turkey was supporting jihadists. To Erdoğan, the Kurds were the real terrorists.

Serious concerns persist about freedom of expression and assembly in Turkey. The 1991 law on the fight against terrorism is used to silence Turkey's perceived critics and enemies.[41] Article 8 of the Anti-Terror Act applies selectively to restrict freedom of expression. Article 301 of the penal code, which makes it a crime to denigrate Turkishness, is used against political opponents.[42]

Corruption is rampant. On December 17, 2013, Erdoğan was recorded instructing his son, Bilal, to launder tens of millions of dollars of ill-gotten assets, including instructions to buy luxury apartments on the Bosporus.[43] In addition, WikiLeaks revealed that his son-in-law, Berat Albayrak, who was Energy Minister at the time, colluded to sell oil from Syria, the proceeds of which, at its peak, generated $3 million a day for ISIS.[44]

Turkey became an outlier in Europe. The European Parliament (EP) voted to suspend talks with Turkey over its EU membership on November 24, 2016. When the AKP wanted to send ministers to campaign for the referendum in Germany and the Netherlands, they were disallowed because of security concerns. Erdoğan responded by calling Chancellor Angela Merkel a "Nazi" and described the Dutch government as Nazi remnants and fascists.[45] A minister in the Erdoğan government threatened that Turkey would launch jihad in Europe and release fifteen thousand refugees each week if the AKP was not allowed to campaign.

Unable to visit and discouraged by the Trump administration's erratic approach to Turkey, I focused on outreach to the US Congress and legislative bodies in Europe. On April 5, 2017, I testified at a Congressional conference, "Turkey's Democracy Under Challenge," convened by the Subcommittee on Europe of the House International Affairs Committee. *In 2018,* the Kurdish Institute of Paris invited me to testify before the French Senate; I also spoke before the British House of Commons. From 2016 to 2018, I was a speaker at the European Parliament's annual conference on Turkey, organized by the Green Party.

In November 2019, I lobbied Congress to enforce the Countering America's Adversaries Through Sanctions Act and impose sanctions on Turkey for purchasing the S-400 missile system from Russia. The purchase violated the core NATO principle of interoperability between weapons systems of its members. The S-400s came with Russian technicians, which risked compromising sensitive technology. Speaking on Capitol Hill at the 9th Annual Religious Freedom reception on November 29, 2019, I called on the United States to cancel Turkey's participation in the F-35 Stealth Fighter training program and impose sanctions.

The US Senate voted to approve sanctions on December 11, 2019. After vehemently protesting sanctions legislation, Erdoğan appeared unperturbed. Sanctions are intended to force the regime to change its behavior. However, Erdoğan has proved to be beyond reform.

Turkey today is not the country I once knew. Most of my Turkish friends have passed away or have been intimidated into silence. US policymakers must understand Turkey as it is, not how it used to be, or how they wish it were. Steely-eyed realism is necessary when re-evaluating US-Turkey relations.

Notes

1 Encyclopedia Britannica https://www.britannica.com/event/Sykes-Picot-Agreement (accessed April 5, 2020).

2 Encyclopedia Britannica https://www.britannica.com/event/Treaty-of-Sevre (accessed April 5, 2020).

3 YouTube, September 26, 2018, https://www.youtube.com/watch?v=z7dG65 KGh7Y (accessed April 4, 2020).

4 Washington Kurdish Institute, https://dckurd.org/2018/07/25/sheikh-said-of-piran/ (accessed April 7, 2020).

5 John Tirman, "Ataturk's Children," *Boston Review,* www.photius.com/thus.ata turk.html (accessed April 5, 2020).

6   Soner Cagaptay, "Reconfiguring the Turkish State in the 1930s," Harvard 2002.

7   Ceng Sagnic, "Mountain Turks: State Ideology and the Kurds in Turkey," *Society and Justice*, July 2010, https://core.ac.uk/download/pdf/36771618.pdf.

8   Cited by the author in *The Kurdish Spring: A New Map for the Middle East* (New Brunswick/London: Transaction Publishers, 2015).

9   David Phillips, "An Uncertain Ally: Turkey Under Erdoğan's Dictatorship," 2017.

10 Fabrice Balance, "The Kurdish Path to Socialism in Syria," *Washington Institute for Near East Policy*, May 16, 2017, https://www.washingtoninstitute.org/policy-analysis/view/the-kurdish-path-to-socialism-in-syria.

11 "Background Briefing," *Human Rights Watch*, https://www.hrw.org/legacy/backgrounder/eca/turkey/2004/10/2.htm (accessed April 5, 2020).

12 United States Department of State, Bureau of Counterterrorism, https://www.state.gov/foreign-terrorist-organizations/ (accessed April 7, 2020).

13 Ali Younes, "Analysis: What does the Adana Deal Mean for Turkey and Syria?" *Al Jazeera*, October 23, 2019, https://www.aljazeera.com/news/2019/10/analysis-adana-deal-turkey-syria-191022194719603.html.

14 Janet Biehl, *Bookchin, Öcalan, and the Dialectics of Democracy* (Compass Press, n.d.), http://new-compass.net/articles/bookchin-%C3%B6calan-and-dialectics-democracy (accessed April 5, 2020).

15 Cited by the author in *Unsilencing the Past: Track Two Diplomacy and Turkish Armenian Reconciliation* (Berghahn Books, 2004).

16 "Former Congressmen Sign Deal to Push Turkish Issues," *Asbarez*, February 3, 2000, http://asbarez.com/42021/former-congressmen-sign-deal-to-push-turkish-issues/.

17 "Turkey-Israel Relations: A Timeline," *Anadolu Agency*, June 27, 2016, https://www.aa.com.tr/en/middle-east/turkey-israel-relations-a-timeline/598666.

18 Mavi Marmara, "Why Did Israel Stop the Gaza Flotilla?" *BBC News*, June 27, 2016, https://www.bbc.com/news/1020372.

19 Mine Eder, *"Turkey,"* 2016, *The Middle East*.

20 "Erdoğan Triumphs—With Plenty of Help from His Enemies," *The Economist*, https://www.economist.com/europe/2002/11/07/erdogan-triumphs-with-plenty-of-help-from-his-enemies (accessed April 7, 2020).

21 The European Institute, https://europeaninstitute.org/index.php/282-euro pean-affairs/ea-may-2016/2160-perspectives-erdogan-the-magnificent-and-his-eu-streetcar (accessed April 4, 2020).

22 "Turkey's Charismatic Leader," *BBC World News*, November 4, 2002, http://news.bbc.co.uk/2/hi/europe/2270642.stm.

23 "Turkish PM Quits for Erdoğan," *CNN*, March 11, 2003, https://www.cnn.com/2003/WORLD/europe/03/11/turkey.elections/.

24 Cited by the author in "An Uncertain Ally: Turkey Under Erdoğan's Dictatorship," 2017.

25 "The Wise Men of Turkey," *Rudaw*, July 4, 2013, https://www.rudaw.net/english/opinion/07042013.

26 Interview by the author with Dogu Ergil, April 5, 2020.

27 Daniel Dombey, "Turkey Spy Chief Summoned over PKK Talks," *Financial Times*, February 9, 2012, https://www.ft.com/content/12733aa0-5328-11e1-8aa1-00144feabdc0.

28 Ezgi Basaran, "Turkey Coup: Who was Behind Turkey Coup Attempt?" *BBC News*, July 16, 2016, https://www.bbc.com/news/world-europe-36815476.

29 Marc Champion, "Coup was a 'Gift from God,'" *Bloomberg News*, July 17, 2016, https://www.bloomberg.com/news/articles/2016-07-17/coup-was-a-gift-from-god-says-erdogan-who-plans-a-new-turkey.

30 Amnesty International, "The Aftermath of the Failed Turkey Coup: Torture, Beatings, and Rape," January 12, 2018, https://www.amnesty.org.uk/after math-failed-turkey-coup-torture-beatings-and-rape.

31 "Turkey Pro-Kurd HDP Party Condemns Arrest of Leaders," *BBC News*, November 16, 2016, https://www.bbc.com/news/world-europe-37875605.

32 "Erdoğan Says HDP Lawmakers are Terrorists," *Ahval News*, March 6, 2019, https://ahvalnews.com/hdp/erdogan-says-pro-kurdish-hdps-lawmakers-not-supporters-are-terrorists.

33 "Turkey Election: Ruling AKP Regains Majority," *BBC News*, November 15, 2015, https://www.bbc.com/news/world-europe-34694420.

34 David L. Phillips and Kelly Berkell, "The Case for Delisting the PKK as a Foreign Terrorist Organization," *Lawfare*, February 11, 2016, https://www.law fareblog.com/case-delisting-pkk-foreign-terrorist-organization.

35 Tim Arango, Sebnem Arsu, and Ceylan Yeginsu, "Police Storm Park in Istan-

bul, Setting off a Night of Chaos," *New York Times*, June 15, 2013, https://www.nytimes.com/2013/06/16/world/europe/protesters-in-turkey.html.

36 "Turkey 'Sledgehammer' Coup Plot Trial Collapses," *BBC News*, March 31, 2015, https://www.bbc.com/news/world-europe-32136809.

37 Gulen Solaker and Daren Butler, "Turkish MPs Elect Judicial Board under New Erdoğan Constitution," *Reuters News*, May 17, 2017.

38 Carlotta Gall, "Turkey Frees Pastor Andrew Brunson, Easing Tensions with U.S.," *New York Times*, October 12, 2018, https://www.nytimes.com/2018/10/12/world/europe/turkey-us-pastor-andrew-brunson.html.

39 "Biden Apologizes to Turkish President," *New York Times*, October 5, 2014.

40 "The Case of Can Dündar and Erdem Gül," *Columbia University*, https://globalfreedomofexpression.columbia.edu/cases/case-journalists-can-dundar-erdem-gul/ (accessed April 7, 2020).

41 Law on Fight Against Terrorism of Turkey, 1991, https://www.legislationline.org/download/id/3727/file/Turkey_anti_terr_1991_am2010_en.pdf.

42 "Turkey: Article 301: How the Law on Denigrating Turkishness is an Insult to Free Expression," *Amnesty International*, March 1, 2006, https://www.amnesty.org/en/documents/eur44/003/2006/en/.

43 Consatanze Letsch, "Leaked Tapes Prompt Calls for Turkish PM to Resign," *The Guardian*, February 25, 2014, https://www.theguardian.com/world/2014/feb/25/leaked-tapes-calls-erdogan-resign-turkish-pm.

44 Robbie Gramer, "Latest WikiLeaks Dump Sheds New Light on Erdoğan's Power in Turkey," *Foreign Policy*, December 7, 2016, https://foreignpolicy.com/2016/12/07/latest-wikileaks-dump-sheds-light-erdogan-turkey-berat-albayrak-redhack-hackers-oil/.

45 Emma Anderson, "Erdoğan Calls Merkel's Stance on EU Membership Nazism," *Politico*, September 16, 2017, https://www.politico.eu/article/turkey-germany-recep-tayyip-erdogan-calls-angela-merkels-stance-on-eu-membership-nazism.

CHAPTER 8

BETRAYAL OF THE SYRIAN KURDS

Turkey was the original backer of Islamist fighters in Syria. As we have seen, Turkey's National Intelligence Agency (MIT) established the "jihadi highway" between Sanliurfa and Raqqa, providing weapons, money, and logistical support to 40,000 foreign fighters transiting through Turkey to join ISIS in Syria. When President Bashar al-Assad used chemical weapons (CW) to attack Ghouta in September 2013, Turkey intensified its collaboration with ISIS, taking over the US train-and-equip program and turning the Free Syrian Army (FSA) into a Turkish-controlled jihadi militia that committed war crimes with impunity.

In March 2014, Turkish-backed Islamist proxies invaded Kessab, an Armenian enclave in northwest Syria, and murdered hundreds of Armenians and other Christians, desecrating and destroying many churches.[1] The rampage continued in the autumn of 2015 during the battle for Kobani, a medium-sized city in Syria on the border with Turkey. By this point, ISIS and the FSA were one and the same. Turkey's support for ISIS in the battle for Kobani was a turning point in Syria's civil war. ISIS tightened the noose around Kobani, overrunning its surrounding villages, beheading villagers, raping women, and using suicide bombers and vehicle-borne improvised explosive devices (IEDs) as they advanced towards the city center. ISIS fighters used Turkey as a staging ground to attack Kobani from behind. Kurds with the People's Protection Units (YPG) and female fighters in the Women's Defense Units (YPJ) fought valiantly against overwhelming odds.[2] Without US intervention, however, they were no match for the well-equipped and zealous ISIS attackers.

International media observed the battle from Suruç on the Turkish side of the border. Turkish tanks were perched on the hills above Kobani. Border guards waved through Turkish trucks that delivered weapons to support the ISIS operation. Prominent former officials from the State Department and Pentagon resisted calls for action. Ryan Crocker, the former US ambassador to Syria, Iraq, and several other countries, cautioned against intervention, maintaining that Kobani had no strategic value. Pentagon spokesman John Kirby called for strategic patience.[3]

As the noose tightened around Kobani, I was in regular contact with Hamdi Ulukaya, owner, founder, chairman, and CEO of Chobani, the top-selling yogurt brand in the US. Hamdi was born to a Kurdish dairy-farming family in Erzincan, a small village in Turkey. In 1994, he immigrated to the US to take business courses and study English. Hamdi is a self-made billionaire businessman, philanthropist, and visionary, who granted 10 percent of Chobani's shares to the company's employees. Thirty percent of Chobani's two thousand employees are immigrants or refugees. In 2016, Forbes Magazine honored him as "The Socially Responsible CEO."[4]

Hamdi pledged $2 million to help Kurds who were displaced by the conflict. He warned, "Either we will be watching the massacre there and will live on with a guilty conscience or we will save people." Although Hamdi asserted he was "not interested in the political aspect of the situation,"[5] he was outraged as the calamity in Kobani worsened and mobilized his political contacts. For someone who professed to be non-political, Hamdi was remarkably well connected. He reached out to Senator Charles Schumer (D-NY) and other prominent personalities on Capitol Hill, urging action by the Obama Administration. I was receiving frontline bulletins through my Kurdish network, relying on colleagues in London who were well informed about developments. Hamdi and I exchanged information on developments in Kobani during our regular calls. We met regularly at the Mercer Hotel in New York's West Village to discuss strategy and coordinate activities. About 40,000 jihadists from approximately eighty countries had already made their way through Turkey to the front lines in Syria. What started as a revolution had turned into a proxy war.

With 80 percent of Kobani under ISIS control and the city on the verge of collapse, the Obama Administration finally heeded calls for intervention. US officials concluded that the city's fall would lead to the violent execution of its defenders. They were concerned that images of ISIS beheading Kurds would be broadcast by ISIS media and exploited to recruit foreign fighters. On October 5, 2015, the US launched more than two hundred sorties using warplanes and drones to bomb the ISIS front lines. US C-130 transport planes dropped twenty-seven bundles of weapons, ammunition, and medical supplies to the YPG. I reached out to the Kurdistan Regional Government (KRG) in Erbil to encourage their participation and learned that these supplies came from the Peshmerga, the battle-hardened Kurdish fighters of the KRG. Erdoğan was under intense pressure and succumbed to US demands, allowing 150 Peshmerga to cross Turkish territory and enter Syria where they joined the fight.[6]

Kobani became a symbol of resistance. The Kurds fought bravely in house-to-house combat. Forty percent of Kobani's defenders were women. Stan Salett, a friend/adviser/donor who served in the Kennedy Administration and was active in Maryland state politics, suggested I contact the Democratic Union Party (PYD) to propose an advocacy campaign that would highlight the role of female fighters. The message was sent via Michelle Allison, an active member of the London Kurdish network. Members of the YPJ were fierce symbols of freedom and women's rights in Rojava, a Kurdish region in North and East Syria (NES). The Rojava experiment—grass-roots democracy, emancipation of women, and environmental sustainability—was compelling. However, the US deferred to Turkey's concerns about Syrian Kurds exercising too much autonomy.

I invited Salih Muslim, co-chair of the PYD, to attend a conference at Columbia University. He submitted his visa application with my invitation letter to the US Embassy in Stockholm and waited several years, with no reply. Traveling from NES would require passage either through Turkey or via Damascus. Both Turkey and Syria were hostile to the Kurds in Syria.

On the one hand, I applauded US support for the Kurds. On the other, I criticized the Obama Administration for succumbing to Turkish pressure and preventing the PYD from participating in the United Nations (UN)-led mediation called the Geneva Process. Peace negotiations need to be inclusive. Kurds controlled 30 percent of the territory in Syria. If they were not seated at the table, they could not be a force for stability and reconciliation during the peace-building phase.

ISIS could not be defeated with air power alone. Based on their tenacious defense of Kobani, the US Department of Defense realized that the YPG and YPJ could effectively serve as boots on-the- ground for the US-led Global Coalition to Defeat ISIS. After Kobani, Kurdish fighters pivoted east and attacked Tal Abyad, a strategic border crossing between Turkey and Syria in Hasakah Province. MIT was using Tal Abyad as a trans-shipment point to supply ISIS in its self-declared capitol of Raqqa. The Kurdish offensive against Tal Abyad lasted from May to July 2015. US Special Forces trained the Kurds as spotters to call in US air strikes against ISIS positions.[7]

Erdoğan resisted US efforts to expand security cooperation with the Kurds, calling the YPG a "direct threat" to Turkey.[8] He demanded that US officials choose between the Kurds, whom he viewed as terrorists with ties to the Kurdistan Workers' Party (PKK), and Turkey, America's NATO ally. He insisted that the PKK and the PYD were one and the same and blamed the US for a "sea of blood" in Syria. Erdoğan demanded, "I told you many times, are you with us or are you with the terrorists?"[9] To address Turkey's concerns, the Pentagon integrated Arabs into a hybrid force called the Syrian Democratic Forces (SDF). Arabs were a fig leaf. At its core, the SDF was a Kurdish force led by General Mazloum Kobani, a Syrian Kurd with historic ties to the PKK.

In August 2016, Turkey invaded Jarabulus in northern Aleppo province. Operation "Euphrates Shield" was carried out in the region between rebel-held Azaz to the west and the Euphrates River to the east.[10] Turkish troops were joined by jihadis in the FSA. It was a decisive military victory for Turkey and a public relations fiasco. Jarablus fell without a shot. The Turks collaborated with ISIS fighters who changed out of their terror garb and joined brethren in the FSA ranks.

The events in Jarablus did not deter the coalition from attacking Raqqa, seat of the ISIS Caliphate. US Special Forces supported the SDF during heavy street-to-street fighting on the city's western front line. Close air support from the US turned Raqqa to rubble. ISIS used civilians in Raqqa as human shields. The city was wired with booby traps and improvised explosive devices (IEDs), inflicting mass casualties as the SDF advanced.[11]

. . . . .

After the fall of Raqqa, Secretary of State Rex W. Tillerson announced that US forces would remain in Syria to keep up the pressure on ISIS and Al-Qaeda and to counter Iranian influence. In a speech at Stanford University on January 17, 2018, Tillerson articulated US concerns and goals of US policy towards Syria. He warned, "US disengagement from Syria would provide Iran the opportunity to further strengthen its position. As a destabilized nation and one bordering Israel, Syria presents an opportunity that Iran is all too eager to exploit." Tillerson endorsed a UN-brokered resolution of the conflict and the complete elimination of Syria's CW stockpiles. Both the US and Turkey believed that a "stable, unified and independent Syria ultimately requires post-Assad leadership in order to be successful." Tillerson opined, "A murderer of his own people cannot generate the support required for long-term stability."[12] According to Tillerson, stabilizing Syria would enable the return of displaced persons and facilitate the return of refugees. By this time, more than three million Syrians had taken refuge in Turkey. Erdoğan initially supported sanctuary for Syrians, but he did not anticipate the war would last so long or that so many would flee.

At Stanford, Tillerson announced the creation of a Border Security Force (BSF) to be comprised of 30,000 SDF members. The BSF would exist until US goals had been achieved. Erdoğan was incensed and accused the US of planning to form a "terror army" in Syria. Threatening the BSF, he declared: "Our mission is to strangle it before it's even born."[13] Erdoğan warned that Turkey would attack Afrin, west of the Euphrates; liberate Tal Abyad; and establish a security belt in Syria all the way to the border with Iraqi Kurdistan.

Erdoğan was true to his word. Backed by Turkish warplanes, tanks, and armored vehicles, the FSA invaded Afrin in January 2018. It beheaded Kurdish defenders and raped and mutilated the bodies of Kurdish women in the YPJ, cutting off their breasts and posing for selfies with their body parts. The FSA coerced a young Syrian boy to decapitate a Syrian soldier and then used his head as a soccer ball.[14]

I was invited to Qamishlo, the de facto capitol of NES to participate in a "Conference on War Crimes in Afrin" in December 2018. I reached out to Masrour Barzani, the KRG's Interior Minister, who offered transport and a security detail to take to me from Erbil to Fishkabour, a transit town on the Iraqi side of the Little Zab River. My arrival was delayed by a mishap on the road. The vehicle took a shortcut near Sinjar, close to where ISIS attacked Yezidi villages, murdered thousands of men, and seized Yezidi women as sex slaves. Our car ran over a spike strip, a device to puncture the tires of wheeled vehicles. We were immobilized for several hours, while new tires were purchased. Sinjar, not far from the Syrian border, is a dangerous place to be immobilized; it was rife with ISIS looking for trouble.

Anticipating a chaotic scene at the border, I expressed concern to Barzani's office and was assured, "Don't worry. We've done this before." At the border crossing, my name was on a list, and I was ushered into the

VIP waiting room so the KRG official could do paperwork authorizing my crossing. There I ran into an old friend, Bernard Kouchner, France's former foreign minister and a long-time Kurdish advocate, who was also traveling to the conference. We had known each other for many years through our shared interest in the Kurdish issue. Kouchner had written the foreword to my book, *The Kurdish Spring*. In addition, Kouchner and I had spent time together in Kosovo, where he served as Special Representative of the Secretary General, after NATO's intervention.

In separate vehicles, we crossed a pontoon bridge to Syria and reunited at the PYD guesthouse in Qamishlo. Bernard was agitated and worried that the US would abandon the Kurds and that Turkey would invade, putting Rojava at risk. In his opening keynote speech at the Conference on Afrin War Crimes, organized by the Rojava Center for Security Studies, his mood was dark and depressed. Speaking after Bernard, I made a point to acknowledge his role, hoping the acknowledgement would lift his spirits. "The Kurds have no better friend than Bernard Kouchner, who has been your advocate for decades."

After the conference, we visited displaced people from Afrin who had relocated to a Christian village in the NES that had been purged by ISIS. The people we met were still traumatized by their experience. Several of the women sobbed quietly as we spoke. One of the community leaders told us about her flight from Afrin. She and her daughter were running down a road to avoid a Turkish artillery attack. A missile landed next to them, instantly killing the teenage girl. The mother held onto her daughter's arm, all that was left of her. Others shared horrific stories of Turkey's bombardment and crimes by the FSA.

I was invited to give a lecture at Rojava University the day before the conference. The main hall was packed, standing room only. My old friend, Salih Muslim, was seated in the front row. I presented a paper on power sharing and the range of constitutional arrangements that decentralize power from the center to the periphery. I said that after the war, Syria would look a lot like Bosnia, with a weak central government and power distributed to the regions. The paper was translated into Arabic and distributed to attendees. I couldn't help but worry that Salih Muslim and other friends in the audience were in peril. At a moment's notice, Turkey could attack NES and destroy their utopian experiment in communal living.

The US established observation posts along the Turkish-Syrian border. The mere presence of US troops helped prevent a Turkish invasion. It also deterred Assad's Syrian Arab Army and Iranian and Russian troops from seizing territory controlled by the Kurds. The SDF held 30 percent of Syria's territory. The autonomous region was an island of relative tranquility amid Syria's chaos and conflict.

Leaving NES on December 15, 2018, I retraced my steps across the pontoon bridge and the Little Zab River. Looking in the rearview mirror at the reception area on the Syrian side, my thoughts drifted to the woman from Afrin holding her daughter's dismembered arm. I thought about Salih Muslim, who had struggled his whole life and lost a son fighting the Syrian regime. Mohammed, my handler and translator, was such a gentleman and so devoted to Rojava. These exceptional people were targeted by Turkish and Syrian forces, as well as by ISIS.

During a conference break, I met Commander Nesrin Abdullah of the YPJ. She was short and stocky but beautiful in her army fatigues and combat boots. The YPG and YPJ were indispensable partners of the US in fighting ISIS. The Kurds paid dearly. More than 11,000 Kurdish fighters died, and about 23,000 were seriously wounded battling ISIS at America's behest.[15] The US owed them a huge debt, or at the very least, our gratitude and loyalty.

· · · · ·

Trump and Erdoğan had a phone conversation on December 14, 2018, in which Erdoğan urged Trump to pull out of Syria, pointing to the near-total defeat of ISIS. Irritated by Erdoğan's constant complaining about the safe zone and US complicity with Syrian Kurds, Trump capitulated to Erdoğan's demand. Trump agreed that the US would withdraw fully and finally from Syria. "OK, it's all yours. We are done," Trump told Erdoğan.[16]

Secretary of Defense James Mattis was flabbergasted that Trump went off-script and urged him to reconsider. He told Trump it was the wrong decision at the wrong time. The US still needed the SDF to eject ISIS from its last Syrian strongholds. When his appeal was ignored by Trump, Mattis resigned in protest. His resignation letter did not mention Syria or the Kurds. It focused instead on the need to respect allies and confront strategic adversaries.

I condemned Trump's declared withdrawal in a statement to the international media, and predicted slaughter in the region:

> As soon as the US folds its tent and leaves, Turkey will immediately begin an air bombardment followed by a ground attack by the [Ankara-backed] Free Syrian army. Thousands will die, thousands will be displaced and will be given no haven within Syria. They will be turned away at the Turkish border .... For more than three and a half years, they have been our boots on the ground and were the point of the spear in retaking Raqqa. Who is going to fight for us in the future when we throw our allies under the bus? [17]

Acceding to Erdoğan's demand was an example of Trump siding with authoritarian foreign leaders over the advice of US officials. Brett McGurk, the Special Presidential Envoy for the Global Coalition to Counter ISIL, submitted his resignation a few days later. When Trump was informed, he asked: "Who's Brett McGurk? I never heard of him."[18]

I worked the media to shame Trump for his decision. To anyone who would listen, I maintained that America's retreat would create a void, giving advantage to Assad, Russia, Iran, and ISIS. *The Jerusalem Post* published my article, suggesting that America's withdrawal would benefit Iran and put Israel at risk.[19]

The Pentagon slow-walked the withdrawal of US troops. Despite Trump's agreement, the US maintained its operations in NES. Erdoğan was furious that Trump refused his request for a bilateral meeting at the UN General Assembly in September 2019. As a consolation, Secretary of State Mike Pompeo arranged a call between Trump and Erdoğan on October 6, 2019. The purpose of the call was to discuss a US-Turkey trade deal and Turkey's acquisition of S-400 surface-to-air missiles from Russia. Trump was unprepared for the conversation, ignoring his briefing book as usual. About halfway through the call, Erdoğan pivoted to his priority agenda. He criticized the safe-zone mechanism to which Turkey and the United States had agreed and repeated his threat to take unilateral action to invade and neutralize the SDF. Like a broken record, Erdoğan insisted that the SDF was a terror group; the SDF and the PKK were one and the same.

Erdoğan was motivated by both political and security factors. Picking a fight with Kurds plays well in Turkey's domestic politics. His Justice and Development Party (AKP) had suffered stinging electoral defeats in local elections during the spring and summer of 2019. Turkish voters resented Erdoğan's Syria policy, which had caused millions of Syrian Arab refugees to seek sanctuary in Turkey. Turks were increasingly agitated by the cost of supporting Syrian refugees and blamed the AKP-led government for creating a crisis that was expensive and had discredited Turkey in the eyes of the international community. Fighting the Kurds was a distraction from local elections and Erdoğan's mismanagement of Turkey's economy, which was suffering from the collapse of foreign direct investment and the devaluation of the Turkish Lira.

Erdoğan repeatedly threatened to flood Europe with refugees unless the European Union provided more funds for refugee relief. He also wanted the European Council to fast-track Turkey's membership negotiations, which had been suspended by the European Parliament over human rights concerns in the aftermath of the 2016 "coup." Erdoğan vowed to resettle 2.5 million refugees on Kurdish lands in violation of customary international law, which requires safe, voluntary, and dignified returns.[20] He also demanded a 20-mile-wide buffer zone in Syria to protect against terrorist attacks by the SDF. His concerns were contrived; the SDF had never attacked Turkey.

During the call on October 6, Erdoğan again threatened to take matters into his own hands and launch a unilateral cross-border attack. Commander of the Central Command General Joseph Votel reflected on US efforts to "placate our Turkish allies," which proved unsuccessful. Turkey "repeatedly reneged on agreements with the U.S." during multiple rounds of negotiations on a security mechanism at the border.[21]

According to an adviser who listened to the conversation, "The president has always professed to believe that Turkey and Erdoğan's massive military capability can contain ISIS." Trump was convinced that the United States was shouldering too much responsibility for stabilizing Syria, bearing inordinate costs and taking extraordinary risks. Trump also believed that Turkey would protect eastern Syria from Assad and his allies. According to the adviser, Trump "just wants out. He doesn't want to be there. He doesn't want to pay."[22] Trump acted precipitously, surprising even his closest advisers, and announced that the observation posts would be dismantled and US forces withdrawn. Although US troops in NES only numbered between fifty and one hundred, their presence had effectively served as a trip wire to prevent Turkey from attacking. Trump gave a green light for Erdoğan to attack, pledging that US troops would get out of the way: US forces "will no longer be in the immediate area."[23]

As a candidate in 2016, Trump pledged to extricate the United States from "endless and ridiculous wars." He tweeted: "[It's time] to bring our soldiers home." On October 16, 2019, Trump asserted that Turkey, Russia, the Kurds, and Europe should "figure the situation out."[24] Trump's decision reversed years of bipartisan US policy. It ignored advice from Pentagon and State Department officials and input from both parties in Congress and from US allies. Ironically, the same week that Trump ordered US forces out of Syria, he announced that the United States would send two thousand troops to Saudi Arabia.[25]

US troops who worked with the SDF called Trump's decision "sickening" and a "disgrace." Abandoning the Kurds was a "dagger to the heart."[26] According to General Mazloum Kobani, "The United States asked us to dismantle our fortifications, block our tunnels, withdraw our heavy weapons and our forces as part of a safe zone agreement, and we did this because we were told it was the only way to keep the Turks out. Now they are being invited by America to come in."[27]

Trump backtracked under strong criticism. He suspended negotiations over a $100 billion trade deal with Turkey and instructed the Treasury Department to impose sanctions, including a 50 percent tariff on Turkish steel. Trump's attempted balancing act was too little and too late.

Erdoğan acted fast before Trump changed his mind yet again. Erdoğan affirmed, "We are determined to take our operation to the end. We will finish what we started." On October 8, he ordered Turkish warplanes and artillery to attack Kurdish positions across the border. Bombings and artillery barrages hit hundreds of targets in just the first few days, concentrated on Tal Abyad and Ras al-Ain. Turkish troops with tanks and armor massed in Akçakaleon on the Turkish side of the border. They were joined by at least two thousand members of the FSA who invaded Syria on October 9, 2019.[28]

As it advanced, the FSA killed civilians and executed prisoners. The Secretary-General of the pro-Kurdish Future Syria Party, Hevrin Khalaf, and ten Kurds were executed on the side of the M4 Highway. Her executioners were a part of an Islamist jihadi group, Ahrar al-Sharqiya, under control of the Turkish military. A video depicts the execution by FSA gangsters. Shouting "Allahu Akbar," they kicked Khalaf's body and sneered, "This is the corpse of pigs." One of the victims, his hands tied behind his back, was forced to kneel and was shot in the back of his head. An FSA member fired repeatedly, crying out, "Film me shooting him with a sniper rifle—pigs ... kill them."[29] Other video footage showed the FSA executing three Kurdish fighters on the highway between Hasakah and Manbij. I joined my voice to a chorus of condemnation, criticizing both Erdoğan and Trump.

Vice President Mike Pence, Mike Pompeo, and National Security Adviser Robert C. O'Brien went to Ankara to negotiate a cessation of hostilities. Pompeo insisted, "We need them to stand down, we need a cease-fire, at which point we can begin to put this all back together again."[30]

Turkish artillery knowingly attacked US forces, just three hundred meters from the Security Mechanism Zone in Kobani. Artillery rounds were fired on both sides of the outpost, creating a "bracketing effect." The Turkish Defense Ministry denied that its forces had fired on US troops, claiming that Turkish troops were targeting Kurdish fighters nearby. The Pentagon scoffed at Turkey's denial, claiming that it gave Turkey "explicit grid coordinate details." According to Brett McGurk, "This was not a mistake. Turkey knows all of our locations."[31]

The Pentagon was deeply concerned about the danger to American personnel. By seizing the M4 Highway, the Turks blocked their escape route. Chairman of the Joint Chiefs of Staff Mark Milley maintained, "We retain the right of self-defense," raising the specter of an unprecedented armed confrontation between NATO allies.[32] The US Department of Defense was increasingly concerned about the control of approximately fifty US tactical nuclear weapons at Incirlik Air Force Base, about 250 miles from the Syrian border in southeastern Turkey. Without a plan to remove them, the nuclear weapons were held hostage by Erdoğan, who vowed to acquire a nuclear arsenal.

Trump's actions in Syria both betrayed the Kurds and undermined US interests. After the Kurds removed ISIS from its last stronghold in Baghouz in March 2019, Trump pronounced, "ISIS is 100% defeated."[33] He later recalibrated his message, indicating that the caliphate was defeated. Speaking on Capitol Hill, I criticized Trump for prematurely declaring victory. The ISIS caliphate may have been destroyed, but ISIS was still a force to be reckoned with. It had 18,000 fighters across Iraq and Syria and a war chest of $400 million. Many ISIS members and their families were detained by the Kurds in northeastern Syria. The al-Hol camp contained 74,000 detainees, including ISIS brides and children who were ripe for further radicalization.

The SDF warned US officials that hardcore ISIS detainees might escape. "That would destroy all that has been achieved in terms of stability over the last years."[34] Trump dismissed these concerns and washed his hands of responsibility. He lambasted European governments for refusing to repatriate their citizens. If ISIS fighters escape, Trump predicted, "They will be escaping to Europe."[35] Turkey's attack caused a severe humanitarian crisis. The UN Office for the Coordination of Humanitarian Affairs said that at least 160,000 people fled their homes between October 9 to 16, including 70,000 children.[36]

On October 9, 2019, Trump sent a confusing yet threatening letter to Erdoğan, writing, "Don't be a tough guy. Don't be a fool! Let's work out a good deal! You don't want to be responsible for slaughtering thousands of people, and I don't want to be responsible for destroying the Turkish economy—and I will." The letter ended with an informal salutation, "I'll call you later." Erdoğan was enraged that the letter violated diplomatic protocol and lacked "niceties." The pro-Turkish government media reported, "President Erdoğan received the letter, thoroughly rejected it and put it in the bin."[37]

With US acquiescence, Turkey established the so-called safe zone it had long sought. Trump boasted that the negotiation resulted in a "great deal" that was "good for everybody." The deal, in fact, was a huge setback for the United States and was deadly for the Kurds. The agreement gave Turkey almost everything it wanted. Turkey agreed to "pause" its military action for 120 hours but rejected the term "cease-fire."[38] The agreement assigned control of a 22-mile buffer area on the Syrian side of the border, 75 miles long, to Turkey.

Lavishing praise on Erdoğan as a "friend" and "hell of a leader", Trump explicitly sanctioned ethnic cleansing of the Kurds. Parroting Erdoğan, Trump indicated that the area needed to be "cleaned out."[39] Pence and Pompeo also adopted Turkey's talking points, claiming that the SDF is worse than ISIS. They echoed Turkish propaganda that blamed the Kurds for attacking Christians in northern Syrian when, in fact, the Kurds had protected them Turkish-backed jihadis.

· · · · ·

Kurds in Syria are blessed by exceptional leadership. Ilham Ahmed is co-chair of the Syrian Democratic Council (SDC) Executive Committee. Although she does not speak English, Ilham addresses her audiences with great authority. I joined her on a panel at the National Press Club in February 2019. The translation was poor, but she impressed a seasoned audience with her knowledge and political savvy.

The Washington Kurdish Institute worked with Senator Chris van Hollen (D-MD) to arrange a meeting for Ilham with a bipartisan group of US senators. She made a strong case for continued US involvement in NES, arguing that premature withdrawal of troops would make ISIS resurgent and give a green light to Turkey's Islamist gangs to continue abusing civilians with impunity.

Ilham came to New York at my invitation. Tom Kaplan, chairman of Justice for Kurds (JFK) hosted a breakfast with JFK board members and other prominent persons, including former Senator Joe Lieberman (D-CT). Lieberman is close to Senator Lindsey Graham (R-SC), who serves on the Senate Foreign Relations Committee and is one of Trump's strongest defenders in Congress. Usually an apologist for Trump, Graham blasted him for announcing the US withdrawal, calling it "shortsighted and irresponsible." According to Graham, "This impulsive decision by the President has undone all the gains we've made, thrown the region into further chaos. Iran is licking their chops. And if I'm an ISIS fighter I've got a second lease on life. So to those who think ISIS has been defeated you will soon see."[40]

Ilham took New York by storm. I arranged for her to meet *The New York Times* editorial board. She engaged UN officials investigating Khalaf's murder and presented evidence on the plight of women and children to the Women's Refugee Commission, proposing a study on humanitarian access for Kurds in Syria and Iraq. The day culminated with a conference at Columbia University. The audience was spellbound by her account of events and practical recommendations for US engagement. When we parted after dinner, Ilham seemed soulful and melancholic. She had been tirelessly traveling the world to make her case to policymakers and opinion leaders in Europe and the US. She and the Syrian Kurds are up against great odds, especially with Erdoğan committed to killing them.

Introducing Ilham, Tom Kaplan quoted the adage, "Kurds have no friends but the mountains." He assured Ilham that Kurds indeed have many friends in New York, as evidenced by the group assembled to meet her. Ilham is a heroine of the Kurdish cause, not alone in her campaign to gain justice for Kurds and shame the international community into defending the Kurds and upholding their Rojava principles. Ilham is a relentless advocate. The Kurdish struggle continues.

Notes

1   Sara Elizabeth Williams, "The Invasion of Kassab: We were Evicted," *Al Jazeera*, April 30, 2014, https://www.aljazeera.com/news/middleeast/2014/04/invasion-kassab-were-evicted-2014427135553170283.html.

2   Mona Mahmood, "We are So Proud – The Women Who Died Defending Kobani against ISIS," *The Guardian*, January 30, 2015, https://www.theguardian.com/world/2015/jan/30/kurdish-women-died-kobani-isis-syria.

3   Brett LoGiurato and Michael B. Kelly, "The ISIS Siege of Kobani Exposes a Critical Flaw in Obama's Syria Plan," *Business Insider*, October 8, 2014, https://www.businessinsider.com/obama-isis-strategy-kobani-kobane-syria-2014-10.

4   https://thekurdishproject.org/hamdi-ulukaya/ (accessed April 5, 2020).

5   Maya Rhodan, "Chobani Founder to Donate $2 Million to Help Syria Refugees," *Time Magazine*, October 8, 2014, https://time.com/3482934/chobani-yogurt-syria-turkey-refugees/.

6   Mary Casey-Baker, "Peshmerga and FSA Fighters Join Kurdish Forces in Kobani," *Foreign Policy*, October 29, 2014, https://foreignpolicy.com/2014/10/29/peshmerga-and-fsa-fighters-join-kurdish-forces-in-kobani/.

7   "Kurdish Forces Seize Border Town of Tal Abyad, Cutting off Key ISIS Supply Line," *The Guardian*, June 16, 2015, https://www.theguardian.com/world/2015/jun/16/kurdish-fighters-cut-key-supply-line-to-islamic-state-capital-raqqa.

8 "US Expresses Concern about Kurdish Offensive in Syrian Kurdistan," *Ekurd Daily*, September 16, 2015, ekurd.net/U-s-expresses-concern-about-kurdish-offensive-in-syrian-kurdistan-2015-06-13.

9 "Turkey's Erdogan blames the US for a Sea of Blood in the Region," *NECN*, February 10, 2016, https://www.necn.com/news/national-international/turkey-upbraids-us-over-support-of-syrian-kurds/1990591/.

10 Vijay Prashad, "What to Expect From Turkey's Coming Invasion of Syria," *Salon News*, October 8, 2019, https://www.salon.com/2019/10/08/what-to-expect-from-turkeys-coming-invasion-of-syria_partner/.

11 Anna Barnard and Hwaida Saad, "Raqqa, ISIS Capital, Is Captured, U.S.-Backed Forces Say," *New York Times*, October 17, 2017, https://www.nytimes.com/2017/10/17/world/middleeast/isis-syria-raqqa.html.

12 Julian Borger, "US Military to Maintain Open-Ended Presence in Syria, Tillerson Says," *The Guardian*, January 17, 2018, https://www.theguardian.com/us-news/2018/jan/17/us-military-syria-isis-iran-assad-tillerson.

13 Patrick Wintour, "Erdogan Accused the US of Planning to Form a 'Terror Army' in Syria," *The Guardian*, January 15, 2018, https://www.theguardian.com/world/2018/jan/15/turkey-condemns-us-plan-for-syrian-border-security-force.

14 "Kurdish Fighters Outraged over Mutilation of Female Fighter," *The Guardian*, February 2, 2018, https://www.theguardian.com/world/2018/feb/02/syrian-kurds-outraged-over-mutilation-of-female-fighter.

15 Robin Wright, "How Trump Betrayed the General Who Defeated ISIS," *The New Yorker*, April 4, 2019, https://www.newyorker.com/news/dispatch/how-trump-betrayed-the-general-who-defeated-isis.

16 Jeremy Diamond and Elise Labott, "Trump Told Turkey's Erdogan in Dec. 14 Call about Syria, 'It's all Yours. We are Done,'" *CNN*, December 24, 2018, https://www.cnn.com/2018/12/23/politics/donald-trump-erdogan-turkey/index.html.

17 Julian Borger, "Mattis Resignation Triggered By Phone Call Between Trump and Erdogan," *The Guardian*, December 12, 2018, https://www.theguardian.com/us-news/2018/dec/21/james-mattis-resignation-trump-erdogan-phone-call.

18 "Very Telling, That Trump Doesn't Know His own Anti-ISIS Point Man, Former Official Says," *Washington Post*, December 23, 2018, https://www.washingtonpost.com/.

19 David Phillips, "Abandoning the Kurds Gives Iran Free Reign in Syria," The Jerusalem Post, December 6, 2018, https://www.jpost.com/opinion/abandoning-the-kurds-gives-iran-free-rein-in-syria-575516.

20 "Erdogan Says 2 Million – 3 Million Syrian Refugees can be Resettled in Safe Zone," Reuters, September 18, 2019, https://www.reuters.com/article/us-syria-security-erdogan/erdogan-says-2-million-3-million-syrian-refugees-can-be-resettled-in-safe-zone-idUSKBN1W31A3.

21 Diana Stancy Correll, "Withdrawing from Northern Syria Could 'Not Come at a Worse Time,' Votel Says," Military Times, October 9, 2019, https://www.militarytimes.com/flashpoints/2019/10/09/withdrawing-troops-from-northern-syria-could-not-come-at-a-worse-time-votel-says.

22 Karen DeYoung, Missy Ryan, Kareem Fahim, and Sarah Dadouch, "Republicans Assail Trump's Decision to Pull Troops from Northern Syria as Turkey Readies Offensive," Washington Post, October 8, 2019, https://www.washingtonpost.com/world/national-security/trump-administration-to-pull-troops-from-northern-syria-as-turkey-readies-offensive/2019/10/07/a965e466-e8b3-11e9-bafb-da248f8d5734_story.html.

23 Eric Schmitt, Maggie Haberman, and Edward Wong, "President Endorses Turkish Military Operation in Syria, Shifting U.S. Policy," New York Times, October 7, 2019, https://www.nytimes.com/2019/10/07/us/politics/trump-turkey-syria.html.

24 Amberin Zaman, "Confusion Reigns as Trump Authorizes Troop Withdrawal from Turkish-Syrian Border Towns," Al-Monitor, October 7, 2019, https://www.al-monitor.com/pulse/originals/2019/10/turkey-syria-border-us-troop-withdrawal-trump-confusion.html.

25 Alex Ward, "Trump says He's Ending the US Role in Middle East Wars. He's Sending 1,800 Troops to Saudi Arabia," Vox News, October 11, 2019, https://www.vox.com/world/2019/10/11/20909932/trump-iran-saudi-arabia-troops-esper.

26 David Ignatius, "Trump's Betrayal of the Kurds is Sickening to U.S. Soldiers," Washington Post, October 14, 2019, https://www.washingtonpost.com/opinions/for-us-soldiers-its-a-dagger-to-the-heart-to-abandon-the-kurds/2019/10/14/f0a1db60-eecf-11e9-89eb-ec56cd414732_story.html.

27 Amberin Zaman, "Confusion Reigns as Trump Authorizes Troop Withdrawal from Turkish-Syrian Border Towns," Al-Monitor, October 7, 2019, https://www.al-monitor.com/pulse/originals/2019/10/turkey-syria-border-us-troop-withdrawal-trump-confusion.html.

28 Ben Hubbard and Carlotta Gall, "Turkey Launches Offensive against U.S.-Backed Syrian Militia," *New York Times,* October 9, 2019, https://www.ny times.com/2019/10/09/world/middleeast/turkey-attacks-syria.html.

29 Fazel Hawramy, "Turkey-Backed Proxy Forces Appear to Commit War Crimes in Northern Syria," *Rudaw News,* December 12, 2019, https://www.rudaw.net/english/middleeast/syria/121020196.

30 Natasha Turak and Tucker Higgins, "Pompeo and Pence will Meet with Erdogan after Turkish Leader Backs off Refusal," *CNBC News,* October 16, 2019, https://www.cnbc.com/2019/10/16/pompeo-says-he-and-pence-expect-to-meet-turkeys-erdogan-despite-refusal.html.

31 Stancy Correll, "Withdrawing from Northern Syria could 'not Come at a Worse Time,' Votel Says," *Military Times,* https://www.militarytimes.com/flashpoints/2019/10/09/withdrawing-troops-from-northern-syria-could-not-come-at-a-worse-time-votel-says/ (accessed April 9, 2020).

32 Ben Wolfgang, "Top U.S. General Warns Turkey: We Retain the Right of Self-Defense," *Washington Post,* October 11, 2019, https://www.washington times.com/news/2019/oct/11/us-forces-could-still-be-risk-syria-defense-se cret/.

33 Jennifer A Dlouhy and Glen Carey, "Graham Says Trump's 'Biggest Lie' is of Islamic State's Defeat," Bloomberg News, October 7, 2019, https://www.bloomberg.com/news/articles/2019-10-07/trump-says-of-syria-it-s-time-u-s-gets-out-of-endless-wars.

34 Ben Hubbard, "American Pullback is Viewed as Potential Boon to Assad and ISIS," *New York Times*, October 8, 2019, A8.

35 Zachary Basu, "Trump on Potential ISIS Escapees: "They will be Escaping to Europe," *Axios*, October 9, 2019, https::/www.axios.com/trump-isis-escap ees-syria-turkey-kurds-a74c803c-6b5b04006-af45-6ff750b29a68.html.

36 Reliefweb, October 15, 2019, https://reliefweb.int/report/syrian-arab-repub lic/regular-press-briefing-information-service-15-october-2019-update.

37 Jamie Ross, "Erdogan Threw Trump's Bizarre 'Tough Guy' Letter in the Trash, Says Report," *Daily Beast,* October 17, 2017, https://thedailybeast.com/erdo gan-threw-trumps-bizarre-tough-guy-letter-in-the-trash-says-report.

38 Saphora Smith and Dartunorro Clark, "U.S., Turkey Agree to Cease-Fire to Allow Kurdish Forces to Retreat," *NBC News,* https://www.nbcnews.com/politics/politics-news/pence-set-make-ceasefire-case-erdogan-after-release-tough-guy-n1067976 (accessed April 7, 2020).

39 Mary Papenfuss, "In Chilling Echo of Ethnic Cleansing, Trump Says North Syria Needed to be 'Cleaned out,'" *HuffPost,* October 17, 2019, https://www.huffpost.com/entry/trump-erdogan-kurds-ethnic-cleansing-syria-ceasefire_n_5da8e1eae4b0bc924759b575.

40 Devan Cole, "Graham Rips into Trump for Removing Troops from Syria," *CNN,* October 7, 2019, https://www.cnn.com/2019/10/07/politics/lindsey-graham-donald-trump-syria-troops/index.html.

CHAPTER 9

TRACK TWO DIPLOMACY: UNSILENCING THE PAST

Ambassador Richard Holbrooke suggested I get top-secret security clearance to work more effectively with US officials. Not only would the clearance provide me with access to classified information. Being affiliated with the government would also enhance my credibility. He complimented my ability to build coalitions between governments and non-governmental organizations and to marshal resources from the public and private sectors, affirming my value to the State Department.

The Bureau for European and Canadian Affairs offered to hire me as a Special Government Employee (SGE). I was given a fancy title as senior adviser, but without any representational or policymaking responsibility. In many ways, the SGE designation was ideal. I was not embedded in the system, which would require me to get approval every time I made a move. My assignment relied on good relations with the Department. Instead of waiting in a queue, I could simply contact my high-powered sponsor and get things done. Holbrooke understood that I am more of a maverick than a team player (not unlike him). After his distinguished service in the Balkans, especially in negotiating the Dayton Peace Accords in 1995, Holbrooke took a break from government service. He re-emerged in 1998 as special envoy to Cyprus and the Balkans on a pro-bono basis as a private citizen. Holbrooke recruited me as a member of his team.

· · · · ·

The Greek military junta engineered a coup against Cypriot President Makarios in 1974. Citing the 1960 Treaty of Guarantee, Turkey's Prime Minister Bulent Ecevit launched a military invasion of Cyprus that summer. The operation displaced thousands of Greek Cypriot citizens and divided Cyprus, with 38 percent of the island under Turkish control. Properties were seized and families divided; many civilians disappeared.

In 1983, Turkey declared the Turkish Republic of Northern Cyprus (TRNC) that encompassed over one-third of the island. A Berlin-like wall separated north from south. Other than Turkey, no country recognizes the TRNC as a sovereign and independent state.[1] To counter Turkish aggression, the US Congress imposed an arms embargo on Turkey in 1987. The United Nations Security Council (UNSC) formally rejected claims of the TRNC.

Greece and Turkey were both NATO members, but intractable rivals. In January 1996, competing groups raised the Greek and Turkish national flags on the tiny uninhabited island called Imia by Greeks and Kardak by Turks. As permitted by the International Convention on the Law of the Sea, Greece extended its continental shelf from six to twelve miles. Turkey viewed the move, which limited its access to the Aegean Sea, as a *casus belli*. Routine dog fights between Greek and Turkish warplanes occurred, putting the countries on a war footing.

I made my first trip to Cyprus in September 1998. I was studying the briefing book provided by the US Embassy in Nicosia. It contained mostly trivia, but I was struck by instructions for ordering coffee. When asked what kind of coffee, say "medium (*metrio*)." Coffee preference could reveal a political bias. Drinking Turkish coffee in Greek Nicosia was strictly taboo. Actually, the kinds of coffee are quite similar: thick with grounds on the bottom.

The Greek side of Cyprus was bustling with economic activity. The other side was like an Istanbul slum. Holbrooke felt that economic issues could mobilize the Greek and Turkish Cypriot business communities to put pressure on President Glafco Cleridis and Turkish Cypriot leader, Rauf Denktash. I worked closely with Ambassador Tom Miller, a straight-talking and savvy diplomat who was Special Coordinator for Cyprus. Miller had a distinguished career, serving as ambassador three times over his twenty-nine-year career in the Foreign Service.

Holbrooke and Miller invited a dozen Greek Cypriots, a dozen Turkish Cypriots, and a dozen Greek and Turkish business leaders to a conference in Brussels hosted by Columbia University and the Peace Research Institute, Oslo. The conference, "In Economic Cooperation Lies Mutual Benefit," was held in November 1997. The Norwegian government covered the costs.

Holbrooke explained the project in his opening remarks: "Track two is separate from substantive negotiations. The whole point is to get people together who are not in governments to talk with each other about things they can do on a people to people basis. The process itself does not resolve core issues—strategic, political and historical—that divide peoples. But it does create bridges of understanding, which break down the barriers."[2]

There was an old telephone switchboard at the UN headquarters in Nicosia. The operator manually inserted telephones wires to connect callers. The system used an old cable to connect emergency calls between people in the north and the south. I thought that upgrading the system could enable more communication between Cypriots on both sides and took the idea to Holbrooke. He jumped on the idea and arranged engineers to computerize the system, which enabled up to one million calls each year. We announced the resumption of phone service at a meeting of the Brussels Business Group on May 5, 1998. The line was flooded with calls, though not all callers were friendly. Angry Greek Cypriots called their old numbers in the north to harangue the Turkish Cypriots who occupied their homes.

The Brussels Business Group was the catalyst for more than fifty bi-communal projects. These projects had intrinsic value but could not replace official diplomacy. Even with his creativity and capacity, Holbrooke was stymied by the opposition of Denktash and recalcitrance of Clerides. He tried wining and dining them with jars of caviar, but they stubbornly resisted compromise.

With progress between Cypriots at an impasse, we focused on thawing relations between Greece and Turkey. Rapprochement accelerated through "earthquake diplomacy" after an earthquake struck Turkey on August 17, 1999.[3] In response, Greece, led by Foreign Minister George Papandreou, deployed search teams and trained rescue dogs. Greece sent thousands of tents, mobile hospital units, ambulances, medicine, water, clothes, food, blankets, and fire extinguishing planes.[4] The Greek Ministry of Health set up centers to collect blood donations, as did a hospital in Thessaloniki. The Orthodox Church of Greece raised funds for earthquake victims in Turkey. When the Mayor of Athens visited the earthquake site, he was met on the tarmac by the Mayor of Istanbul.

Less than a month later, Greece was hit by an earthquake of its own, and Turkey reciprocated with aid. A Turkish military transport was the first to deliver life-saving equipment. Turks rushed to hospitals and community centers, donating blood to help victims in Greece.

The natural disasters changed bilateral dynamics and mutual perceptions. Assistance from Greece was widely reported in Turkish media with headlines such as "Friendship Time," "Friendly Hands in Black Days," and "Help Flows in from Neighbors." Greek Foreign Minister George Papandreou applauded "human solidarity in the face of national tragedy. People have dared to think what we politicians thought was impossible. They have gone beyond our diplomatic maneuvers. In a glorious moment, they have taken diplomacy into their own hands."[5]

Track two is supposed to complement official diplomacy. However, it is not a substitute. In the case of Greek-Turkish relations, Greece lifted long-standing objections to Turkey's European Union candidacy. Bilateral agreements were reached in the fields of trade, tariffs, illegal immigration, counterterrorism, environmental protection, and cultural and educational exchanges. We set up working groups of Greeks and Turks in these fields to move the process along.

We maintained close coordination with concerned governments. We also worked with Greek and Turkish media to shape public opinion and encourage the engagement of a broad cross-section of civil society. Developing relations between project participants was critical to overcoming obstacles created by governments.

A "shared history" project between Greek and Turkish scholars focused on recording events during the waning years of the Ottoman Empire. The "Burning of Smyrna," as it is known by Greeks, or the "Fire of Izmir," as described by Turks, was a defining moment in the histories of both peoples. I invited scholars from Sabanci, Panteion, Aegean, and Yannina universities to a "Seminar on the Construction of National Memory in Greece and Turkey." Over the course of a year, scholars exchanged research materials and oral histories, wrote parallel accounts of the event, and co-authored papers.

· · · · ·

Marc Grossman was intrigued by the shared history approach and asked if I could undertake a similar project with Turkish and Armenian historians. Turkey's conflict with Armenia, its much smaller neighbor to the east, involve both current and historical issues. World War I and the end of the Ottoman Empire witnessed the brutal elimination of almost the entire Armenian Christian population of Turkey.

Armenian and most international scholars characterize the events between 1915 and 1923 as the "Armenian Genocide." As of 2020, governments and parliaments of 32 countries, including the United States, Germany, France, Italy, Canada, Russia and Brazil, had formally recognized the Armenian Genocide. However, the Republic of Turkey is in denial. Furthermore, it objects to efforts by Armenia and Armenians to gain international recognition. Turkey leads an extensive worldwide denial campaign. Turks use the term "shared suffering" to describe the contraction of the Ottoman Empire and the loss of life during its waning years.

Turkey officially recognized Armenian independence in 1991, but closed its border and denied diplomatic relations. It demanded that Armenians stop using the term "Genocide". It also favored Azerbaijan in the Nagorno-Karabakh conflict, a territory within Azerbaijan that is controlled by Armenians but is internationally recognized as part of Azerbaijan. Beginning in 1994, there was much bloodletting in Nagorno-Karabakh.

Each year on April 24, Armenians gather at the Genocide Memorial in Yerevan to remember what happened to their ancestors. The Genocide is a bond between Armenians in Armenia and the broader Armenian diaspora. Every Armenian was touched by tragedy. Turkey's denial is salt in the wound. The worldwide Armenian community cannot fully heal and move on until Turkey acknowledges the Genocide and apologizes. Some Armenians also demand reparations.

The United States and other countries have many good reasons to see these conflicts resolved and relations normalized. Except for Ronald Reagan, US Presidents have refused to use the "G-word". Presidential candidates, including Barack Obama, promised to recognize the Genocide and then found ways of avoiding the term. As a senator and presidential candidate, Obama repeatedly described the killings of Armenians as genocide. His surrogate, Samantha Power who became the US Ambassador to the United Nations, recorded a video urging Armenian-Americans to vote for Obama with assurance that he'd keep his word. Instead of calling it a genocide, Obama used the Armenian language term *Meds Yeghern* after becoming president. His artful choice of words did not go far enough to satisfy many Armenian-Americans

Turkey deploys a team of lobbyists to thwart Congressional recognition of the Genocide. Many of its advocates are former members of Congress like Robert L. Livingston, who was the main lobbyist for Turkey in blocking Congressional efforts to pass an Armenian genocide resolution.[6] His firm, the Livingston Group, was paid $12 million to lobby against Genocide resolutions. Livingston and other advocates for Turkey tout the special relationship between Turkey and the United States. Turkey was the eastern flank of NATO during the Cold War. US and Turkish troops fought side-by-side during the Korean conflict. Turkey presented itself as a moderate and secular bridge to Central Asia and the broader Muslim community. Turkey was an indispensable ally during the 1991 Gulf War as a staging ground for US air strikes on Iraq. It also received more than one million Kurdish refugees who had been displaced by Saddam Hussein's counterattack. The US and Turkey worked together to assist refugees through Operation Provide Comfort. Operation Northern Watch, which used facilities in Turkey to enforce a no-fly-zone in northern Iraq, preventing fixed-wing aircraft from air space north of the 36th parallel.

Turkey refuses to establish diplomatic relations with Armenia until territory taken by Armenians in Azerbaijan is returned. It also demands that Armenians abandon their efforts to affirm the Armenian Genocide in parliaments around the world, including the US Congress.

Grossman introduced me to Van Krikorian, an Armenian-American who is currently co-chair of the Armenian Assembly of America (AAA). Krikorian is an insightful lawyer with a strong moral compass. In the early 80s, he had sued the State Department and won the first federal court decision confirming US recognition of the Armenian Genocide. With that and other wins, he earned the respect of people like Ambassador Grossman and others in Washington. For his good work, Krikorian also has special standing among Armenian leaders.

Ambassador Grossman and I met Krikorian in Manhattan to propose a dialogue between Turks and Armenians. Recently hired as an SGE at the State Department, I was introduced by Grossman as "our track two guy." I presented background on the Greek-Turkish dialogue and the shared history project. Though Krikorian listened courteously, he was adamant that there was only one version of history and that the Armenian Genocide was indisputable. Any distortion of the facts would divide the Armenian community and exacerbate tensions between Turks and Armenians.

After hearing Krikorian's "red lines," we agreed to go forward with discussion on a Turkish-Armenian issues. To Krikorian and the Armenian community, reconciliation was a zero-sum game that could only be achieved by Turkey's admission of the Genocide. Grossman warned me that it would be the most difficult project of my life. Optimistic and a bit naïve, I agreed to give it a go.

．　．　．　．　．

We tried to engage the Turkish History Foundation as a project partner. However, its director was beholden to the Turkish authorities, which made it difficult to work together. I learned some important lessons from the first failed effort. First, it is essential for the convener to retain control over decision-making during the sensitive start-up of a dialogue project. Second, initial meetings should be convened at a neutral site. And third, it is much easier for people with opposing views to work together once good personal relations are established. Additionally, individuals are restricted by the formal positions of the groups they represent. They are typically beholden to a board of directors or to funders. Governments also pressure them to conform activities.

Rather than seek an institutional partner, I invited Turks and Armenians in their individual capacity to a "Discussion between Turkish and Armenian Civil Society Representatives" at the Diplomatic Academy of Vienna where I was an Adjunct Professor of Preventive Diplomacy. The initial group of discussants would meet on a trial basis. We gathered on June 10, 2000, to discuss expectations, agenda, and procedures.

I first met each delegation privately in order to better understand their pre-dispositions and build confidence in my role as convener. The Turks adamantly rejected use of the term "Genocide" in our deliberations, whereas Armenians insisted that the whole purpose of the dialogue was to make the Turks understand that the events constituted genocide and to gain their recognition of the events as such.

Participants were stiff and uncomfortable when we sat down for the first time at the Diplomatic Academy. It was the first structured dialogue between Turks and Armenians in almost a century. As we went around the table to introduce ourselves, Halil Berktay, a Turkish scholar at Sabanci University, put the Armenians at ease by using the term "Armenian Genocide." We discussed Turkish and Armenian official records, encyclopedias and textbooks. We reviewed the status of official relations between the governments of Turkey and Armenia, and explored a role for scholars and civil society representatives. I was careful at first not to refer to the events as genocide. As chairman, it was important that participants perceived no bias on my part.

That evening we attended a concert of Bruckner's "Grosse Messe." After the concert, we ran into Turkey's ambassador to Austria. Seeing Turks and Armenians together, he asked what we were doing there. Ozdem Sanberk, a gentlemanly former Undersecretary of State in Turkey's Foreign Ministry, replied, "We came for the concert." We were all impressed by his adroit handling of the encounter. Our meeting was supposed to be discreet; we did not want to blow our cover.

The following morning, we reviewed important themes that arose during our discussion. We also discussed practical matters and next steps. We agreed to meet again, which was significant given the project's level of difficulty. We also decided to expand the small circle to include persons with closer ties to their governments. Ultimately, we wanted our dialogue to serve as a laboratory that could influence official positions. Armenian participants in the project were sincere about dialogue. However, some Turks saw it as an opportunity to deflect official efforts aimed at Genocide recognition.

Sanberk questioned whether the project was viable with Turkey under threat and duress. He asked the Armenians to use their influence to defeat genocide recognition in the United States and other countries. Predictably, the Armenians refused. Genocide recognition by Turkey was their goal; global recognitions built toward that result. Sanberk also suggested we discuss the "occupation" of territories in Azerbaijan by Armenians. Former Foreign Minister Alex Arzoumanian rejected this proposal, maintaining we should focus on bilateral issues. He argued that broadening the agenda would sink the whole endeavor.

After the Vienna ice-breaker, the governments of Turkey and Armenia took a keen interest in the dialogue. Both sent representatives to engage in the process, participating in their private capacity. A new group initially consisting of four Armenians and six Turks emerged at the core of the dialogue project.

Sanberk was joined at the next meeting by Gunduz Aktan, another former Undersecretary at the Turkish Foreign Ministry with close ties to Turkey's National Security Council. Turkey's former foreign minister Ilter Turkmen also attended, as did Ustun Erguder, an urbane academic and former President of Bogazici University. Sadi Erguvenc, a military man who was commander of Incirlik Air Force Base during the Gulf War, also joined.

On the Armenian side, Krikorian was joined by David Hovhanissian, a "minister at-large" for regional issues and former ambassador to Syria. Alex Arzoumanian, a former foreign minister and UN ambassador, and Andranik Migranian, a senior foreign policy adviser to Boris Yeltsin and a leader of the Armenian community in Russia, also participated. Migranian and Aktan were both ultranationalists who balanced each other.

. . . . .

While relying on our project partners to keep their governments informed, I established relations with Armenian Foreign Minister Vartan Oskanian and a senior adviser to Turkish Foreign Minister Ismail Cem who worked at Turkey's embassy in Washington. In addition, I kept senior State Department officials apprised; Ambassador-at-Large and Special Adviser to the Secretary of State for the Newly Independent States of the Former Soviet Union Stephen Sestanovich and his deputy, Dan Fried, were regularly informed of our efforts. The US ambassadors in Ankara and Yerevan were also in the loop.

At the same time, I was asked to work on track two efforts surrounding the Nagorno-Karabakh conflict. Elected Nagorno-Karabakh officials were supportive, but Azerbaijan was adamantly opposed with Azerbaijan's President Heider Aliev suppressing civil society contacts with Armenian counterparts. The Azerbaijan element was a roadblock to normalization throughout the region.

The next Vienna meeting on April 30, 2001 was businesslike. Turkish participants explained why Turkey reacted so strongly to international recognition of the genocide. Turks refuse to acknowledge the Genocide because acknowledgement contradicts their noble self-image. It is humiliating to be judged in the court of international public opinion for events that occurred before the Republic of Turkey came into being. In addition, Turkey fears that recognition would lay the groundwork for reparations or territorial claims. "Western Armenia" includes Mount Ararat on the border with Armenia in modern-day Turkey. Turkish nationalists believe the country is surrounded by hostile powers seeking to destroy it.

We discussed the historical, psychological, and legal issues affecting our work. Armenians wanted to talk about the consequences of genocide while Turks turned a blind eye. Aktan explained, "We Turks do not look to our past. We never heard of our sufferings. Instead we look to the future. The Republic was formed upon the amnesia of this pain."[7] Even well-educated Turks have a selective reading of history.

According to Aktan, Armenians were killed because they rebelled against the Ottoman Empire. They were not targeted as a racial, religious or ethnic group, which would meet the definition of genocide, as established by the 1948 International Convention of the Prevention and Punishment of the Crime of Genocide. Aktan suggested that the best way to resolve differences would be to submit arguments to the International Court of Justice in The Hague. He admonished the Armenians to abandon their recognition campaign, warning: "Passage of another resolution will generate great hostility towards Armenia."[8] He asked, "How do you think it makes us feel to be accused of Genocide?" Fast on his feet, Arzoumanian responded: "How do *you* feel? *We* were the ones who were genocided."

The Turks resisted my proposal to formalize terms of reference for the project. They did not want an agenda and timetable. The two sides had very different motivations. These Turks reasoned that just showing up would win some points that could undermine Armenian efforts to gain international recognition. Armenians, however, were focused on tangible outcomes. They needed to demonstrate progress. We agreed on "the importance of building confidence through an incremental approach and a flexible work plan." We concurred that all matters would be closely held by participants and would not be disclosed to the public. It was also decided that we would institutionalize our work through establishment of the Turkish-Armenian Reconciliation Commission (TARC).

Our next meeting in Geneva was hosted by the Center for Humanitarian Dialogue on July 9, 2001. We anticipated that news of TARC would leak, so we decided to be pro-active with the media. I planted a news item with Doug Frantz of *The New York Times* and arranged for him to interview Elie Wiesel, which we hoped would lend moral authority to our efforts.

Migranian took a hard line. "We need to come to an understanding on the Genocide and other issues that divide us." If not, he warned, "We will continue to raise the Genocide in parliaments around the world."[9] Sanberk threw fuel on the fire by asking how TARC would address the "occupied territories" in Azerbaijan. Ilter Turkmen suggested we move forward and not wait for the big issues to be resolved.

When Hovhanissian called Foreign Minister Oskanian to update him on the decision to go public, Oskanian shockingly denied all knowledge of the project and told Hovhanissian he was attending in his private capacity. Hovhanissian was visibly shaken after the call. To his credit, Armenian President Robert Kocharian made clear that TARC was initiated with the government's knowledge.

We invited Geneva-based media representatives to a briefing. Ilter Turkmen made a bland opening statement, but the press drilled down, asking how TARC would address the Armenian Genocide. Turkmen gave a vague diplomatic answer, which Krikorian supported. Aktan jumped in with incendiary remarks. Sanberk fueled the controversy by questioning why Armenian grievances were prioritized while the suffering of Muslims was forgotten. Turkmen blandished, "It seems we get along much better when the media is not present."[10]

· · · · ·

The headline of *Milliyet* read, "A Historic Breakthrough." A public opinion poll on August 29, 2001, involving 2,458 Turks found that 38.5 percent favored dialogue with Armenians; 36.9 percent were against; and 24.7 percent had no opinion.

The reaction of Armenians was more uneven. TARC's detractors accused it of negotiating whether the Genocide actually occurred, insisting that TARC was established to undermine international recognition. Representatives of the Dashnak nationalist party accused TARC of undermining Genocide recognition by considering two sides to the events of

1915-23. They asserted that Armenian members of TARC were paid to participate, which was not the case. They called TARC a secret process that lacked transparency.

Despite the controversies swirling around TARC, Turkish and Armenian civil society representatives were keen for contact. Through American University, I launched the "Track Two Program on Turkey and the Caucasus." We financed and provided management assistance to a range of activities, starting with on music and culture. Other cultural activities included restoration of the Akhtamar Church on an island in the middle of Lake Van. We launched a journalist exchange program and fostered cooperation between parliamentarians, mayors, women's groups and NGOs. We also sponsored the Turkish Economic and Social Studies Foundation to conduct joint research on mutual perceptions with the Armenian Sociological Association. Ahmet Ertegun, a distinguished Turkish-American and chairman of Atlantic Records whose father served as a Turkish diplomat, took an active interest in TARC.

Dialogue projects typically secure financing as work progresses. In this instance, however, we started with a large grant from the State Department's Bureau of Educational and Cultural Affairs (ECA). Helena Finn, acting Assistant Secretary of State at ECA, introduced me to Ambassador Bill Taylor, who managed Congressionally appropriated funds for the Freedom Support Act (FSA). Armenia was eligible for financing through the FSA. Britain, Austria and the Swiss authorities also contributed to the project's costs.

·   ·   ·   ·   ·

The 9/11 terror attacks changed the tone of our discussions. Turkey presented itself as a moderating influence over the Muslim world and agreed to lead the International Security Assistance Force (ISAF) for Afghanistan. Turks in TARC were already inflexible. Absent pressure from the United States, they dug in their heels. Turks came to the table bolstered by the knowledge that Turkey's indispensable role in the fight against terrorism gave them the upper hand. Track two does not occur in a vacuum. It is always affected by domestic and international politics.

We invited hardliners, former Turkish ambassadors Mumtaz Soysal and Omer Lutem, to our Istanbul meeting in mid-September 2001. When

Armenians explained the grief of being driven from their homes, Lutem retorted, "Anatolia was never an Armenian homeland. You were just visitors." Arzoumanian pointed out that Armenians were in Anatolia long enough to build four thousand churches, to which Soysal responded, "We tried to destroy them all, but there were just too many." Lutem threatened, "If Armenians insist on Genocide, Turkey will inflict hurt on Armenia. Is that what you want?"

The Armenians were shocked by words designed to hurt and diminish them, but they did not sink to the level of Lutem and Soysal.[11] I brought the discussion back to practical measures such as opening the border between Turkey and Armenia for normal travel and trade. We emphasized resuming railroad services between the city of Kars in Turkey and the Armenian city of Gyumri, involving the chambers of commerce from both sides.

We also instituted rules on media interaction to control posturing outside the meetings. The personalities and group dynamics in track two always need to be taken into account. Meetings are often intense; some rise to the occasion, showing flexibility, while others fall back on their entrenched positions. At one of those points, David Hovhannisian intervened by asking everyone to answer the question "Who are we?" It was perfect to reset the discussion. Aktan, however, could not resist legal semantics and put salt in the wound with his acerbic comments.

I suggested we meet experts on truth and reconciliation to discuss all of the outstanding issues. Ted Sorensen, President Kennedy's legendary former aide proved invaluable in this next phase of work. He was on the board of the International Center for Transitional Justice (ICTJ). In New York, ICTJ made lengthy presentations and met with the sides separately to discuss options going forward. Aktan proposed that TARC request that ICTJ conduct an analysis on the applicability of the Genocide Convention. The Armenians were surprised by Aktan's request and did not hesitate to accept the offer. The term "applicability" was subject to interpretation, including the legislative intent of the Convention.

We negotiated the final language of TARC's request to the ICTJ and finally agreed: "TARC requests that ICTJ facilitate the provision of an independent and third party analysis of the applicability of the 1948 Genocide Convention to events in the beginning of the twentieth century [and that] this analysis would be made available to TARC on a confidential basis."

Despite the confidentiality clause, Migranian felt that confidentiality only applied to the outcome of the study rather than the agreement to conduct the study. When Migranian went public, other TARC members took the liberty of discussing the project with their respective medias. The Turks went around my back and lobbied Sorensen to disallow "legislative intent" in the analysis. When Aktan could not influence ICTJ, he attacked its credentials. The initiative was on the verge of collapse.

Armenian members announced that TARC was suspended, but we discreetly continued to work. I invited Kirkorian and Turkmen to my home in upstate New York for a friendly meeting. Krikorian wanted Aktan and Sanberk to resign, but Turkmen said that he too would have to step down if they were pushed out. Drawing on their positive chemistry, they wisely agreed on a way forward.

I visited Yerevan and Istanbul to discuss next steps. Migranian told the Armenian press, "Phillips is holding consultations with Armenian and Turkish participants in an attempt to salvage the initiative. The outcome of those contacts will determine when, under which format and with whose participation the commission will resume its work."[12] *Yerkir*, a Dashnak publication, published a photo of me on the front page with the headline: "Enemy of the Armenian Nation Visits Yerevan." John Ordway, the US Ambassador to Armenia, hosted a dinner for me, signaling Washington's support.

TARC did not disband, but it took a break. It had become apparent that there was a gap in expectations between the Turks and Armenians. Armenians pushed to achieve results, while Turks wanted to slow down the process. There were more problems in between meetings than at the meetings themselves. Krikorian maintained there might be only one chance and was determined to proceed with the ICTJ analysis.

The ICTJ insisted it would only participate if both Turks and Armenians reiterated their request. At a meeting in Bodrum, Turkey, we negotiated a memorandum of understanding describing arrangements with ICTJ. In New York on September 10, 2002, Krikorian and Aktan with his lawyers presented arguments to the panel convened by the ICTJ. Krikorian highlighted the legislative intent of Rafael Lemkin, a lawyer who initiated the Convention on the Prevention and Punishment of Genocide and coined the term genocide. When asked to explain the term, Lemkin offered: "Genocide is what happened to the Armenians." Krikorian's first witness was Samantha Power, who went on to become President Obama's UN Ambassador.

Aktan made his case for defensible homicide. His lawyers reiterated other theories and worn-out Turkish arguments. The panel included Sorensen, Alex Boraine then an NYU law professor, and Paul van Zyl, a brilliant young lawyer from South Africa who had worked with Boraine on the Truth and Reconciliation Commission. Nearly two years after the initial idea, ICTJ issued its report on February 4, 2004.

Turks welcomed part of the finding, which concluded:

> International law generally prohibits the retroactive application of treaties .... The [1948] Genocide Convention contains no provision mandating its retroactive application. To the contrary, the text strongly suggests that it was intended to impose prospective obligations on the states party signatory to it. Therefore, no legal, financial, or territorial claim arising out of the Events could successfully be made against any individual or state under the Convention."

To the liking of Armenians, ICTJ also found:

> The crime of genocide has four elements: (i) the perpetrator killed one or more persons; (ii) such person or persons belonged to a particular national, racial or religious group; (iii) the perpetrator intended to destroy in whole or in part that group, as such; and (iv) the conduct place in the context of a manifest pattern of similar conduct directed against the group or was conduct that could itself effect such destruction.

> There are many accounts of the Events, and significant disagreement among them on many issues of fact. The core facts common to all various accounts establish that three of the elements listed above were met .... For the

purposes of assessing whether the Events, viewed collectively, constituted genocide, the only relevant area of disagreement is on whether the Events were perpetrated with the intent to destroy in whole or in part, a national, ethnical, racial, or religious group, as such.

We believe that the most reasonable conclusion to draw from the various accounts of the Events is that at least some of the perpetrators knew that the consequence of their actions would be the destruction, in whole or in part, of the Armenians of Eastern Anatolia, as such, or acted purposefully towards this goal, and therefore possessed the requisite genocidal intent. Legal scholars, as well as historians, politicians, journalists and other people would be justified in continuing to so describe them [as genocide]."[13]

Neither side was totally satisfied, which is what I hoped for. Conflict resolution can be achieved when neither side feels totally vindicated. Thereafter, I have always used the term genocide to characterize the events. The opinion was published in English, Turkish and Armenian. The Armenian journalist, Hrant Dink, who was prosecuted in Turkey for using the term Armenian Genocide, pointed to the ICTJ study in their defense. The finding is still widely cited.

TARC concluded its work after more than three years with the publication of joint recommendations to the governments. Critics are correct that TARC failed to facilitate the opening of the border between Turkey and Armenia. However, TARC was a game-changer. It was a lightning rod that allowed direct contact between Turks and Armenians to proceed safely. It registered multiple practical achievements, including a jointly issued legal opinion from ICTJ affirming that genocide had occurred.

. . . . .

Abdullah Gul became President of Turkey in 2007 and Serge Sarkisyan became President of Armenia the following year. Official contact increased and with quiet but effective international mediation, Armenia and Turkey endorsed Protocols to normalize diplomatic relations and open the border. In October 2009 in Zurich, the documents were signed in the presence of Russian Foreign Minister Sergei Lavrov, US Secretary of State Hillary Clinton, French Foreign Minister Bernard Kouchner, and EU High Commissioner Javier Solano. Under extreme pressure from Azerbaijan and its domestic Azeri population, Turkey refused to implement the Protocols.

To set the record straight on rapprochement initiatives between Turkey and Armenia, I reached out to Dan Fried, the Assistant Secretary of State for European Affairs, and proposed a diplomatic history. Fried put me in touch with Michael Ambühl, Switzerland's State Secretary of Foreign Affairs and the principal mediator between the governments of Turkey and Armenia. With Fried's recommendation, Ambühl agreed to get together.

When Ambühl and I met at Lumi's Restaurant in New York on February 7, 2012, he pulled a stack of papers from his large briefcase. Piled high, the stack was about 18 inches. He apologized for not making copies, but said I could study the materials and take notes. The files included several years of email correspondence between Turkey's Ambassador Ertuğrul Apakan and Armenia's Ambassador Arman Kirakossian, as well as messages from US officials. It was a treasure trove of information.

The materials described discussions leading up to signing of the Protocol on the Establishment of Diplomatic Relations and the Protocol on the Development of Bilateral Relations on October 10, 2009. The correspondence revealed information on the work of Turkish and Armenian diplomats, as well as the role of Swiss mediation. The Protocols represented an unprecedented advancement in relations between Turkey and Armenia. However, Turkey's failure to ratify was a significant bilateral, regional, and international setback.

My monograph—"Diplomatic History: The Turkey-Armenia Protocols", was published by the Future of Diplomacy Project at Harvard's Kennedy School and Columbia's Institute for the Study of Human Rights. It evaluated TARC's role and the contribution of other civil society actors to reconciliation and advancing the Protocols. It recounted difficulties along the way, including the signing ceremony itself in 2010. The ceremony was scheduled for 5pm in the main hall (*Aula*) at the University of Zurich. Ten minutes before the event, Nalbandyan asked to see the Turkish statement, which highlighted the creation of a historical commission to uncover the facts. Nalbandyan not only objected to the joint commission, but to Davutoğlu's commentary on Azerbaijan and demands for Armenian forces to withdraw from "occupied territories."

He refused to sign, keeping the VIP delegates waiting. Clinton played an indispensable role persuading Nalbandyan to sign the Protocols. The ceremony was finally held at 8pm, three hours later than planned. Swiss Foreign Minister Calmy-Rey was the only speaker. If Germany and France could overcome their enmity after the Second World War, she said, then Turkey and Armenia could also overcome their differences and join the European family.

The AKP-led government delayed submitting the Protocols to the Turkish parliament for ratification. With progress delayed, Armenia's Constitutional Court issued a contentious finding on the Protocols that Turkey used to cast doubt on the deal and reintroduce Azerbaijan into the discussion. A series of political and procedural disputes undermined progress.

Eric Rubin, the Deputy Assistant Secretary of State with responsibility for the Caucasus, invited me to brief an inter-agency group of US officials working on Turkey and Armenia. The US Government prepares a diplomatic history of events, but it usually draws exclusively on State Department sources and takes many years. My diplomatic history was different. The Swiss authorities were its primary source, and it was published just a couple of years after the events. My personal involvement through TARC was invaluable to that research and analysis.

The Protocols may be dormant, but they still provide a roadmap for the way forward. When Erdogan is removed from office, a more conciliatory government in Ankara may then address the age-old problem of Turkey-Armenia relations and Genocide recognition.

. . . . .

Since the demise of the Protocols, Turkey regressed domestically and internationally. In 2017, my book, *An Uncertain Ally: Turkey Under Erdogan's Dictatorship* described how Erdogan's Turkey became an outlier to the values of the Western alliance. US attitudes towards Turkey shifted in 2019 when Turkey and its jihadist proxies invaded North and East Syria, threatening US Special Forces and their allies fighting ISIS. Turkey occupied Kurdish lands, committed atrocities, and targeted Armenians and Syriac Christians. Congress also objected to Turkey's purchase of S-400 missiles from Russia in violation of NATO principles and procedures. More and more policy-makers and opinion-leaders questioned Turkey's suitability as an ally.

To diffuse the clamor for sanctions and Genocide recognition, Turkey's ambassador called for a historical commission to review the facts and foster a dialogue between the sides. Having led a commission with comparable terms of reference, I issued a statement that was distributed to every member of Congress, providing information on previous efforts. As TARC's chairman, I was qualified to set the record straight.

On October 29, 2019, the House of Representatives passed HR 296 by an overwhelming margin of 405 to 11. The bill required the United States to commemorate and recognize the Armenian Genocide; reject association of the US government with all forms of its denial; and to promote public education of the Armenian Genocide.[14] The Senate followed suit on December 12, passing the resolution "without objection."

I called Krikorian to congratulate him. He had devoted his life to Genocide recognition and justice for Armenian victims. However, he was subdued in the wake of the legislative triumph. Recognition by Congress of the Armenian Genocide was worthy of celebration after so many years and so much work, but he was pre-occupied with what would come next. President Trump did not follow the lead of Congress. He deferred to Tayyip Erdogan, who lashed out at Armenians and summoned surrogates to attack them. He was right to be concerned. Public opinion, including evangelicals in the US, were turning against Turkey.

Krikorian and I live in New York and have continued to interact since TARC. He has been generous with his expertise, helping other partner organizations. Despite the scarring TARC experience, Krikorian keeps perspective and a good sense of humor. We have remained close colleagues and friends.

Notes

1   Deputy Prime Ministry and Ministry of Foreign Affairs, Turkish Republic of Northern Cyprus, "Historical Background," https://mfa.gov.ct.tr/cyprus-ne gotiation-process/historical-background/ (accessed May 11, 2020).

2   Remarks by Richard C. Holbrooke, Brussels, November 1997.

3   A. Barka, "The 17 August 1999 Izmit Earthquake," *Science*, 1999.

4   Niels Kadritzke, "Greece's Earthquake Diplomacy," *Le Monde Diplomatique*, June 2000.

5   Statement by George Papandreou, *Taksim Roundtable*, October 3, 1990.

6   Marilyn W. Thompson, "An Ex-Leader in Congress Is Now Turkey's Man in the Lobbies of Capitol Hill," New York Times, October 17, 2007. (https://www.nytimes.com/2007/10/17/washington/17lobby.html) (accessed May 11 2020)

7   Gunduz Aktan, "The Pot Calling the Kettle Black," *Turkish Daily News*, October 20, 2001.

8   Meeting notes, April 30, 2001.

9   Meeting notes, July 9, 2001.

10 Ibid.

11 Meeting notes, September 24, 2001.

12 *Mediamax*, April 22, 2002.

13 Legal analysis prepared by the International Center for Transition Justice, February 4, 2003.

14 "US House says Armenian mass killing was genocide," BBC, October 30,2019. (https://www.bbc.com/news/world-europe-50229787) (accessed May 11, 2020)

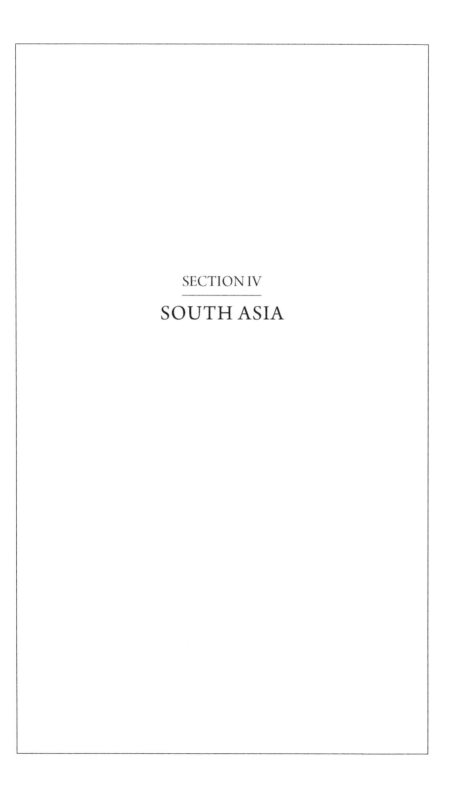

SECTION IV

SOUTH ASIA

CHAPTER 10

THE LADY

A scrum of taxi drivers waited outside the airport in Yangon, which was named Rangoon at the time. It was 1982, and I had just graduated from college and was traveling on holiday to Thailand and Burma with a school friend. We picked a rather unremarkable driver. Kyaw wore thong sandals and a longyi, the traditional wrap for both men and women. We traveled together for about a week, during which time he shared his story.

Kyaw was previously Burma's Minister of Mines. He was removed from his post during a purge of educated Burmese who might pose a threat to the military junta. Kyaw had a PhD from a Canadian university and was desperate to leave Burma to resume his career. However, travel and overseas employment was strictly forbidden by the Burma Socialist Programme Party (BSPP).

I offered to help and asked Kyaw for his curriculum vitae. I re-organized his biographical information into a more standard format. The mining industry was unfamiliar to me, but I wrote the California Mining Industries Association and requested a roster of their members. I wrote a letter to the heads of about twenty companies, inquiring about employment opportunities on Kyaw's behalf. A few of the mining companies wrote back and expressed interest. I was keeping Kyaw abreast of my efforts; he was enthusiastic during our initial communications. At a certain point, however, he sent a hurried message. He wouldn't be able to write again; I should take care of everything and inform him.

His mail must have been monitored; I wrote again but never heard back. Kyaw was probably detained and instructed to abandon his efforts to find a job overseas. The BSPP was renamed the State Law and Order Restoration Council. In 1988, it was renamed again as the State Peace and Development Council. Whatever the name, Burma's military rulers ran a brutal police state. I assumed that Kyaw, with whom I lost contact, was a victim.

. . . . .

Aung San Suu Kyi, known as "The Lady," is the daughter of General Aung San, a nationalist revolutionary and the father of the nation. Aung San, who founded the "Tatmadaw," Burma's modern-day armed forces, was re-vered for resisting British colonial rule. Suu Kyi showed me a photo of her father on the grand piano at her home in Yangon and reverentially said, "I always liked a man in uniform."[1] Aung San was assassinated during the transition period in July 1947, six months before Burma became inde-pendent.

Suu Kyi left Burma in 1969 to study in the United Kingdom, where she received graduate degrees from the University of Oxford and the School of Oriental and African Studies at the University of London. She mar-ried Michael Aris and they had two children, Alexander and Kim. She re-turned to Yangon in 1988 to find the country in turmoil. Burmese monks, students, and workers were protesting in the streets and demanding the removal of General Ne Win, the leader of the all-powerful military gov-ernment. She said on August 26, 1988, "I could not as my father's daugh-ter remain indifferent to all that was going on."[2]

Su Kyi was greeted by enthusiastic supporters across the country calling for free and fair elections. She was a real threat to the military junta. Her National League for Democracy (NLD) swept elections in 1990. How-ever, the results were annulled by the military government, and she was placed under house arrest a year later. She would spend fifteen of the next twenty-one years as a prisoner in her home in Yangon, called "The Rose Garden." Located at 54 University Avenue, it is surrounded by high walls, guarding her privacy.

Suu Kyi was awarded the Nobel Prize for Peace in 1991. In its statement, the Nobel Committee commended her as a champion of humankind, giv-ing hope to the world, and proving through her actions that democracy will prevail over autocracy. Suu Kyi was unable to visit Oslo, so Aris and her sons accepted the Nobel Prize for Peace on her behalf.

Burma, since renamed Myanmar, held elections on November 7, 2010, resulting in the replacement of direct military rule with a military-backed civilian government. The junta tried to micromanage the country's tran-sition but feared that releasing Suu Kyi would unleash popular demands for democracy that it could not control. The NLD swept bi-elections in April 2012, winning forty-three of forty-five contested seats.[3] The follow-ing month, Suu Kyi left Myanmar for Oslo and the United States.

She belatedly accepted her Nobel Prize in person with stirring remarks:

> I am standing here because I was once a prisoner of
> conscience. As you look at me and listen to me, please
> remember the often repeated truth that one prisoner
> of conscience is one too many. Those who have not yet
> been given access to the benefits of justice in my country
> number much more than one. Please remember them
> and do whatever is possible to affect their earliest, un-
> conditional release.

She explained that knowledge of the Prize was consolation during her isolation in house arrest:

> I thought of that great mass of the uprooted of the earth
> who have been torn away from their homes, parted from
> families and friends [and] forced to live out their lives
> among strangers who are not always welcoming.[4]

Suu Kyi found comfort in her Buddhist practice, meditating on the meaning of suffering and memorizing Buddhist sutras. According to Suu Kyi,
"I meditated, I read, I listened to the radio, I exercised. I think I was the
healthiest prisoner of conscience in the world."[5]

. . . . .

US Ambassador Derek Mitchell, Barack Obama's special representative
and policy coordinator for Burma, facilitated my initial meeting with
Suu Kyi. I had contacted Ambassador Mitchell to see how I could help
Burma's transition. Burma not only had a democracy deficit, which resulted in the systematic abuse of its people, but was also rife with ethnic
conflict. Myanmar has 135 ethnic groups, comprising 40 percent of its
population. Ambassador Mitchell introduced me to Zo Tum Hmung,
the Washington, DC advocate for the Chin, a Christian people in Burma's north on the border with India. In turn, I met N'BanLa, chairman
of the Kachin Independence Organization and the United Nationalities
Federal Council (UNFC), a coalition of armed opposition groups. I
worked extensively with the Ethnic Nationalities Affairs Center (ENAC)
that coordinated with the UNFC on power-sharing formulas to achieve
peace in Burma.

When I learned that Suu Kyi was coming to the United States for high-level meetings in Washington, I reached out to Ambassador Mitchell and, through him, extended an invitation for her to visit Columbia University. In Washington, she met with President Barack Obama and Secretary of State Hillary Clinton and received a gold medal from Congress. I helped her schedule activities in New York.

Hosted by Columbia's President Lee C. Bollinger, Suu Kyi spoke at the World Leaders Forum on September 23, 2012. The event was only for members of the Columbia community, faculty and students. Suu Kyi was such a celebrity that tickets were fully allocated in just seventeen minutes after the website went live. No visitor to the World Leaders Forum was ever in such demand. Everybody wanted to meet "The Lady."

In addition to her event on campus, I arranged an interview with NBC's Ann Curry, an Asian-American anchor and good friend. I also asked Curry to chair the discussion at the Low Library, the largest and most prestigious venue on the Columbia campus. Bollinger welcomed her with a rose, which he explained was a symbolic gesture in honor of their mutual friend Vaclav Havel, the late president of the Czech Republic. Havel was a strong advocate for Suu Kyi's release and had written how he longed to give Suu Kyi a rose but, due to her imprisonment, was never able to meet her. Havel died in 2011.

Bollinger explained:

> Havel understood so well that you provided hope to op-
> pressed people not only in your own country, but around
> the globe demonstrating how to endure both physical
> isolation and personal hardship by keeping one's eyes
> and heart firmly fixed on what others may see as an un-
> reachable horizon, sustained by the knowledge that dem-
> ocratic change is not only possible, but inevitable when
> enough people finally choose to make it so.[6]

Suu Kyi focused on the students in attendance. Dressed in a traditional ethnic outfit of the Karen, one student stepped up to the microphone to ask a question but was overwhelmed by the moment and was speechless. He finally asked what Burmese who have left their country could do to help. Suu Kyi said that they should not feel ashamed if they chose to settle abroad. She added, "You are our present as well as our future. And you should be our treasure and our joy." According to Suu Kyi, "Principles matter ... and one thing, best things, about living a principled, duty-conscious life is that you learn to take responsibility for your own actions, and do not to keep blaming others for whatever happens to you."

Suu Kyi told the audience that a law was being drafted to make Burmese universities more open and progressive. She welcomed cooperation with universities abroad to help raise the standards of teaching in Burma. Curry interjected, introducing me as the Columbia representative who had arranged Suu Kyi's visit, and indicating that I would coordinate future cooperation. I was thrilled by this awesome responsibility.

After the event, I took my daughters out for ice cream at Ciao Bella on the Upper East Side. We ran into Luis Ubinas, President of the Ford Foundation, and his wife Deborah Tolman. He asked what I was doing in a tie and jacket on a Saturday afternoon. I told him about the event and Luis volunteered, "We've been looking to support work in Burma. Can we help?" I asked for a couple of hundred thousand dollars. On Monday morning, I was contacted by Maya Harris, a Vice President at the Ford Foundation and sister of Senator Kamala Harris. Within weeks we received an unrestricted grant to launch activities in Myanmar.

Before Suu Kyi's talk at the Low Library, I hosted a lunch for about twenty faculty, friends, and donors. Bob Thurman, my Tibetan Buddhist Studies professor at Amherst College and chair of Columbia's Religion Department, was there. I contacted faculty colleagues and recruited them for our "Myanmar Assistance Program," which sought to support Myanmar's political transition and its peace process with armed ethnic groups. Columbia's system-wide response was unprecedented. Activities involved the Columbia Law School, School of Journalism, School of International Policy Administration, Graduate School of Architecture, Planning and Preservation, Mailman School of Public Health, and the Global Center/ East Asia. A multi-disciplinary team visited Myanmar by year's end and connected with Myanmar partners. Subsequently, Myanmar was flooded with would-be collaborators, but Columbia was one of the first. Moreover, we had money for activities in Myanmar. Our quick-impact projects were designed to achieve a political objective: demonstrate measurable progress to avoid backsliding, which the junta could use to justify its return to power.

Derek Mitchell became US Ambassador to Burma in 2012. He was optimistic about Myanmar's reforms and political transition and pushed to lift US sanctions. In her address to a joint session of the US Congress, Suu Kyi indicated, "We think that the time has come to remove all of the sanctions that hurt us economically." Myanmar's access to trade benefits had been suspended in 1989 over human rights abuses by the military junta. During Suu Kyi's visit to the White House. President Obama announced that he was adding Myanmar to the Generalized System of Preferences. However, he refused to ease restrictions on a blacklist of more than one hundred companies and individuals with links to the military junta who trafficked in jade and rubies from conflict areas. Long-time campaigners for human rights in Burma were cautious. Human Rights Watch issued a statement that sanctions targeting military officials "shouldn't be fully lifted until the democratic transition is irreversible."[7]

Although the NLD won a landslide victory in 2015, Suu Kyi was banned from serving as president by Myanmar's constitution. According to Chapter 3, section 59(f) of the constitution, the president must be someone who "he himself, one of the parents, the spouse, one of the legitimate children or their spouses not owe allegiance to a foreign power. [They shall] not be subject of a foreign power or citizen of a foreign country ... [or] be persons entitled to enjoy the rights and privileges of a subject of a foreign government or citizen of a foreign country." Since her sons were both British citizens, Suu Kyi was disqualified. Chapter 3, section 57(d) states the president must "be well acquainted with the affairs of the Union such as political, administrative, economic and military." However, Suu Kyi had no military experience. Chapter 4, section 109(b) reserved 25 percent of seats in the upper and lower houses for defense personnel. The constitution requires concurrence of more than 75 percent of legislators to change the constitution. Furthermore, the constitution reserves the right for the president to appoint the ministers for defense, home affairs, or border affairs.[8] These undemocratic requirements effectively barred Suu Kyi from exercising full executive powers. Although she was not allowed to become president, Suu Kyi would become the de facto leader as "state counselor."

On my initial assessment trip in December 2012, my flight from Yangon to the administrative capital of Naypyidaw was cancelled, so I hired a taxi and went by car. I briefed Suu Kyi at her home in Naypyidaw on my meetings in Myanmar, and we discussed ways that Columbia could assist. It was important to get her buy-in and facilitation with potential Myanmar partners.

Suu Kyi was a major proponent of the rule of law. She requested that Columbia provide training and technical assistance to the Parliament's Rule of Law Committee. In February 2013, Professor Sarah H. Cleveland from the Columbia Law School visited Naypyidaw for a seminar, which was chaired by Suu Kyi and attended by sixty Members of Parliament. The seminar addressed international experience in constitutional reform, including civil-military relations. Cleveland and other Columbia faculty conducted a similar seminar in Yangon, organized by Myanmar Egress, a think-tank with close ties to the transitional government.

J. Cobb Mixter, my research assistant at Columbia and the Council on Foreign Relations, provided "Legislative Training" to lawmakers and military representatives in Naypyidaw. After being my intern and research assistant, Mixter had a high-flying career as staff director of the Asia-Pacific Sub-committee of the House International Affairs Committee and as Deputy Assistant Secretary for Congressional Affairs at the Treasury Department. It was gratifying to watch Mixter rise and excel in the system.

Training highlighted the role of Parliament in democratic governance, including techniques for legislative oversight, bill drafting, and conducting a hearing. Creating a parliamentary research service was also discussed. We hired a translator who was not very skilled. When it was apparent that the translator was struggling, Suu Kyi stepped in to facilitate the discussion. Although she was a global icon, Suu Kyi was still hands-on.

Columbia also focused on civil society, not only political elites. With "Justice for All" (JFA), a local non-governmental organization (NGO), we developed a training manual on human rights law and advocacy, which was published in Burmese with financing from the State Department's Bureau for Democracy, Rights and Labor. JFA held twenty-four seminars around the country with workers, farmers, lawyers, and political activists. The seminars were also held in ethnic areas where violent conflict was underway. JFA's Kyaw Min San proved to be one of Columbia's best local partners.

In July 2013, Suu Kyi introduced me to Tin Tun, Rector at the University of Yangon. We finalized a University Partnership Agreement with the

University of Yangon and worked with Khin Mar Yee, Chair of the Law Department. Columbia developed a human rights curriculum, which we transferred to the University of Yangon, Mandalay University, and other universities around the country. Contact between Myanmar and overseas universities had been severely restricted by the junta. Although the restrictions were lifted, we faced an attitudinal roadblock getting Myanmar academics involved. With funding from the Open Society Foundation, we managed to overcome these obstacles by regularly visiting Myanmar and forging personal relationships with key faculty. To cement good relations, we arranged for Khin Mar Yee to spend a semester at Columbia Law School. The experience left a deep and positive impression. Beginning in January 2014, Ben Fleming, an Assistant Professor at the Columbia Law School, conducted a nationwide assessment of opportunities for legal education that led to partnerships with Yangon University, Mandalay University, Mawlamyaing University near Kayan State, and Taungyi University.

Columbia also developed media training to assist Myanmar's nascent independent media. My friend, Shelley Hack, who was one of "Charlie's Angels" and had worked on independent media in Bosnia, was the point person. When the Journalism Department and UNESCO developed a curriculum for teaching journalists, Columbia provided a critique of the UNESCO curriculum. Professor Joshua M. Friedman, former dean of Columbia's Journalism School, led seminars on journalism with instructors at Yangon University.

Professor Alfred C. Stepan, the former dean of Columbia's School of International and Public Affairs, taught courses on international relations and political science in December 2013. He also advised Tin Tun on establishing a Political Science Department.

I facilitated arrangements and financing for Wafaa al-Sadr from Columbia's Mailman School of Public Health to work with the Ministry of Health (MoH) on the prevention and treatment of HIV-AIDS, tuberculosis, and other communicable diseases. When the Memorandum of Understanding (MoU) between Columbia and the MoH inexplicably stalled, I went to Naypyidaw and obtained the ministry's signature on the MoU. Just showing up compelled the MoH to finalize arrangements.

In November 2013, Columbia organized a "National Women's Dialogue: Peace, Security and Development in Myanmar" with Myanmar's Gender Equality Network (GEN). The 2011 Nobel Peace Laureate Leymah Gbowee and filmmaker Abigail Disney attended, as did three hundred Myanmar women. Inexplicably, Suu Kyi did not show up for her keynote address.

Sarah Costa, my wife and head of the Women's Refugee Commission (WRC), also attended the conference. The WRC and GEN conducted a "Workshop on Livelihoods and Preventing Violence against Women" in Yangon for grassroots women's organizations working in conflict areas around the country, including Rakhine and Kachin states in November 2013.

My trusted right-hand, Danielle Goldberg, coordinated with GEN. In addition, she transferred Columbia's "Curriculum on Social Harmony and Conflict Resolution" to Myanmar women with the Concord Institute. Goldberg also held workshops with on conflict resolution with youth from war-torn regions, which focused on civil society's role in peace building.

Each of these projects relied on Myanmar partners from NGOs and universities. We kept both the US and Myanmar governments informed. Columbia benefitted from cooperation with Ambassador Mitchell and his staff and from financing from US Government sources, the Ford Foundation, and the Open Society Foundation. The importance of local partnerships defined our work worldwide. Myanmar was the first instance, however, where we adopted a "whole of university" approach.

· · · · ·

While Columbia's teams fanned out across the country, I retained responsibility for developing recommendations for constitutional power sharing and work on Myanmar's armed ethnic conflicts. Since ethnic conflicts often had a religious dimension, I also focused on inter-religious dialogue.

Armed ethnic groups in Myanmar have struggled for self-determination since the early twentieth century. At a critical point in the struggle for independence from Great Britain, Aung San convened the Panglong Conference in February 1947.[9] Panglong was held in Shan State, and leaders of the Shan, Kachin, and Chin ethnic minorities attended. They agreed to unite their struggle for independence and foresaw Burma as a unified republic after independence.

Zo Tum Hmung, an ethnic Chin born in Burma, brought Chin leaders, Pu Liak Uk and Dr. Za Hlei Thang to Columbia. I conducted a daylong seminar on international standards for minority rights, constitutional power sharing, and international autonomy models. Myanmar participants asked me to visit Chiang Mai, Thailand, for a follow-up seminar with the UNFC leadership. I assembled a team of Columbia experts including Al Stepan, who is recognized worldwide for his work on democratic transitions. The meeting, which was chaired by UNFC General Secretary Khu Oo Reh and attended by representatives of different ethnic groups, was held in June 2013.

Zo wanted to institutionalize cooperation, so we worked together with UNFC leaders to launch the ENAC, and Zo became its executive director. The organization was a think-tank focused on federalism and other issues of priority concern to ethnic groups. Pon Nya Mon, ENAC's current executive director, wrote, "I am also so glad to know that you were part of the team to get ENAC up and run and sustain it."[10] Zo and I arranged start-up financing from the National Endowment for Democracy and the Open Society Foundations.

At Zo's urging, I wrote a "Negotiations Manual: Towards Sustainable Peace in Myanmar" that was translated into Burmese and presented to the UNFC during a return trip to Thailand. There I met Gawlu La Awng, head of the Kachin Independence Organization's Technical Advisory Team. Zo and I went to Myitkyina, the capital of Kachin State, in March 2014. Negotiation training was conducted for KIO teams, while battles raged with the Tatmadaw in the remote jungles of Kachin State near Ruili on the border with China.

Lincoln A. Mitchell, a Columbia professor with expertise in political party building, joined me in Myitkyina. He spoke with Kachin political parties and civil society groups about getting organized for the next election. Instead of fighting the Tatmadaw, he emphasized that the KIO could achieve its goals by strengthening its capacity and building coalitions with other ethnic-based parties. He also spoke about relations with the NLD and outlined a strategy for getting Suu Kyi more involved in ethnic interests.

U Aung Min, Myanmar's Senior Minister, chief peace negotiator, and confidant of President Thein Sein, was kept informed of our efforts. With financing from the European Commission, he and other senior ministers established the Myanmar Peace Center to coordinate in-country activities and manage external relations with foreign experts. Through his adviser, Kyaw Yin Hlaing, we arranged for Aung Min to visit Columbia for a conference to discuss the peace process on April 24, 2013. I found Aung Min stiff, remote, and overly cautious during our meetings in Yangon. However, he had a totally different demeanor on campus in New York. He sent the right message, declaring emphatically that the reform process launched by Suu Kyi was "irreversible."[11] He also set the right tone; he was animated, enjoying the interaction with students. After we adjourned, he was surrounded by attendees. Aung Min was in no hurry to depart, spending at least an hour chatting with guests.

Suu Kyi launched a peace process at a conference in Naypyidaw on August 31, 2016. Burmese President Htin Kyaw and United Nations (UN) Secretary General Ban Ki Moon joined two thousand delegates from across the country. Suu Kyi gave a motivational address to open the conference:

> This is a unique opportunity for us to accomplish a great task that will stand as a landmark throughout our history. Let us grasp this magnificent opportunity with wisdom, courage and perseverance and create a future infused with light.

She put forth an ambitious agenda: end violent conflict, rein in the armed forces, build confidence between the state and ethnic groups, and encourage equitable and sustainable development in lands where ethnic minorities reside. Despite Myanmar's rich natural resources, ethnic areas in the north and east are the poorest in the country. The Tatmadaw take advantage of violent conflict to extract minerals and forest products. As delegates met in Naypyidaw to talk about peace, the Tatmadaw were battling armed ethnic groups in Kachin, Shan, and Karen states. More than 240,000 ethnic people, mostly Kachin and Shan, had fled the fighting and were internally displaced. Another 100,000 refugees, mostly Karen, were afraid to leave their refugee camps in Thailand and return to Myanmar.[12]

The Myanmar Government and its foreign friends relentlessly pursued a comprehensive nationwide ceasefire agreement (NCA). It wanted every armed ethnic group to disarm, demobilize, and reintegrate (DDR) into society to set the stage for a peace agreement. I felt this approach was flawed and debated with Ambassador Mitchell, Norway's Ambassador

Hilde Haraldstad, and others who backed this strategy. DDR is typically written into a peace agreement. It is not a pre-condition for negotiations. Groups that agreed to the NCA wanted to see a peace dividend. However, waiting for everyone to agree meant they had to wait longer, giving spoilers an opportunity to gain greater sway. The NCA was never finalized; Myanmar's ethnic conflicts continued.

Ethnic conflicts also had a sectarian dimension. Major areas of conflict in Karen, Kachin, and Chin states were populated by Christians. Burmans, referred to as Bamar, were deeply resentful of other religious groups, which included Muslims. On each of my visits to Yangon, I met Al Haj U Aye Lwin, who heads the Islamic Center of Myanmar.

In January 2013, I was accompanied by Bob Thurman. With Aye Lwin's assistance, we met protagonists of the conflict between Buddhists and Muslims in Rakhine State and with mainland Muslims. We asked Bikkhu Bodhi, an American scholar and friend of Thurman's, to adapt Goldberg's curriculum on social harmony and conflict resolution to "Theravada Roots of Conflict Resolution." Theravada Buddhism is widely practiced in Southeast Asia and codified in the Pali Canon. We felt that highlighting Buddhist teachings on compassion and kindness might mollify hardline nationalist monks.

Thurman led an "Inter-Faith Dialogue: The Religious Roots of Social Harmony" with Aye Lwin, The Venerable Sitagu Sayadaw, a Buddhist community leader, and The Reverend Kyaw Hlaing Bwa from the Myanmar Institute of Christian Theology. In January 2014, we convened about sixty top-tier religious leaders, officials, and educators. While we were inside releasing a joint statement that condemned hate speech and the use of religion to justify violence, Ashin Wirathu, a radical monk and leader of the "Saving Myanmar Movement," convened a press conference outside the plenary during which he espoused his racist ideology toward Muslims.

· · · · ·

We were focused on Buddhist violence against Muslims in central Burma. However, the more dangerous flashpoint was in Rakhine State in Burma's northwest. In a spasm of violence, thousands of Rohingya Muslims were killed and about 900,000 were driven from their homes to neighboring Bangladesh beginning in August 2017. The UN denounced the "brutal security operation" and called it a "textbook case of ethnic cleansing."[13] According to Amnesty International, "The situation on the ground is dire, the scale unprecedented, and the need to act—immediate and imperative."

Like many ethnic and sectarian conflicts, the problem is rooted in history. The dispute between Rakhine Buddhists and Rohingya goes back centuries. The Sultan of Bengal surrendered control of the Rakhine Kingdom in 1531. At the time, Rakhine extended from the Ganges to the Ayeyarwaddy River, including the Chittagong region in modern-day Bangladesh. The Rakhine Kingdom remained independent until 1826, when it was ceded to Britain after the First Anglo-Burma war.

In the Second World War, Rakhine was a battleground between Japan and Britain, with Britain arming the Rohingya and Japan siding with Rakhine Buddhists. In the 1870s, unskilled Bengali laborers migrated to Lower Burma, modern day Myanmar. After the war, Britain imported more Rohingya workers. Their influx intensified after India's partition in 1947, and with the birth of Bangladesh in 1971.

Myanmar's 1982 Citizenship Law accorded citizenship and identity cards to those whose parent or grandparent belonged to an "indigenous race." Only those whose ancestors lived in Burma prior to 1823 or whose parents were citizens can themselves be citizens. Myanmar's Rohingya were classified as stateless people, denied citizenship in Myanmar and rejected by Bangladesh.

In the *Huffington Post*, I called for the Myanmar government to allow immediate and unfettered access by humanitarian organizations to Western Rakhine State so they could provide food, medicine, shelter, and protection. I challenged the international community to expand assistance to Bangladesh, which was overwhelmed by the influx of refugees and lacked the resources and capacity to manage the crisis. I also suggested a systematic registration process to expedite an orderly arrangement for their safe and dignified return to Myanmar in the future. Since history is central to the formation of national identity, a historical dialogue to discuss historical legacy and memory could be an effective tool for conflict prevention.

Suu Kyi's adamant denial of crimes against the Rohingya was profoundly disappointing and disheartening. Instead of using her moral authority as a Nobel Peace laureate and the bully pulpit as state counselor, she commended Myanmar's security operations.[14] She claimed that the military's action was a counterterrorism response to coordinated Rohingya militant attacks against dozens of police stations. However, the government's reaction was totally disproportionate. Clearance operations sought to accomplish a broader goal: to rid Myanmar of its "Bengali" people.

Criticism of the Myanmar government intensified because it forsook transparency. UN agencies were barred from providing humanitarian aid, and journalists were blocked from entering Rakhine State. Responding to charges of murder by the Tatmadaw, Suu Kyi claimed that "fake news" was aimed at discrediting Myanmar and her administration, calling it "a huge iceberg of misinformation."[15] The Myanmar government blamed conflict escalation on the Arakan Rohingya Salvation Army (ARSA), though some Burmese Muslims questioned its role.

Most Bamans have a deep contempt for Rohingya. In their racist worldview, Rohingya are vermin to be expelled or exterminated. Not only does the Myanmar government refuse to recognize them as citizens; it also denies their identity by refusing to use the term Rohingya. A case was brought against Myanmar at the International Court of Justice. Suu Kyi could have sent international barristers to represent Myanmar but elected instead to present the defense herself. As she entered the courthouse, Rohingya advocates, shouted: "Liar, liar, shame, shame."[16] In a rebuke to Suu Kyi, the ICJ's initial ruling in January 2020 ordered Myanmar to "take all measures within its power" to protect Rohingya Muslims from genocide.

. . . . .

After the killing and expulsion of Rohingya, I reached out to activist leader, Kyaw Hsan, who had studied at Columbia, and asked him to facilitate my arrangements in Rakhine State. We received an official letter authorizing my visit to camps for internally displaced persons (IDPs). However, we were stopped at the camp gates on the outskirts of Sittwe, the capital of Rakhine State. Efforts by the police to create uncertainty and doubt about atrocities were simply a power play by local authorities to show they were in charge and could delay or detain me. The camp was ringed by a barbed wire fence. Rohingya were packed into longhouses, a breeding ground for virus and sickness. With hollowed glazes and empty eyes, they looked like concentration camp detainees in World War II.

Genocide took its toll on Myanmar's international relations. The US government used the Global Magnitsky Human Rights Accountability Act, passed years earlier by the US Congress, to impose sanctions on military and police commanders for their involvement in extrajudicial killings, enforced disappearances, arbitrary arrests, and torture against civilians from ethnic minority communities. Sanctions included an asset freeze and a travel ban.

Suu Kyi established a commission of advisers to support implementation of Kofi Annan's recommendations for Rakhine. Governor Bill Richardson, the American representative, resigned after only a few months, calling the commission a "whitewash." He called me from the plane en route from Yangon to Tokyo. As a member of the advisory board of the Richardson Center for Global Engagement, I had written him a personal note admonishing him not to turn a blind eye to ethnic cleansing. He called to let me know that he opposed Suu Kyi's coercion and intimidation. "You were worried that I'd sell out," he chuckled.

Myanmar compounded its image problem as a human rights violator by arresting two *Reuters* journalists, Wa Lone and Kyaw Soe Oo, on December 12, 2017. At the time of their arrests, they were investigating the killing of ten Rohingya Muslim men and boys in a village in Rakhine state. They were prosecuted under the colonial-era Official Secrets Act and kept in jail for five hundred days.

A poster of Suu Kyi by the artist Shepard Fairly was prominently displayed in my office. Huseyin Tunc, a Kurd from Turkey, with whom I've worked extensively on special projects, was troubled when he saw it. Huseyin always talks straight and suggested that I take it down. He pointed out that it was unseemly for someone who is a human rights advocate to display the image of a human rights offender.

I rolled up the poster and tucked it into a corner for safekeeping. I am deeply disappointed in Suu Kyi and concerned about trends in Burma. However, I have not given up. She can still use her power and redeem her reputation with the people of Myanmar and as a force for good in the world.

Notes

1 Meeting notes, private lunch on the occasion of the World Leaders Forum, Columbia University, September 26, 2012.

2 "Aung San Suu Kyi: Myanmar Democracy Icon Who Fell from Grace," *BBC*, January 23, 2020, https://www.bbc.com/news/world-asia-pacific-11685977.

3 Kocha Olarn, "Myanmar Confirms Sweeping Election Victory for Suu Kyi's Party," *CNN*, April 4, 2012, https://edition.cnn.com/2012/04/04/world/asia/myanmar-elections/index.html.

4 Anthony Kuhn, "Aung San Suu Kyi Gives Long-Overdue Nobel Speech," *NPR*, June 16, 2012, https://www.npr.org/2012/06/16/155171944/suu-kyi-delivers-long-overdue-nobel-speech.

5 Omar Kasrawi, "Nobel Laureate Daw Aung San Suu Kyi Speaks at World Leaders Forum," *Columbia News*, September 23, 2012, https://news.columbia.edu/news/nobel-laureate-daw-aung-san-suu-kyi-speaks-world-leaders-forum.

6 Ibid.

7 "US Lifts Decades-Long Trade Sanctions against Myanmar," *BBC*, September 14, 2016, https://www.bbc.com/news/world-africa-37365835.

8 Anne Barker, "Myanmar Election: Why Can't Aung San Suu Kyi be President and Why is the Country in Leadership Limbo?" *ABC*, November 10, 2015, https://www.abc.net.au/news/2015-11-10/myanmar-election-explained/6928542.

9 Martin Smith, *Burma—Insurgency and the Politics of Ethnicity* (London: Zed Books, 1991).

10 Email from Pon Mya Mon to the author, March 21, 2019.

11 "U Aung Min on Irreversible Reforms and Daw Aung San Suu Kyi's Role," *VOA Burmese*, April 24, 2013, https://www.youtube.com/watch?v=nrk0p0m MeeE.

12 Hannah Beech, "Aung San Suu Kyi Seeks Elusive Peace in Burma with Panglong Summit," *Time*, August 31, 2016, https://time.com/4473849/aung-san-suu-kyi-burma-panglong-summit/.

13 Stephanie Nebehay, "U.N. Sees 'Textbook Example of Ethnic Cleansing' in Myanmar," *Reuters*, September 11, 2017, https://www.reuters.com/article/us-myanmar-rohingya-un/u-n-sees-textbook-example-of-ethnic-cleansing-in-myanmar-idUSKCN1BM0SL.

14 David L. Phillips, "Historical Dialogue about the Rohingya in Myanmar," *Huffington Post*, September 20, 2017, https://www.huffpost.com/entry/his torical-dialogue-about-the-rohingya-in-myanmar_b_59c2a9e8e4b0ffc2ded b5a70.

15 "Rohingya Crisis: Suu Kyi Says 'Fake News Helping Terrorists,'" *BBC*, September 6, 2017, https://www.bbc.com/news/world-asia-41170570.

16 Shoon Lei Win Naing and Toby Sterling, "Suu Kyi Tells U.N.'s Top Court Charge of Rohingya Genocide is 'Misleading,'" *Reuters*, December 11, 2019, https://www.reuters.com/article/us-myanmar-rohingya-world-court/suu-kyi-tells-u-n-s-top-court-charge-of-rohingya-genocide-is-misleading-idUSK BN1YF06P.

CHAPTER 11

VICTOR'S JUSTICE IN SRI LANKA

Sri Lanka's Tamil population suffered discrimination by the Government of Sri Lanka (GSL), following the country's independence from Britain in 1948.[1] Unmet Tamil grievances over land, language, and citizenship led to an armed rebellion by the Liberation Tigers of Tamil Eelam (LTTE) starting in July 1983. In addition to greater rights, the LTTE demanded a separate state called "Tamil Eelam."

Although Sri Lanka's ethnic Tamils represented 12.6 percent of the population, as opposed to the majority ruling Sinhalese who were nearly 75 percent, the LTTE was a formidable fighting force. Led by Velupillai Prabhakaran, it controlled 90 percent of the Northern Province and 30 percent of the Eastern Province by 2001. In addition to 30,000 troops under arms, the LTTE had a navy called the "Sea Tigers," a small air force, and a capable intelligence operation. It pioneered suicide terrorism, used women for suicide attacks, and conscripted child soldiers. The LTTE was classified as a "terrorist organization" by thirty-two countries, including the US. The Tamil struggle for an independent state of Tamil Eelam lasted nearly forty years and led to the deaths of more than 100,000 people.[2]

The dream of an independent Tamil Eelam ended tragically at the battle for Mullaitivu in May 2009. When the Tamil Tigers had their backs to the sea, the Sri Lanka Air Force dropped leaflets urging hundreds of thousands of civilians to come to government-controlled "safe zones," but there was nothing safe about them; it was a trap. Civilians were shelled by artillery and mortar fire, killing thousands. Ignoring appeals from the United Nations and the International Committee of the Red Cross, the Sri Lanka Army (SLA) attacked hospitals and medical clinics, shelled humanitarian operations and food distribution points, and obstructed food delivery and medical treatment to civilians.[3] The LTTE also violated international humanitarian law by using civilians as human shields and allegedly firing on civilians who were attempting to flee.

In the final hours, Tamil Tigers retreated to a narrow finger of land extending into the sea called Mullivaikal. Artillery blasts rained down from all sides; the sand was soaked with blood. Some LTTE fighters made a mad dash to get off the beach but were wiped out by the SLA; Prabhakaran was apprehended and shot.

· · · · ·

Sri Lankan President Kumaratunga asked Norway to facilitate a dialogue with the LTTE in 1999. At first, the GSL insisted on a ceasefire as a pre-condition for negotiations. However, the LTTE refused to negotiate until the GSL lifted its economic embargo and removed its label as a terrorist organization.

Norway's Special Representative Erik Solheim based his mediation on principles of impartiality, local ownership, and internationalization. He brokered an initial meeting in Thailand with subsequent meetings in Norway, Switzerland, Germany, and Japan. Negotiations were at an impasse until the LTTE deferred its demands for an independent state and instead focused on federalism that would provide local self-rule while ensuring the territorial integrity of Sri Lanka.

A ceasefire agreement (CFA) was finalized on February 22, 2002. Committees were established on De-escalation and Normalization, Immediate Humanitarian and Rehabilitation Needs, and Political Matters. That year, the Government of Sri Lanka agreed to remove the LTTE from its terror list. Soon after the CFA, Norway internationalized its efforts by launching the Sri Lanka Monitoring Mission (SLMM) using personnel from Nordic countries – Norway, Denmark, Finland, Iceland, and Sweden. The SLMM lasted from 2002 until 2008.

Mahinda Rajapaksa was elected President of Sri Lanka in 2005 as the candidate of the United People's Freedom Alliance. Following in the footsteps of President George W. Bush, he embraced the "Doctrine of Preemption," which justified unilateral preemptive war against adversaries before they could attack. Despite Solheim's skilled mediation and Norway's soft power, ceasefire violations undermined confidence. In 2006, Rajapaksa vowed to crush the LTTE and seek a military solution to the Tamil conflict.

Local media and leading politicians in Colombo accused Norway of bias, fueling skepticism toward Western involvement. The LTTE deputy Muralidharan Karuna claimed that Norway provided funds to the LTTE for purchasing lethal weapons. Documents released by WikiLeaks also revealed that Norway provided high-tech satellite equipment to the LTTE.[4] In April 2009, the GSL formally requested that Norway cease its involvement in the peace process.

According to an after-action report by the Norwegian Agency for Development Cooperation (NORAD), "Norway was being used as a pawn of peace, and should have considered the ethical implications of continuing the role as facilitator and mediator more thoroughly. Soft power may be a suitable approach to bring parties to the negotiation table, but is a much more challenging when trying to reach a settlement."[5]

· · · · ·

A tsunami hit Sri Lanka on December 26, 2004. Between 35,000 and 39,000 people were killed and nearly 500,000 were displaced. Norway, with the support of the international community, proposed a "Post-Tsunami Operational Management System" (P-TOMS), comprising the GSL and the LTTE, with the participation of Muslims who lived in the tsunami-affected area. The Memorandum of Understanding was signed on June 24, 2005 and was an opportunity to advance a political solution to the decades-long conflict. However, the Jathika Vimukithi Peramunai and Sinhala nationalists opposed cooperation with the LTTE and filed a petition in the Sri Lankan Supreme Court challenging the legality of the P-TOMS. The Supreme Court held that the funding arrangements violated the unitary character of the Sri Lankan state, disallowing P-TOMS. Even the tsunami was not able to wipe away entrenched ethnic and political divisions.[6]

Wegger Strommen, Norway's Ambassador to the US, regularly shared information with me on developments in Sri Lanka. Not only were we colleagues, but Strommen and I had become close personal friends. A month after the battle for Mullivaikal, we celebrated our fiftieth birthdays at my apartment in New York City. Many doormen offered congratulations as we walked down Park Avenue with balloons emblazoned with the number "50."

After Norway was expelled from Sri Lanka, its Ministry of Foreign Affairs needed eyes and ears on-the-ground to monitor conditions. Although it was unable to directly influence events, the Norwegian government sought other means to uphold the political and financial interests of both the Tamils and the Sinhalese. In collaboration with Ambassador Strommen, I developed a dialogue project aimed at engaging all sides of the conflict. My background as a US official provided additional credibility. A US-based organization had clout that Rajapaksa could not ignore.

I met regularly with Robert O. Blake, the Assistant Secretary of State for South and Central Asian Affairs, who had previously served as US Ambassador in Colombo, Sri Lanka's capital. His team working on Sri Lanka included a very capable Deputy Assistant Secretary of State named Alyssa Ayres. Blake and I first met when he was an assistant to Ambassador Marc Grossman, and we crossed paths frequently in subsequent years. The State Department renewed my contract as a Special Government Employee, focusing on Sri Lanka, and Norway's Peace and Reconciliation Unit made a multi-year grant to Columbia University for dialogue and reconciliation between the Tamils and the Sinhalese.

· · · · ·

To prepare for my assessment trip to Sri Lanka in 2012, I sought guidance and information from several sources. I spoke with Blake and his team to better understand US goals in the post-Mullivaikal period. Strommen provided background on Norway's historical involvement and its current view of the situation. I also met with Sri Lanka's Permanent Representative to the United Nations (UN), Palitha Kohona, and Visuvanathan Rudrakumaran, a lawyer based in New York who was legal counsel to the LTTE.

In addition to his UN post, Ambassador Kohona was the Permanent Secretary to Sri Lanka's Ministry of Foreign Affairs. He had deep experience in the peace process, having served as Secretary General of the GSL Secretariat for Coordinating the Peace Process and a member of the Sri Lankan delegation at meetings in Geneva and Oslo. Kohona and I enjoyed a good relationship. I attended Sri Lanka's independence celebrations, which he hosted. We also met frequently and dined together.

Rudrakumaran, known as "Rudra," is a razor-sharp lawyer who has spent his life as an advocate of the Tamil people. He was Prabhakaran's legal adviser responsible for international and diplomatic affairs. In 1997, he also led the legal challenge in the US to the LTTE's designation as a Foreign Terrorist Organization. Rudra attended several meetings of the peace process mediated by Norway.

Knowing of his LTTE affiliation, I was cautious about getting together. I checked with the State Department to make sure I was not breaking any rules by meeting him. After getting the green light, Rudra and I met regularly at "The Three Guys" coffee shop on Madison Avenue in New York. To cover myself, I always informed the Bureau of South and Central Asian Affairs of our meetings and sent notes of our discussion to Ambassador Blake and Deputy Assistant Secretary Alyssa Ayres. I was sympathetic to the Tamils and provided information on Tamil demands for accountability.

Rudra provided valuable insight into the Tamil community, including the Tamil National Alliance, ethnic Tamil members of the Sri Lankan Parliament. He was an adamant supporter of independence for Tamil Eelam. After Mullivaikal, he became Prime Minister of the Transnational Government of Tamil Eelam (TGTE).

My first introduction to the Tamil diaspora was at a conference in New York. I was struck by the profound grief of the participants. Each one walked up to the dais, laid a garland, and joined their hands together in prayer for a family member who had died or disappeared. After Mullivaikal, many thousands of Tamils were arrested and confined in camps. There was no registration process, and many people were unaccounted for. To this day, Rudra leads a campaign for accountability of the GSL's war crimes. I was cautious during my remarks at the Tamil conference, choosing my words carefully. Through my presence, I intended to express solidarity with the suffering of Tamils. However, I did not endorse the TGTE's independence bid lest GSL spies were in attendance. Impartiality was an important attribute of my efforts to facilitate a dialogue between the Tamils and the Sinhalese.

The costs of my trips to Sri Lanka were paid by Columbia University using funds from the Norwegian government. Ambassador Blake arranged for the US Embassy in Colombo to make appointments and provide a control officer to manage my itinerary. Upon arrival in Colombo, I received a briefing at the embassy with the country team. Then I set off to Jaffna, the largest Tamil city in northern Sri Lanka.

Jaffna had an overwhelming security presence. My hotel was around the corner from a school for girls. They wore light blue dresses over starched and perfectly pressed white shirts. Many had braided shiny dark hair and new book bags. Despite their immaculate appearance, the girls seemed absolutely joyless. I tried to make eye contact, but they avoided my glance. Many buildings in Jaffna were pockmarked from the fire of automatic weapons or partly collapsed from artillery blasts. Not only the schoolgirls, but Jaffna's entire Tamil population was traumatized the army's attack and occupation. From my discussion with Suresh Premachandran, a Tamil National Alliance (TNA) member in Jaffna, I understood the bitterness and anger that still existed in the Tamil community.

I then traveled to Sri Lanka's south, the heartland of Sinhalese nationalists. They described how the Tamil Tigers had terrorized Sri Lankan civilians for decades. Some Sinhalese were victims of suicide bombings, a technique championed by the Tamil Tigers. All felt the economic impact of Sri Lanka's civil war. It was clear that there was enormous suffering on both sides of the conflict. Although the Tamils were victimized during the final stage of the war, Tamil militants also committed crimes in their struggle for independence.

· · · · ·

Columbia University organized a range of track two activities involving Tamil and Sinhalese civil society. We transferred our curriculum on social harmony to the University of Jaffna, trained their faculty, and worked with students. Curriculum sharing was organized by Bonnie Miller, our blue-ribbon consultant and first-class educator, who worked with Danielle Goldberg, my program coordinator. Columbia cooperated with the Pathfinder Foundation, a think-tank established by a former minister and Member of Parliament, Milinda Moragoda, engaging Tamil and Sinhalese scholars in a shared history project. We worked with Visaka Dharmadasa, founder of the Association of War-Affected Women (AWAW), who lost two sons in the war, to mobilize women as peace-builders. To this end, we brought Leymah Gwobee, the 2011 recipient of the Nobel Peace Prize, for a conference with AWAW on the role of women in political transition. Pakiasothy Saravanamuttu from the Center for Policy Alternatives conducted important research on peace-building models. Jehan Perrera organized a conference with board members of the National Peace Council on "Global Truth-Telling" and published a booklet of my keynote remarks in English, Sinhalese, and Tamil.

In 1982, I had visited Sri Lanka with my father, who supported Oxfam's work with a local community development organization called Sarvodaya Shramadana. Its head, Ari Ariyaratne, had a wonderful expression encapsulating the organization: "We build the road, and the road builds us." During the assessment trip, the US Embassy arranged my meeting with Harsha Navaratne, Chairman of the Sewalanka Foundation. Coincidentally, my father and I had met Harsha many years before. Sewalanka is a national organization working on development in post-conflict communities. Together we organized a "Humanitarian Dialogue" to explore how reconciliation strategies could be incorporated into projects of community-based organizations. The dialogue was convened at the Sewalanka retreat center south of Kandy. That morning, I ate chilies with breakfast. About midday, I broke out in fever and was terribly sick to my stomach. I tried to persevere but finally adjourned the dialogue; I simply could not perform my role as facilitator. Harsha and Vinya Ariyaratne, Ari's son, nursed me back to health.

These partners represented Sri Lanka's best and brightest. However, the wounds of war were deep. I wondered how activities with civil society might advance the goal of peacebuilding. Track two not only encourages adversaries to deal with each other, it is also a way to influence official policymaking. I was seeking partners who could work on reconciliation. Moving from war to peace requires dialogue between former adversaries and an accountability mechanism so that the perpetrators of war crimes can be brought to justice.

As democratically elected members of Parliament representing the Tamil community, the TNA had unique attributes to promote post-conflict peacebuilding.[7] Sampanthan, an older man whose life had been dedicated to the Tamil cause, was chairman of the TNA. He was ably supported by M.A. Sumanthiran, a lawyer based in Colombo who was well schooled and politically savvy. Sampanthan was the leader, but Sumanthiran was the power behind the throne.

Columbia invited a TNA delegation to New York for a seminar on constitutional power sharing. We arranged other activities during their visit, such as a forum at the Asia Society and a conference with the Tamil diaspora. We held extensive discussions on accountability mechanisms through the UN system, the International Criminal Court, and informal bodies, such as a truth and reconciliation commission and a history commission. The International Center for Transitional Justice was a valuable resource.

· · · · ·

My history with the US Government was both an asset and liability. The US was vying for influence in Sri Lanka with regional powers: India and China. India's High Commissioner in Colombo explained his country's complicated relationship with Sri Lanka.

The Indian state of Tamil Nadu has a population of more than sixty million people with ethnic and cultural ties to Tamils in Sri Lanka. In 1991, Prime Minister Rajiv Gandhi was campaigning in Tamil Nadu on behalf of the Congress Party when a female Tamil suicide bomber from Sri Lanka embraced him and exploded a suicide vest that killed him instantly. The LTTE had targeted Gandhi as revenge for ordering Indian troops to intervene in the Sri Lankan civil war on behalf of the GSL. With LTTE dying on the beach at Mullivaikal, Prabharakan hoped that external powers would come to the rescue. However, the chance for Indian intervention on behalf of the LTTE died when Gandhi was assassinated. During our meeting in 2010, the Indian High Commissioner was polite but distant. Ever since Gandhi's death, India walked a fine line between emotional support for the Tamils of Sri Lanka and commercial cooperation with the GSL.

China was overt in its influence peddling. It offered credits to the GSL for purchasing Chinese goods and provided financing for infrastructure projects with no questions asked. US legislators typically condition US aid on human rights criteria. However, human rights are of no concern to the Chinese. The Port of Hambantota in southern Sri Lanka is a Chinese project a few nautical miles from one of the world's busiest shipping lanes in the Indian Ocean. In 2002, China offered $1.1 billion in loans to greatly expand the port. Financing required Sri Lanka to hire Chinese contractors. When the project started to hemorrhage money, the Chinese state-owned operator negotiated a ninety-nine-year lease and physically took control of the port.[8] Ambassador Blake expressed concern that Hambantota may become a forward military base for China's ever-expanding blue-water navy. Through its "Belt and Road Initiative," China provided financing that advanced its interests by making countries beholden to Beijing.

Concern over China's maritime influence drove the strategic interests of India, Japan, and the US. Japan eyed Sri Lanka's deep-water port of Trincomalee as a counterbalance to Chinese influence. Japan has an extensive history of involvement in Sri Lanka. It was one of the largest providers of official development assistance; Japanese banks carried large debts of Sri Lankan concerns on their books. With full understanding of Japan's risk-averse approach to foreign policy, I made a special effort to cooperate with the Japanese government, coordinating outreach through my old friend, Tsuneo Nishida, Japan's Permanent Representative to the UN. I met Japanese officials in Colombo and kept Nishida informed.

In September 2016, Nishida invited me to a Lebanese restaurant near the UN to discuss Sri Lanka. Knowing my focus on reconciliation, he spoke about the need for a reconciliation project between Colombo and the international community. He and Ambassador Palitha Kohona agreed that Japan would sponsor UN ambassadors for a fact-finding trip to Sri Lanka. Nishida requested that I work with the Japanese Embassy in Colombo on arrangements and draft the report to be issued in Nishida's name.

He proposed the title of "Observation of the Progress of Reconstruction in Sri Lanka." I balked at the project title, which lacked a reference to reconciliation. Beyond bricks and mortar, I felt strongly that the study needed to consider governance and human rights in order to be credible. Nishida shared my concerns with Kohona, and they agreed that the study would be titled "Observation of the Progress of National Reconciliation and Reconstruction in Sri Lanka." I was not privy to their discussions, although I imagined that Nishida assured Kohona that he would keep a tight leash on activities.

The Japanese Mission recruited diplomats from Bangladesh, Brazil, Italy, Nigeria, Romania, and South Africa for the project. No US, Indian, or Chinese official was included. Kohona himself wanted to be an official member of the delegation, but I suggested that Nishida keep him at arm's length. Nishida's invitation letter indicated:

> The goal of this project is to encourage the progress of national reconciliation and reconstruction in Sri Lanka through observation from neutral, objective viewpoints. To this end, the Permanent Representatives are expected to visit Sri Lanka in an effort to observe the current de-

velopments in Sri Lanka's reconciliation and reconstruction process. Observation may be the basis for assessing progress towards implementation of the Lessons Learnt and Reconciliation Commission (LLRC) recommendations, challenges with implementation, and requirements for further implementation, including recommendations.

Nishida's letter indicated that the study was being conducted "in association with Columbia University." It also affirmed that, "The Government of Sri Lanka (GSL) provides assistance to the project."[9] My job was to coordinate the visit and draft the report in Nishida's name.

Between December 6 and 8, 2016, we visited Colombo, Jaffna, and Kilinochni for meetings with GSL officials, opposition members of Parliament, civil society representatives, religious figures, Colombo-based businesses, the UN country team, and foreign envoys posted to Sri Lanka. The journey was beset by difficulties from the beginning. First Nishida was not able to travel. North Korea launched a missile through Japanese air space. Nishida was needed to manage the response of the UN Security Council, and stayed in New York. Japan's deputy ambassador was substituted to head the delegation.

After initial consultations at the Japanese Embassy in Colombo, we went to the airport to board a Sri Lanka Air Force plane for travel to Jaffna. To Kohona's embarrassment, the plane did not work, and the delegation had to wait for the GSL to replace it.

To complicate matters further, we received mixed messages from our interlocutors. After a presentation from religious leaders in Jaffna, the Bishop's aide pulled me aside to say there were "government agents" in the meeting. "If we told you what was really going on, we'd be killed."[10] I shared this warning with members of the delegation. Japanese officials were more concerned about their relations with the GSL than any harm that might come to our interlocutors.

The delegation met with the military commander in Killinochi. Midway through the meeting, the commanding officer summoned a dozen young Tamil girls as living proof of reconciliation. He squeezed their cheeks in a paternal way. The girls did not flinch, but they seemed sullen and terrified.

We were informed that many Tamil girls had been raped and turned into sexual slaves of the SLA.

Upon our return to Colombo, the delegation met all three Rajapaksa brothers. They had a family resemblance but were profoundly different in manner and temperament. Basil Rajapaksa, the Minister of Economic Development, seated us around a long table, boardroom style, and presented a detailed, business-like, and efficient technical briefing with power point and photos.

President Mahinda Rajapaksa received us in his garden. He kicked off his sandals and was barefoot. He had a fragrant garland around his neck and played with his Buddhist prayer beads, smiling broadly through his thick black mustache.

Gotabaya Rajapaksa, the Secretary of Defense and Minister for Urban Development, hosted a reception for the delegation. He and I spent most of the reception talking one-on-one. He was very keen to impress me with his charm and likability. Gotabaya had dual citizenship of Sri Lanka and the United States. I surmised that he wanted to enlist me as a character witness should a US court indict him for war crimes. He may also have worried that the US government would impose sanctions, by barring international travel and freezing his assets. He suggested that we meet privately and took my business card, but I never heard from him again.

·   ·   ·   ·   ·

I was busy taking notes in between meetings and organizing information back in my hotel room. By the time we returned to New York, I had already written a draft of the report. The paper was balanced yet hard-hitting. It encompassed reconstruction, reconciliation, accountability, the rule of law, human rights, and military issues. The report gave credit where credit was due while recommending strategies for strengthening Sri Lanka's LLRC and accountability mechanisms.

> Since the war's end in May 2009, Sri Lanka has made great progress on reconstruction, especially rebuilding infrastructure, and with economic development. While it has also made progress with resettlement and reintegration, additional measures are needed to resettle IDPs and reintegrate ex-combatants. Winning the peace re-

quires more than reconstruction. Adhering to international norms of human rights, demonstrating a commitment to the rule of law, and decreasing the footprint of the military in civilian life will help to build confidence of Tamils in the North and East. Priority CBMs include accounting for missing persons, addressing land issues, and holding elections in the Northern Province. Abiding by the constitutional commitment to devolution is essential for the rule of law.

The report concluded that the GSL had a great opportunity to heal society's wounds after defeating the LTTE. However, "majoritarian triumphalism" has created a "trust deficit." We were told by a non-governmental organization representative, "War is over, but conflict is ongoing." He emphasized the need for a "message of care" to create a new, better, and more inclusive and compassionate society, which would go a long way to address the root causes of conflict.[11]

When Nishida returned the draft to me, it had been sanitized of all recommendations on accountability and mention of human rights. Though the report was still a work in progress, Kohona circulated it to members of the UN Human Rights Commission in Geneva, which was considering a resolution on accountability in Sri Lanka. The GSL used the report as evidence of their progress and cooperation with the international community. I received a call from Ken Roth, executive director of Human Rights Watch, expressing his dismay. The GSL was misusing the report to burnish its image, not as the basis for genuine reforms.

Ambassador Blake was also upset. I had shared the original version of the report with the State Department, and he was troubled that Japan doctored the text. The US government issued a demarche to Japan's Foreign Ministry in Tokyo, its ambassador in Geneva, and the Japanese Mission in New York. As damage control, Blake urged me to release the original version of the report.

Nishida invited officials from UN missions to a briefing on the project in the boardroom of the Japanese Embassy. The invitation had already been sent, identifying Nishida, Kohona, and me as keynote speakers. Nishida is an experienced and savvy diplomat who did not want a major confrontation with the US. I informed him of my intention to release the original version and agreed to participate in the conference if the original report was distributed under my name. Nishida assured me that copies would be made available.

He welcomed guests and then called on Ambassador Kohona to speak before turning to me. I noticed that my report had not been distributed. Within earshot of his guests, I refused to present my remarks until the report was distributed. He instructed his staff, and copies were passed out to conference participants. I gave a measured but honest account of our fact-finding trip, summarizing the findings and recommendations. I was seated next to Ambassador Kohona, with whom I had grown friendly over recent years. He was seething with anger during my presentation. "I am so deeply disappointed in you," Kohona admonished. I told him that I too was disappointed by his whitewashing the report.

The Japanese are deeply averse to confrontation, yet Nishida took the whole incident in stride. From his perspective, Tokyo would mend fences with the GSL. More importantly, US-Japan relations were not affected. His deputy pulled me aside and playfully called me a "troublemaker." If the truth is trouble, then bring it on.

· · · · ·

Sri Lanka held presidential elections on January 9, 2015. Mahinda Rajapaksa was defeated by Maithripala Sirisena, a former ally, who won 51.3 percent of the vote. Sirisena won with support from Tamils and Muslims, as well as surprising support from Sinhalese. Many Sri Lankans gave credit to Rajapaksa for defeating the Tamil Tigers and reviving the economy, but they objected to his increasing authoritarianism. Rajapaksa had changed the constitution to allow a third term, which riled the citizens. Rajapaksa accepted the result in a victory for democracy.[12]

President Sirisena proved to be incompetent. Although he joined forces with Ranil Wickremesinghe to defeat Rajapaksa in 2015, their relations soured over economic reform and government administration. Sirisena also claimed there was an assassination plot against him, implicating Wickremesinghe. In a shocking turnaround, Sirisena fired Wickremesinghe as Prime Minister and replaced him with Mahinda Rajapaksa on October 26, 2018. Sirisena dissolved Parliament through a controversial no-confidence vote. However, Sri Lanka's Supreme Court suspended the order. In the midst of a constitutional crisis, the Rajapaksa clan clamored for early elections, demanding that the people decide.[13]

Sri Lanka's constitution required the presidential election by the end of 2019, followed by parliamentary elections. With Mahinda precluded from presidential elections by term limits adopted during Sirisena's rule, the Sri Lanka Podujana Peramuna Party nominated Gotabaya as its candidate for president. Sri Lanka was at a fork in the road: Down one path lay opportunities for reconciliation and accountability with closer ties to India and the United States. Down the other path, preferred by the Rajapaksas, lay a return to centralized government and autocracy with support from China.[14]

Sri Lanka was traumatized by an ISIS attack on Easter 2019 that killed more than 250 people.[15] Gotabaya presented himself as the candidate of law and order, vowing to fight terrorism and put the country back on track. He defeated the UNP's Sajith Premadasa with 52 percent of the vote on November 17, 2019. Gotabaya announced that he would appoint Mahinda to serve as prime minister.

Many Sri Lankans worried about a return to the Rajapaksas' brutal treatment of minorities and dissidents. I was contacted by a civil society activist who feared a reprisal by Gotabaya. I arranged her appointment as a Visiting Scholar at Columbia University so she could continue her research. My real motive was to get her out of harm's way.

Mahinda blamed Norway for favoring the LTTE. In 2016, I visited Oslo with Governor Bill Richardson. Our study tour included interviews with Norway's peace mediators. Erik Solheim reflected on Norway's efforts, which he acknowledged went on too long and ultimately lacked the appearance of impartiality. Norway's soft power would have worked best when combined with a more confrontational approach by the US. The United States could have played a more proactive role supporting Norway's mediation and through sanctions and other punitive measures prior to the battle of Mullivaikal.

Violent conflict is man-made. Some humanitarian emergencies, however, result from natural catastrophe that can influence the way people view one another and interact. A tsunami devastated the eastern and southern coasts of Sri Lanka on December 26, 2004. It could have galvanized negotiations between the GSL and the LTTE.[16] Unlike East Timor and Aceh, Indonesia, where the tsunami catalyzed a peace process, Sri Lanka's antagonists stuck to their guns even as a giant wall of water swept 30,000 people out to sea and flooded hundreds of acres of coastal land.

Notes

1 Senaka Weeraratna, "Sri Lanka's Independence—A Beneficiary of Japan's Entry to the Second World War which Sealed the Fate of European Colonialism in Asia," *Lankaweb,* February 2, 2017.

2 H.E. Ambassador Tsuneo Nishia, "Observation of the Progress of National Reconciliation and Reconstruction in Sri Lanka," December 31, 2012.

3 "War Crimes in Sri Lanka," *International Crisis Group,* May 17, 2010, http://responsibilitytoprotect.org/War%20Crimes%20In%20Sri%20Lanka.pdf.

4 Hemantha Dayaratne, "An Appraisal of Norway's Role in Sri Lanka," *IDSA Comments,* February 3, 2011. https://idsa.in/idsacomments/Anappraisalof NorwaysRoleinSriLanka_hdayaratne_030211.

5 Report in External Series, NORAD Evaluation report no. 5/2011, "Pawns of Peace. Evaluation of Norwegian Peace Efforts in Sri Lanka, 1997-2009," 2011.

6 Mark Salter, "To End A Civil War—Norway's Peace Engagement in Sri Lanka"; Rohan Edrisinghe et al., eds., *Power-Sharing in Sri Lanka: Constitutional and Political Documents: 1926-2008.*

7 Robert C. Oberst et al., "Government and Politics in South Asia," *Avalon Publishing,* July 9, 2013.

8 "Sri Lanka Signs Deal on Hambantota Port with China," *BBC,* July 29, 2017, https://www.bbc.com/news/world-asia-40761732.

9 Nishida, "Observation of the Progress of National Reconciliation and Reconstruction in Sri Lanka."

10 Author's recollection of the meeting with religious leaders, December 7, 2012.

11 David L. Phillips, "Observation of the Progress of National Reconciliation and Reconstruction in Sri Lanka," December 31, 2012.

12 "Sri Lanka's Rajapaksa Suffers Shock Election Defeat," *BBC,* January 9, 2015, https://www.bbc.com/news/world-asia-30738671.

13 Rathindra Kuruwita and Zaheena Rasheed, "Sirisena, Rajapaksa, Wickremesinghe Fail to End Power Struggle," *Al Jazeera,* November 19, 2018, https://

www.aljazeera.com/news/2018/11/sirisena-rajapaksa-wickremesinghe-fail-power-struggle-181118210835557.html.

14 *Guardian,* December 13, 2018.

15 Kat Lonsdorf," Gotabaya Rajapaksa Wins Sri Lankan Presidential Elections," *NPR,* November 17, 2019, https://www.npr.org/2019/11/17/780241242/gotabaya-rajapaksa-wins-sri-lankan-presidential-elections

16 "US Presidents in Tsunami Aid Plea," *BBC,* January 3, 2005, http://news.bbc.co.uk/2/hi/asia-pacific/4143459.stm#map.

CHAPTER 12

EAST TIMOR IN FLAMES

New York's "West End" was a well-known jazz club on Broadway across from the campus of Columbia University. I arranged to meet Jose Ramos-Horta there in the spring of 1998. Ramos-Horta was co-recipient of the Nobel Prize for Peace with Bishop Ximenes Belo in 1996. The Nobel Committee recognized his work "towards a just and peaceful solution to the conflict in East Timor."[1]

He showed up for the meeting unshaven with beard stubble of about a week. He wore a white dress shirt underneath a Nehru-collar jacket. Every time I met him over the coming years, he was similarly attired, somewhere between elegant and disheveled. His greying beard was always the same length. The studiously unkempt look was consistent with his image as a revolutionary. From 1975 to 1999, Ramos-Horta, the son of a Portuguese woman and an East Timorese man, represented Fretilin, the center-left Revolutionary Front for an Independent East Timor. Falintil, the Armed Forces of National Liberation of East Timor, was Fretilin's armed wing.[2]

Meeting at Columbia was a homecoming for Ramos-Horta. He completed post-graduate courses in American Foreign Policy at Columbia in the 1980s. He was very much a "New Yorker." Ramos-Horta stayed at Shep Forman's apartment on West 86th Street. Forman, a former vice president of the Ford Foundation, raved about Ramos-Horta's intellect and political acumen. Everything he said about Ramos-Horta was true, and then some.

Indonesia's President Suharto was challenged in 1997. Having served as Indonesia's president for thirty-two years, Suharto cultivated an aura of invincibility. When we met at the West End, Ramos-Horta predicted the end of Suharto's rule. According to Ramos-Horta, peaceful pro-democracy protests would intensify. Suharto's security would crack down with unnecessary force.[3] The 1997 Asian financial crisis would cause the rupiah, Indonesia's currency, to collapse, resulting in a national economic meltdown. Suharto would be overthrown and, in the tumult of transition, East Timor would go free. Ramos-Horta's prediction sounded like wishful thinking. It was, however, exactly what happened.

I first met Indonesia's foreign minister Ali Alatas at our family Thanksgiving in the 1970s. My grandmother, Betti Hellinger Salzman, chaired the United Nations (UN) Hospitality Committee and was well connected to the spouses of UN ambassadors from around the world. I met Alatas again on the margins of the UN General Assembly (UNGA) in September 1997. He denied Indonesia's troubles and denounced the prospect of East Timor's independence, warning that East Timor's secession would destabilize the entire Indonesian archipelago and have a ripple effect across Southeast Asia.

From Aceh in the far west on the northern tip of Sumatra to West Papua in the far east, Indonesia consisted of 13,000 far-flung islands. Some parts had a Dutch colonial legacy, while East Timor had been a Portuguese colony. Indonesia is predominantly Muslim. However, East Timor, Flores, Maluku, and Sulawesi are mostly Christian. Ethnic Chinese of Buddhist and Christian background reside in Jakarta and parts of Java. East Timor is totally unique. The vast majority of East Timorese are Catholic, and East Timorese speak their own language, Tetun, rather than Bahasa Indonesian. Although Indonesia's armed forces (TNI) tried to impose order across the vast archipelago, Indonesia risked fragmenting due its lack of national identity and coherence between communities.

· · · · ·

The April 1974 Carnation Revolution was a military coup with popular support to overthrow the fascist-colonial dictatorship in Portugal, which had governed for forty-eight years. In its aftermath, Portugal started to withdraw and negotiate the decolonization of its colonies—Guiné Bissau, Cabo Verde, São Tomé and Príncipe, Mozambique, Angola, and Portuguese Timor. Indonesia, prodded by Australia and the US in the aftermath of its Vietnam War, feared a left-leaning government would fill the vacuum from Portugal's departure. It incited rivalries in East Timor in a bid to divide and conquer.

Portuguese authorities were unable to contain unrest resulting from Fretilin's Declaration of Independence on November 28, 1975, and left Dili for the smaller East Timorese island of Ataúro. Indonesia invaded East Timor on December 7, 1975. The US provided weapons and turned a blind eye to the invasion and occupation. Suharto persuaded National Security Adviser Henry Kissinger that his opposition to left-leaning Sukarno was a critical frontier in the Cold War. Kissinger and President Gerald Ford visited Jakarta the day before East Timor was invaded, leading to speculation that the US had given a green light to the invasion.

On May 31, 1976, a so-called People's Assembly in Dili, organized by Indonesian intelligence, endorsed an "Act of Integration" and East Timor officially became the twenty-seventh province of the Republic of Indonesia on July 17. The UN did not recognize Jakarta's annexation. Moreover, the East Timorese rejected Indonesian rule; Falintil rebelled, which led to repression by the Government of Indonesia (GOI). As many as 200,000 people perished in the ensuing famine and massacres. The international community paid attention when troops fired on mourners at a funeral of a Fretilin supporter in Dili on November 12, 1991. Killing more than 250 people, the incident was called the Santa Cruz massacre.[4]

Despite its betrayal of the East Timorese people, Portugal became East Timor's advocate, raising human rights abuses and East Timor's right to self-determination at the UN Security Council, UNGA, in the UN's Fourth Committee, the Human Rights Commission (UNHRC), and other international forums.

The US was conspicuously absent from the debate about East Timor. US officials refused to meet Ramos-Horta because of Fretilin's leftist ideology. Ramos-Horta's receipt of the Nobel Prize for Peace together with the Dili Bishop Ximenes Belo burnished his credentials and credibility. However, the US government still ignored him. Richard Holbrooke played a pivotal role shifting US policy.

Holbrooke was highly motivated to help East Timor. First and foremost, it was the right thing to do. In addition, Holbrooke aspired to receive the Nobel Prize for Peace and wanted an endorsement from Ramos-Horta. Elie Wiesel advised Holbrooke on winning the Prize, emphasizing the importance of recommendations from previous laureates. Holbrooke should have received the Nobel Peace Prize after his mediation ended the Bosnian war. However, the nomination cycle was closed by November of 1995 when the Dayton Peace Agreement was finalized. His nomination languished on the back burner, even though Nobel laureates and distinguished international personalities supported him. I was affiliated with the Peace Research Institute in Oslo and, because of my Norwegian connections, helped manage Holbrooke's campaign to gain recognition from the Nobel Committee. Although lobbying for the Prize is strictly taboo, I arranged to visit Oslo with Bosnia's Prime Minister Haris Silajdžić to advocate on Holbrooke's behalf.

Geir Lundestad, Secretary General of the Nobel Peace Prize Committee, is a big, burly man of hardy Norwegian stock who is missing his index finger from a hunting accident. Lundestad gave us a tour of the Nobel Committee's offices including the boardroom, the inner sanctum where committee members deliberate nominations. The wall was lined with photos of each Nobel laureate since the Prize was first awarded in 1901. A gap existed in the photomontage. The missing photo was of North Vietnam's Lee Duc Tho, who refused to accept the Nobel Peace Prize, jointly awarded with Henry Kissinger in 1973 for the Paris Peace Talks aimed at ending the Vietnam War. Lundestad explained that the Nobel Prize is recognition not only for an individual's existing contribution to peace. Awarding the Prize may also be aspirational, bestowed to enhance future contributions.

Ramos-Horta was well suited as Holbrooke's advocate. Not only was he a recent recipient, but also his leftist orientation resonated with Lundestad, with whom he shared a progressive worldview. Lundestad had a reputation for being anti-American, which made Holbrooke an unlikely recipient.

· · · · ·

Ramos-Horta's prediction about Suharto's demise was compelling; I contacted Governor Bill Richardson, the US Permanent Representative to the United Nations, to propose a meeting in early March 1998. Richardson checked with the State Department, which blocked the appointment. I shared this development with Holbrooke, who served as Assistant Secretary of State for Asia from 1977 to 1981 and was familiar with America's complicity in Indonesia's invasion of East Timor. He was perturbed to learn that the State Department refused to meet Ramos-Horta.

Holbrooke changed the format of the proposed meeting. Instead of meeting at the US Mission, he invited Ambassador Richardson to his home at 211 Central Park West for an informal, off-the-record discussion. Richardson was accompanied by his aide, Mona Sutphen. Ramos-Horta gave a substantive presentation on injustices committed by the GOI in East Timor and the prospects for political transition in Indonesia.

The US was internally conflicted over its support for human rights and the need for cooperation with Jakarta. Good relations were in America's security and economic interests. Indonesia was a counter-balance to China, which had aggressively staked claim to the Natuna Islands in the South China Sea. Chinese fishermen plied Indonesia's traditional fishing ground, which overlaps with its exclusive economic zone.

Richardson reported the details of his meeting with Ramos-Horta to colleagues at the State Department. His findings must have been positive, as he facilitated a follow-up meeting for Ramos-Horta in Washington. Meeting US officials was a big step in Freitilin's campaign for legitimacy and greater recognition.

Unrepresented peoples lack official credentials and therefore are barred from meetings at the UN. East Timor was the exception. Portugal felt a deep sense of obligation to its former colony and issued credentials to Ramos-Horta and his Fretilin colleagues as members of the Portuguese delegation to the UNHRC, which enabled their access to the Palais des Nations in Geneva.

The Portuguese diplomat, Ana Gomes, was the ringleader. We met in 1992 when she was a Member of the Portuguese Delegation to the UNHRC and had interacted extensively during the demise of Yugoslavia. She was a tireless critic of ethnic cleansing in Bosnia and an activist within the Western and European Group of the UNHRC.

Our friendship was forged during the East Timor crisis. In 1997 and 1998, as Coordinator of the Portuguese Delegation at the UN Security Council in New York, Gomes used Portugal's position as a member of the UN Security Council (UNSC) to hammer on Indonesia for its repression. She was fierce and principled, Jakarta's worst nightmare, calling out the Indonesian government repeatedly for its repression in East Timor and demanding a referendum on East Timor's independence.

Gomes was in close contact with Antonio Guterres, who was secretary-general of the Socialist Party from 1992 to 2002 and Portugal's prime minister from 1995 to 2002. Columbia University planned a study on "Social and Economic Conditions in East Timor," anticipating the need for baseline data that could be used for East Timor's development and reconstruction. Gomes enlisted support from Guterres for a grant of

$200,000 to Columbia. With Portugal's commitment in hand, I went to Oslo to pitch the project to Norwegian officials.

The Christian Unity Party took over Norway's government in 1998. Up to that point, my collaboration was facilitated by Jan Egeland, the deputy foreign minister in the left-leaning coalition government and a leading figure in Norway's Socialist Party. Egeland introduced me to his successor as deputy foreign minister, Wegger Strommen. We met at a fish restaurant on the pier in Oslo with Johan Vibe, who headed the Foreign Ministry's Peace and Reconciliation Unit. I was pleased to receive their support for our East Timor project in the amount of $400,000. The Norwegian government typically requires foreign organizations to work with a Norwegian counterpart; Vibe introduced me to the Fafo Institute for Labour and Social Research, which specialized in household social and economic surveys. Columbia and Fafo launched the project together; I visited East Timor in October of 1998 to initiate field research.

We also cooperated with the UN. Gomes introduced me to Tamrat Samuel who, from his position at the UN's Department of Political Affairs, emerged as the lead UN official on East Timor. Between 1992 and 2000, he was the focal point for the secretary-general's good offices on the "Question of East Timor" and lead negotiator with the GOI. It was invaluable to work with a key person in the UN system and to have the support of member states.

· · · · ·

On May 12, 1998, riot police fired on peaceful protesters, killing four students from Trisakti University in West Jakarta. Their killing led to a spasm of violence as mobs attacked Jakarta's Chinatown burning, looting, and killing and raping ethnic Chinese. Students stormed the Parliament building chanting slogans from its rooftop and demanding that Suharto step down. On May 21, Suharto resigned as president of the Republic of Indonesia. Indonesians were shocked; they thought his demise would never come.[5]

Vice President B. J. Habibie replaced Suharto in 1998. He suggested a "special status" of autonomy for East Timor within Indonesia. His proposal started negotiations under the auspices of UN Secretary General Kofi Annan. Habibie suddenly went further, affirming the GOI's support for independence for East Timor if people rejected autonomy. Violence escalated, with the TNI orchestrating violence by shadowy militias under its control. Indonesia and Portugal signed an agreement in May 1999 to allow East Timorese to vote on their future. Portugal and the UN pushed to conduct the referendum. Australia's Prime Minister John Howard had no alternative and supported it. Under international pressure, the GOI released Xanana Gusmao, the East Timorese Resistance leader, whom it had jailed in 1992. The UN Mission in East Timor (UNAMET) was led by a capable diplomat, Ian Martin, who organized a referendum in East Timor on August 30, 1999.

Almost 99 percent of East Timor's electorate participated in the ballot. The referendum was the culmination of twenty-four years of occupation by Jakarta, which followed centuries of colonial rule by Portugal. Indonesian officials were shocked when 78.5 percent rejected autonomy. Habibie never dreamed that a majority of East Timorese would actually vote for independence. Had Habibie anticipated the strong support for independence, he never would have allowed the vote to happen.[6]

During the run-up to the referendum, the TNI and their militias launched a campaign of violence to intimidate voters. Opposition Indonesian politicians such as Megawati Sukarnoputri were strongly opposed to independence. Repression intensified in response to the referendum's result, as the TNI, since renamed ABRI, sponsored a campaign of terror by its anti-independence militias. As violent conflict intensified, East Timorese desperately sought protection at the UNAMET compound where about 2,500 people, mostly women and children, sheltered. Ian Martin tried to protect them. He reported, "Significant numbers of militia members are still roaming the streets with impunity. Dili is a ghost town with not very much left to loot."[7]

Ana Gomes was sent to Jakarta in January 1999 as Portugal's diplomatic representative. She coordinated with the Portuguese Mission in New York, led by ambassador Antonio Monteiro and other relevant UN officials. Gomes was a strident advocate of humanitarian intervention. Holbrooke, who had become US Ambassador to the UN, supported intervention, coordinating advocacy with Ramos-Horta. Camping out on the third floor of the UN outside the Security Council chambers, Ramos-Horta pleaded for urgent action by the international community. When he wasn't lobbying member states, Ramos-Horta was working the international media. Intervention in East Timor would require authorization from the UNSC, so international public opinion was important.

Conditions worsened on the ground. East Timor only had a population of 850,000; yet during the ensuing three-week campaign of violence, 2,600 people were killed; nearly 30,000 were displaced; and up to 250,000 were forcibly driven across the border to Kupang and Atambua in West Timor. Wanton violence was part of the Indonesian plan to divide East Timor, annexing territory to West Timor and leaving a rump state. ABRI undercut political authorities such as Habibie and Alatas, who sincerely sought a political settlement of the longstanding problem.[8]

After the US intervened to prevent genocide in Kosovo during the spring of 1999, President Bill Clinton appreciated that conflict prevention required a credible threat of force. The Pentagon froze its International Military Assistance and Training Program with Indonesia and suspended weapons sales, over the strong objection of General Wiranto, head of ABRI. The US also threatened economic sanctions, suggesting it would veto a $43 billion aid package from the International Monetary Fund, which Indonesia desperately needed.

Clinton was in New Zealand at the Asia-Pacific Economic Cooperation Council meeting from September 9 to 13, 1999. He knew the international community had no appetite for intervening without a UN Chapter 7 resolution authorizing all necessary measures. António Guterres urged Clinton to act, threatening to withdraw Portuguese troops from Kosovo. According to Guterres, the Portuguese people would not understand international inaction to stop the violence in East Timor. Clinton spoke directly to Habibie, wagging his finger: "You must invite an international peacekeeping force to East Timor." He warned further, "I have made clear that my willingness to support future economic assistance from the international community will depend upon how Indonesia handles the situation from today."[9]

Habibie succumbed to international pressure and agreed to a UN-backed peacekeeping operation. On September 15, the UNSC adopted Resolution 1264, authorizing measures to restore peace and security to East Timor, as well as humanitarian operations. The resolution also mandated peacekeepers to protect UNAMET.

Boots on the ground were needed to enforce Resolution 1264. Australia committed to lead a coalition of the willing, which became the International Force for East Timor (INTERFET). Under the command of Australian Major General Peter Cosgrove, INTERFET included 11,000 troops, half of whom were Australian. Another twenty countries sent personnel, starting September 20, 1999. Canberra's fast action prevented the situation from spiraling out of control and saved many lives. The US provided intelligence and logistical support but no troops. I called Australia's Ambassador Penny Wensley, whom I knew from Geneva, to express appreciation for Australia's leadership.

On September 28, Xanana Gusmao and Ramos-Horta held a press briefing at UN headquarters. They conveyed three primary messages:

1. The TNI's scorched-earth policy had taken a devastating toll. Funds were urgently needed for humanitarian assistance and help to rebuild the country.

2. The security situation was dangerous in the western part of the country and Dili. INTERFET should accelerate and expand its deployment.

3. A transitional period with international assistance would pave the way for independence.

East Timor was on its way to becoming an independent and sovereign state.[10]

.　.　.　.　.

Ramos-Horta was like a conquering hero when he returned to East Timor on April 17, 2000. He had been away for twenty-four years, mythologized by East Timorese as their champion and voice to the outside world. He flew back to Dili from Darwin on an Australian C-130 transport plane. There was room on the trip for three guests. He invited Kerry Kennedy; Michael Richardson, an editor at the International Herald Tribune; and myself.

I flew to Sydney, then Alice Springs, and Darwin on the north coast. It was so exciting to be a part of Ramos-Horta's triumphant return. Australian personnel calmly managed arrangements on their end. However, the airport in Dili was absolute bedlam, with tens of thousands of people to greet Ramos-Horta. Their country had been burnt to the ground, but they were jubilant. East Timor was poor to begin with, more so after Indonesia's scorched-earth policy, but now the people were free, and it was time to celebrate.

Ramos-Horta was mobbed at the airport. There was convoy of four-wheel drive vehicles, and he made sure I got in the second car. It would have been so easy to get separated and lost in the crowd. We drove to the Freitilin office downtown for an initial round of meetings. Two days later, we left the city for villages in the countryside. When we inspected a Frenamo military formation at their headquarters, they hoisted their flag while the band played an anthem. We were greeted by dancing girls who presented us with hand-woven scarves as a welcome gesture. Traditional dancers performed a welcome dance at every stop. Ramos-Horta held a ceaseless series of meetings with Xanana and Mari Alkati, who was Secretary General of Freitilin and would become prime minister in 2002.

We rose with the sunset one morning and drove through villages that were still smoldering. The car stereo played a cassette of "The End" by the Doors. The experience was surreal, driving through razed villages, listening to music from the film "Apocalypse Now." I thought about General Kurtz, a character in the film, who referred to "the horror, the horror."

Indonesia's destruction of East Timor was indeed horrible, but it merely motivated Ramos-Horta to struggle more on behalf of his people. The world wanted East Timor to succeed, and he was pivotal to its success. As a measure of the international community's commitment to East Timor, Secretary General Kofi Annan appointed Sergio Vieira de Mello as his Special Representative and head of the UN Transitional Authority for East Timor (UNTAET). It was led by De Mello, a Brazilian diplomat with thirty-four years as an international civil servant who was one of the best and brightest of the UN system. UNTAET's task was to prepare East Timor for independence.

De Mello hired me as a Senior Adviser for Humanitarian Advocacy at the UN's Office for the Coordination of Humanitarian Affairs (OCHA). Before I could assume the post, he left for East Timor. I felt abandoned to UN bureaucrats who reflexively opposed advocacy lest it offend the sensibilities of a member state.

Kofi Annan telephoned my first day on the job. He was a family friend and was simply calling to welcome me. The administrator who picked up the phone was shocked by the Secretary-General's call. Instead of enhancing my status at OCHA, colleagues were perturbed that I knew the big boss. They viewed me warily and with distrust during my year on the thirty-sixth floor of UN headquarters.

. . . . .

With the East Timorese economy devastated, Ramos-Horta was focused on reconstruction. Japan and the World Bank convened a donors' conference in January 2000, which resulted in pledges of $517 million. It was a significant sum but just a fraction of what was needed. A follow-up donors' conference was convened in Lisbon on June 23. In his opening remarks, de Mello noted, "East Timor represents a tremendous opportunity for us all. We have the chance in this newly emerging country, to find pragmatic ways to blend Timor's traditional culture and societal beliefs with international norms and practices in a spirit of international development cooperation. We are on the verge of making this a reality, and we now need to reaffirm our resolve to support this enterprise."[11]

At the Lisbon conference, De Mello itemized both achievements and challenges. The international relief effort had delivered tens of thousands of tons of essential humanitarian supplies including shelter, food, water, and sanitation. The UN's humanitarian program facilitated the return and reintegration of over 163,000 refugees. However, 120,000 refugees remained in West Timor in camps under the control of pro-integration extremists, where they lacked security and supplies. With so many homes destroyed by militias, there was a severe housing shortage.

East Timor required jobs. Economic activity was accelerating, measured by the registration of some 2,300 international and Timorese businesses. UNTAET and the World Bank finalized major agreements on health, infrastructure, agriculture, education, and community empowerment.

Peter Galbraith, who introduced me to Kurdish issues in 1988, led negotiations with Australia over oil and gas development in the Timor Gap, waters between the two countries. In July 2001, East Timor and Australia signed a deal dividing earnings from oil and gas fields in the Timor Sea. East Timor was awarded 90 percent of revenues.

Coffee was another potentially lucrative commodity. Holbrooke hosted a lunch for Ramos-Horta at his ambassador's residence at the Waldorf Astoria. William Schultz, the CEO of Starbucks, was one of the guests. Schultz and Ramos-Horta discussed the sale of East Timorese coffee beans. I facilitated follow-up, arranging to send samples to the Starbucks headquarters in Seattle. Starbucks was prepared to source product from East Timor, but tasters concluded that the beans were too bitter. They proposed mixing it with beans from Indonesia and calling it the "Java blend." Ramos-Horta was indignant and rejected the deal. He explained that East Timor spent twenty-four years resisting Javanese domination. He would not condone a Java blend no matter how lucrative.

De Mello focused on handing over governance responsibility as soon as possible. With UNTAET's guidance, the East Timor assembly approved a constitution in February 2002, envisaging a parliamentary system. Independence Day was May 20, 2002. It was a grand event; President Bill Clinton attended the celebrations with President Megawati. Of course, de Mello played a leading role; Gomes, Samuel and other old friends of East Timor also attended. East Timor was renamed "Timor Leste" and became the UN's 191st member.[12]

. . . . .

Ramos-Horta was understandably resentful of Indonesia for its occupation and the destruction it wrought at the end. However, he evolved from an activist into a statesman. I was surprised by his conciliatory approach to bilateral relations with Jakarta. He worked assiduously on arrangements for the return of refugees from West Timor. Regarding transitional justice, he emphasized Indonesia's responsibility for trying generals and senior officials accused of crimes during the 1999 unrest. Indonesia established a special human rights court in 2002 but convicted only one militia leader three years later.

East Timor launched a truth and reconciliation commission (TRC) in January 2002. However, the TRC's first meeting did not occur until August 2005. Advised by Patrick Burgess, an Australian barrister and original member of the International Center for Transitional Justice, East Timorese decided on a body that was purely investigative with no power to prosecute. Its final report concluded that atrocities were committed during Indonesia's twenty-four-year rule and that occupation was directly responsible for the deaths of more than 100,000 East Timorese. However, no action was proposed against the perpetrators. The TRC's final report was presented to the UN, ending a chapter in East Timor's history and setting the stage for reconciliation between the neighboring countries.[13]

Ramos-Horta was a polarizing advocate who became a unifying leader. Gone were the days of his rabble rousing and venom towards Jakarta. He became Foreign Minister after independence in 2002, a position that he filled until 2006. He then served as Prime Minister from 2006 to 2007 and was elected President on May 20, 2007, a position he occupied for five years until 2012.

In a shocking development, East Timorese troops tried to assassinate Ramos-Horta as he returned to his official residence outside Dili on February 11, 2008. An hour later, mutineers attacked the convoy of Prime Minister Xanana Gusmao, who escaped unhurt. The double assassination attempt was a "coup." Ramos-Horta called for calm. "My message to my people is please forgo violence and hatred with weapons, machetes, with arson - we only destroy each other and the country." He was rushed to the hospital in Darwin where he underwent repeated surgeries for gunshot wounds in the chest and back. Ramos-Horta barely survived.[14]

· · · · ·

The independence of East Timor occurred at an important moment in time, after the Kosovo intervention and before Bush's invasion and occupation of Iraq. Good people converged to help the East Timorese realize their dream of independence. They are too numerous to mention here, but some deserve special commendation.

De Mello effectively managed state building in East Timor, addressing its humanitarian emergency and putting it on the path to independence. In Baghdad, he and twenty UN staff were murdered during a car bombing on August 19, 2003. The Government of Brazil established the Sergio Vieira de Mello Medal, recognizing his contribution to peace, security, and bettering the human condition.

Richard Holbrooke never received his much-deserved Nobel Peace Prize, nor did he become Secretary of State, a position for which he was well suited. He worked himself to death as the Obama administration's Special

Envoy for Afghanistan and Pakistan. His heart burst and he died of a torn aorta on December 12, 2010.

My friendship with Ana Gomes spanned several decades and continues to this day. Beyond East Timor, we collaborated on many human rights projects. She led the resumption of Portuguese diplomatic relations with Jakarta and became Portugal's first Ambassador to Indonesia in 2000. Gomes hosted a dinner in Jakarta where I presented a conflict prevention report on West Papua. At the time, I headed the Indonesia Commission of the Council on Foreign Relations.

After four years in Jakarta, Gomes was elected a Member of the European Parliament for Portugal. Over Belgrade's objection, she invited me to present my report on the Kosovo-Serbia dialogue at a forum in the European Parliament. Gomes was a leading member of the Socialist Party in the European Parliament from 2004 to 2019. We sat side-by-side as keynote speakers at the European Parliament's Conference on Kurds in Turkey in 2017. She has retired from diplomacy but remains a political commentator and an outspoken anti-corruption advocate.

Oil and gas in the Timor Gap proved less lucrative than expected. Starbucks did not purchase East Timor's "bitter" coffee beans. The country's economic development is slowly progressing, but its people are far better off than they were under Indonesian rule. East Timor is free and independent. Ramos-Horta's prediction came to pass.

Notes

1   The Nobel Prize, October 11, 1996, https://www.nobelprize.org/prizes/un categorized/the-nobel-peace-prize-1996.

2   Encyclopedia Britannica, https://www.britannica.com/topic/Revolutionary-Front-of-Independent-East-Timor.

3   David E. Sanger, "In the Shadow of a Scandal, U.S. Challenges a Suharto Project," *New York Times,* June 14, 1997, https://www.nytimes.com/1997/06/14/world/in-the-shadow-of-scandal-us-challenges-a-suharto-project.html.

4   Marek Marczyński, "Remembering the Santa Cruz Massacre in Timor-Leste," *Amnesty International,* November 13, 2012, https://www.amnesty.org/en/latest/campaigns/2012/11/remembering-the-santa-cruz-massacre-in-timor-leste/.

5   Richard Borsuk, Marcus W. Brauchli, and Robert KeatleyStaff, "After Presidential Reign of 32 Years, Suharto Hands Power to Vice President," *Wall Street Journal*, May 21, 1998, https://www.wsj.com/articles/SB895651439485261000.

6   Allison Rourke, "East Timor: Indonesia's Invasion and the Long Road To Independence," *The Guardian*, August 29, 2019, https://www.theguardian.com/world/2019/aug/30/east-timor-indonesias-invasion-and-the-long-road-to-independence.

7   Tom Fawthrop, "East Timor Militias Call off Siege of UN Compound," *The Guardian*, September 9, 1999, https://www.theguardian.com/world/1999/sep/10/indonesia.easttimor7.

8   Allison Rourke, "East Timor."

9   The United States Government, September 12, 1999, https://www.govinfo.gov/content/pkg/WCPD-1999-09-20/pdf/WCPD-1999-09-20-Pg1727.pdf.

10 Xanana Gusmao and Jose Ramos Horta, "Press Conference on East Timor," *The United Nations*, September 28, 1999, https://www.un.org/press/en/1999/19990928.etimor.doc.html.

11 "UNTAET Opening Address," *East Timor Donors Conference*, Lisbon, June 22-23, 2000, https://reliefweb.int/report/timor-leste/untaet-opening-address-east-timor-donors-conference-lisbon-22-23-jun-2000·

12 "East Timor Becomes 191st U.N. Member Today," *New York Times*, September 27, 2002, https://www.nytimes.com/2002/09/27/world/east-timor-becomes-191st-un-member-today.html.

13 United States Institute of Peace, https://www.usip.org/publications/2002/02/truth-commission-timor-leste-east-timor.

14 "East Timor President Recounts Assassination Bid," *Reuters*, March 19, 2008, https://uk.reuters.com/artcle/uk-timor-ramoshorta-idUKSYD19344720080319.

CHAPTER 13

THE FREE ACEH MOVEMENT

H asan di Tiro was Aceh's revered sultan (*Wali Nangro*) and undisputed head of the Free Aceh Movement (*Gerakan Aceh Merdeka*), known as GAM, a group seeking independence for the Aceh region of Indonesia.[1] We met in March 2000 at his dreary apartment block in the suburbs of Stockholm, home of Aceh's government in exile. Di Tiro was living in the past, obsessed by history.

On his kitchen table, he kept an album of yellowing newspaper clippings and photographs and a collection of sympathy and support letters he received from world leaders over the decades. He was especially proud of a letter from Henry Kissinger that addressed him in his official capacity: "Wali Nangro." To di Tiro, the letter was evidence of international support for Aceh's independence. Aceh's Minister of State Malik Mahmud and Zaini Abdullah, who was in charge of media and international relations, joined our discussions.

Di Tiro explained Aceh's history of resistance and independence. Due to its strategic location on the Straits of Malacca, Aceh had for centuries been a wealthy center of trade and culture. It was a commercial empire in the sixteenth and seventeenth centuries, trading in gold, pepper, ivory, tin, aloe wood, and exotic spices. Aceh was an independent sultanate for five hundred years until 1873, when the Netherlands sought to extend its colonial rule to all of Sumatra. The fighting lasted forty years, but the Dutch never established legal or de facto control over Aceh.

The Dutch presence in Aceh lasted until World War II, when Aceh was occupied by Japan. The Acehnese joined Indonesian nationalists to resist Dutch colonialism and Japanese occupation. Indonesia became independent on August 17, 1945, two days after Japan's emperor surrendered and the Pacific war ended. In 1949, the Dutch ceded the Dutch East Indies and transferred control to the Republic of Indonesia (RI). The Acehnese struggled to regain independence, but the Darul Islam rebel movement was outmatched by Indonesian government forces. Rebels signed a peace deal in 1962, which granted autonomy to the province. GAM was established on December 4, 1976. Di Tiro rejected autonomy for Aceh as part of Indonesia and demanded outright independence.

· · · · ·

Indonesia is a mosaic of different ethnic and religious groups numbering 220 million people. It spans 13,000 islands over four thousand miles and five time zones. Aceh is situated at the tip of Sumatra in the far west, straddling the Malacca Straits to the north, a vital maritime link between the Pacific Ocean, the South Atlantic, and the Indian Ocean. Aceh's population of four million is devoutly Muslim. Aceh is anecdotally referred to as "the front porch of Mecca."[2]

After coming to power in 1967, President Suharto promoted Indonesia's armed forces to solidify its dual function (*Dwi Fungsi*) as both a social and a political force.[3] Aceh was heavily militarized by the Indonesian Armed Forces (TNI), Special Forces (KOPASSUS), Strategic Reserve Battalions (KOSTRAD), and the National Police (POLRI). The Regional Military Command Structure (KODAM) exploited Aceh's rich natural resources. Pertamina, the national energy company, paid the military to provide security to Aceh's Arun natural gas field located near Lhokseumawe in north Sumatra.[4]

Di Tiro was part of the revolutionary left that dominated the decolonization movement at the time. He was, however, more nationalistic than ideological. Through the Darul Islam rebel movement, he sought to overthrow the Indonesian state ideology of "Pancasila," articulated by President Sukarno on June 1, 1945, which is based on five principles: nationalism, internationalism or humanism, consent or democracy, social prosperity, and belief in one God.[5] Pancasila was enshrined in the constitution and adopted by Suharto. Beginning in 1965, his rise to power included brutal anti-communist purges resulting in the deaths of up to one million people. Declassified US diplomatic cables reveal the US government's extensive involvement in the purges, backing Suharto's strident opposition to communism.[6]

Di Tiro and Malik Mahmud learned of my extensive involvement in East Timor and asked me to provide information on statutory and constitutional arrangements for devolving power and enhancing local control of natural resources. I developed a curriculum for training the Aceh government-in-exile, focusing on international models of regional autonomy with relevance to conditions in Aceh. We gathered with Zaini Abdullah and GAM staff members in their boardroom for a short course on power sharing. My training was not prescriptive for the Aceh case. Rather, I presented a range of options informed by relevant international experience.

Across Indonesia, including Aceh, people suffered under Jakarta's restrictive rule and demanded the right to self-determination. I emphasized that self-determination does not necessarily mean independence. There are a range of options for protecting and promoting minority and group rights that do not involve breaking up the state. My presentation also highlighted different strategies for enhancing local control over government, culture, and the economy.

We started with a conversation about constitutions, which provide a basis for the rule of law, distributing governance responsibilities and defining the relationship of individuals and groups to one another and the state. To institutionalize the "politics of accommodation," constitutional power sharing addresses expectations in post-conflict countries emerging from ethnic or religious conflict and undergoing political transition.

Constitutions typically address the vertical separation of powers and the horizontal distribution of responsibilities. Vertical separation involves national-subnational arrangements as defined through confederation, federation, asymmetric federal arrangements, or provisions for regional or cultural autonomy. Horizontal separation of powers involves the relationship between different branches of government.

Di Tiro, Malik, Zaini, and I discussed definitions of sovereignty in international law. According to the 1933 Montevideo Convention on Rights and Duties of States: "The State ... should possess the following qualifications: (a) a permanent population; (b) a defined territory; (c) government; and (d) capacity to enter into relations with other States."[7] We also discussed the legal basis and historical evolution of self-determination. We agreed that territorial questions should be settled in the interests of the populations concerned. When identity is denied or suppressed, ethno-politics results and conflict often ensues. Economic disparities or the uneven exploitation of natural resources typically aggravates divisions.[8]

A group may seek to exercise its right to self-determination, including the right to constitute its own state, when its aspirations are thwarted or denied. However, self-determination does not necessarily mean separatism. The right of self-determination can be realized through autonomy arrangements that fall short of secession and do not threaten territorial integrity.

Unitary State

We discussed different associational arrangements. A unitary state is governed by a single unit, the central government, which exercises final authority. In a unitary state, subnational units are created and abolished and their powers may be broadened and narrowed by the central government.

Federal State

Federal arrangements accommodate differences among populations divided by ethnic or cultural cleavages yet seek a common, often democratic, political order. In federal states, sovereignty is shared between the central government and subnational units. The central government usually retains powers regarding defense, foreign policy, and fiscal affairs.

Confederation

A confederation is the union of autonomous or semi-autonomous political units, which band together to enhance their individual interests through common action. Confederations are often established by treaty between its members who have equal status.

Devolution

Addressing ethnic conflicts—center-periphery, majority-minority, or powerful-powerless—involves a resolution of competing claims that preserves both the identity of an aggrieved group, as well as the existing state structure. Like federation, symmetrical devolution allocates the same powers to all sub-national units. Asymmetrical devolution varies in power and status.

Special measures complementing a bill of rights may be needed to uphold group and minority rights in situations with a long history of conflict. The two overriding issues are equality/non-discrimination and the protection and promotion of minority rights.[9] Autonomy is one way to achieve a group's rights. Autonomy can encompass governance, culture, and economy.

Instruments of self-government manage affairs at the local level. They may include judicial bodies with due regard to customs or customary laws. The role of police and security is also a governance concern.

Cultural autonomy includes provisions for the use of local languages in education and before administrative bodies. Traditional local names, street names, and other topographical indicators are permitted. Cultural autonomy includes religious practice,[10] access to media,[11] and cultural development,[12] including the display of emblems and the right to observe cultural or religious festivals.

Autonomy also addresses economic development. While states must ensure that minorities may participate fully in the economic progress and development of their country,[13] states are obligated to ensure the effective participation of minorities in the development of their land and natural resources.[14]

Di Tiro and Malik urged me to share information on decentralization and autonomy with Indonesian government officials. They also encouraged me to work with a local partner in Aceh.

· · · · ·

After Abdurrahman Wahid succeeded B. J. Habibie as president of Indonesia in October 1999, he embraced "reformasi" and power sharing to maintain Indonesia's unity. He also adopted security reforms, demilitarizing Aceh and removing external forces from the province. GAM fighters who abandoned violence and separatism were offered amnesty.[15]

In the spring of 2000, representing Columbia University, I proposed a conference on "International Autonomy Models" to Indonesia's UN Ambassador Nugroho Wisnu Murti. He relayed Columbia's offer to Ryaas Rasyid, the newly appointed minister of regional autonomy. He requested Columbia organize a conference on decentralization, whereby power can be transferred from the central government to provinces and sub-provinces.

To move forward with the conference, I had to first overcome the distrust of some Indonesian officials who knew of my involvement in East Timor. They suspected that my support for regional autonomy was a Trojan horse for collapsing the country. My home at the time was on 68th Street between Fifth and Madison Avenues, directly across the street from Indonesia's consulate. Some East Timor activists petitioned New York City and arranged for the street to be renamed "East Timor Way." Indonesian officials thought I was behind the name change.

Marty Natalegawa was the spokesman of Indonesia's Foreign Ministry during the Timor crisis. He was a suave, British-educated diplomat of great intellect and charm. He was a rising star in the ministry who would become Permanent Representative of Indonesia to the United Nations between 2007 and 2009 and Foreign Minister, a post he held until 2015, which overlapped with Indonesia's presidency of the UN Security Council.[16] Ambassador Natalegawa and I had jousted in a friendly and respectful fashion during the East Timor crisis. In 2000, I reached out to him about autonomy models. The US and Indonesia had guarded relations, dating back to 1961 when President Sukarno helped found the Non-Aligned Movement (NAM) along with India and Yugoslavia. The NAM represented developing nations that sought a "third way" between the West and Communist Bloc in the Cold War. With Jakarta distrustful of US intentions, I had some explaining to do.

The Ministry of Autonomy accepted my offer to convene a conference and cover in-country costs. Robert S. Gelbard was US Ambassador to Indonesia from 1999 to 2001.[17] We had a troubled relationship, dating back to his work as Special Envoy for Implementation of the Dayton Peace Agreement. I called Ambassador Gelbard to inform him of my discussions with the Government of Indonesia (GOI) and assured him that I had undertaken the autonomy initiative in my capacity at Columbia University, not as a Special Government Employee (SGE). He knew that Indonesia's intelligence agency was monitoring his phone and was clearly irritated that I had disclosed my SGE status on an open line.

The Bali Conference on Regional Autonomy in September 2000 included US specialists and experts from South Africa, Brazil, and Switzerland. Ann Marie Murphy, a Senior Research Scholar at the Columbia's Weatherhead East Asian Institute, made a valuable contribution.[18] The conference was a useful forum for sharing information on how different countries had successfully managed power-sharing challenges. We discussed lessons learned that could inform Jakarta's approach to regional autonomy.

In addition to intellectual substance, we enjoyed Indonesian cultural activities. Minister Ryaas Rasyid hosted a welcome dinner and a traditional Balinese dance performance. The stage was circled by flaming tiki torches as Balinese dancers performed the Ramayana, a Hindu epic about the monkey God Hanuman. Balinese dance includes dramatic gestures using fingers, hands, eyes, and the head. I was seated in the front row and some of the dancers kneeled next to me. When I crossed my legs, they gave me dirty looks. I did not know that showing the bottom of one's feet is offensive to Indonesians and many other people in Southeast Asia.

· · · · ·

I kept US officials informed throughout the process. The State Department introduced me to Karen Brooks, Director for Asian Affairs at the White House National Security Council.[19] Karen was razor sharp and spoke perfect Bahasa Indonesian, which she learned living in the country. She was focused on conditions in Aceh and introduced me to Suraiya IT, an Acehnese civil society representative who had good relations with both the GAM and Indonesian officials. We agreed on the importance of engaging civil society in peace talks.

The Center for Humanitarian Dialogue (HDC) initiated talks between the GAM and RI officials in 1999.[20] The HDC, also known as the Henri Dunant Center after the founder of the International Committee of the Red Cross, is a non-governmental organization founded by international luminaries like Sergio Viera de Mello and led by Martin Griffiths. HDC is based at an elegant facility on Lake Geneva with a conference room that opens onto a veranda and garden adjoining the water. In between meetings, we would go outside to stroll the grounds to view the city of Geneva and surrounding mountains. I served as a member of HDC's international program advisory board upon its founding.

When HDC initiated talks on Aceh, GAM was functioning like a parallel government, controlling 75 percent of the province. HDC mediated the "Joint Understanding on Humanitarian Pause for Aceh," signed by Ambassador Hassan Wirajuda and Dr. Zaini Abdullah of GAM on May 12, 2000.[21] The Humanitarian Pause called for a three-month ceasefire, allowing the free movement of humanitarian personnel and supplies to remote villages. It also called for confidence-building measures aimed at setting the stage for a peaceful resolution of the Aceh conflict.

The humanitarian pause led to a temporary lull in the conflict. However, fighting resumed when government officials accused GAM of failing to control their fighters in the field. The spiral of deadly violence prompted a decision by Exxon Mobil to suspend operations of the Arun natural gas fields in March 2001.[22] Shutting down the production of liquid natural gas was a blow to both Indonesia's national economy and Aceh's provincial economy.

To incentivize talks, HDC convened the parties with a group of "Wise Men" in July 2001. The Wise men included General Anthony Zinni, a retired Four Star US Marine Corps General; Surin Pitsuwan, Thailand's former foreign minister; Tan Sri Musa Hitam, Malaysia's former deputy prime minister; and Budimir Loncar, the former foreign minister of Yugoslavia. Experts like William Ury of Harvard University's Negotiations Project were also included as resources for the negotiators. The Wise Men group was established to complement rather than replace HDC's role as mediator.[23]

A forum for engaging civil society was missing from HDC's mediation toolkit. Griffiths proposed that I undertake a civil society dialogue to reinvigorate the peace process. With HDC financing, I coordinated a "Civil Society Peace Conference" with Suraiya IT at American University in Washington, DC. Brooks helped arrange visas for about sixty Acehnese to visit the United States. US officials placed great importance on working with civil society in order to prevent the radicalization of Acehnese in the aftermath of terror attacks on September 11.

The conference's opening dinner was held on October 6, 2001, with introductory remarks by Acehnese leaders. I presented on autonomy as a tool for conflict resolution. Participants included Azwar Abubakar (Vice Governor of Aceh), Imam Syuja (Chair of Muhammadiyah organization, Aceh Chapter), Hasballah Saad (Former Indonesian Minister of Human Rights), Nasir Jamil and Ghazali Abbas (parliamentarians), Radhi Darmansyah (Farmedia), and Juanda Jamal from a local NGO named. GAM was represented by Zaini Abdullah, among others.

During the next morning's coffee break, we watched on CNN as US and British warplanes attacked the Taliban in Afghanistan. Although the outbreak of war was a huge distraction, the Acehnese participants focused on the business at hand. After much discussion, we agreed to establish a civil society task force led by Imam Syuja. The task force also included academics and representatives from youth, women's, and development organizations. Suraiya was the pivotal link as task force coordinator. We agreed to meet again in Banda Aceh in order to deepen civil society's engagement and impress upon GAM commanders the support of civil society for peace. In a track two process, the agreement to reconvene is always a pivotal next step.

A delegation from the civil society task force met me at the Banda Aceh Airport in December 2001. The next day we gathered in a seminar room of the Swiss Bell Hotel to discuss the work of the task force. That evening, Suraiya took us to the home of her sister, Muslihah, who operated the Jambo Geumuloh Restaurant, which was perched on stilts above the water in Lambaro Skep. Aceh is surrounded by water, with the Indian Ocean to the west and north and the Strait of Malacca to the east. In the southeast, it is connected via a land bridge to North Sumatra. Medan, the capital of North Sumatra, is notorious for organized crime dealing in teak and gemstones. The people of Aceh are open and friendly. Although women are wrapped in hijabs and conservative clothing, they are quick to smile and shake hands. In North America, I greeted Suraiya with a hug. In Aceh, however, I was respectful of the region's conservative social mores and merely shook her hand.

I met several GAM representatives in Banda Aceh. Malik and Zaini told me they had total control of GAM fighters in the field, even though they lived in Sweden. I pressed local GAM representatives on the dynamic of relations with the Stockholm-based Acehnese government in exile. Typically, diaspora representatives believe they have more control over local actors than they actually do. There is often a gap between outsiders, who live in relative prosperity without security risks, and in-country representatives, who are subject to arrest, imprisonment, and torture. Any deal negotiated in Geneva would need buy-in from civil society in Aceh. Our civil society task force was an important bridge between efforts by the international community and local Acehnese.

Suraiya took me to the University of Banda Aceh for a lecture on "Power-Sharing, Minority Rights Standards, and Autonomy Options." A big banner was displayed with my name, the topic, and Columbia University's logo. The conference center, called a "high house," was a structure that was open on four sides and built onto tall posts to protect against flooding. It was packed with members of the civil society task force and others from Banda Aceh's communities. I went off-script and appealed to them to take action for peace by holding both the GAM and government officials responsible for the country's conflict. I quoted a Swahili proverb: "When the elephants are at war, the grass suffers most." Acehnese swarmed the dais after my talk, lingering to discuss details of a notional peace agreement.

When we returned to the hotel, people at the front desk were perturbed. My talk had been infiltrated by BIN (*Badan Intelijen Negara*), the State Intelligence Agency. Its representatives came to the hotel and asked for my passport. Fortunately, it was in my briefcase; otherwise it would have been seized by state security. Suraiya told me to pack my bags and go to the airport immediately. Seated next to me was an Indonesian man wearing sunglasses and gold rings with ostentatious gemstones. I assumed he made his money as a member of the Medan mafia. After a brief stop in Medan, I was relieved to get back to Jakarta, check into my hotel, and go for a swim in the pool.

. . . . .

With the humanitarian pause in tatters, HDC initiated discussions with GAM Commander Abdullah Syafei. Many civil society representatives were frustrated that their views were not more fully considered during negotiations between GAM and the GOI. Civil society leaders were brought to Geneva in order to pressure the GAM to compromise.

President Megawati Sukarnoputri appointed seasoned cabinet members, which increased the credibility and gravitas of the negotiations. The former chief negotiator for the Aceh talks, Hassan Wirajuda, was named foreign minister, and General Susilo Bambang Yudhoyono became Coordinating Minister for Political and Security Affairs on August 9, 2001, and later President from 2004 to 2014. Wirajuda and Bambang were experienced policymakers, known for their pragmatism, not ideology.[24]

Talks facilitated by HDC led to a Cessation of Hostilities Agreement (COHA) on December 9, 2002.[25] Alongside the COHA, a tripartite monitoring mission was established, coordinated by HDC with personnel from Thailand, the Philippines, and Norway. Internationalizing HDC's efforts burnished its credentials, leading to a dramatic reduction in violence by both sides.

Both sides repeatedly violated the COHA, risking a renewal of armed conflict. To reinvigorate diplomacy, HDC convened the parties in Tokyo on May 17 and 18, 2003. They agreed to establish a Joint Council to resolve problems, but the initiative collapsed immediately over the details of demilitarization. A few hours later, the GOI cracked down and declared martial law in Aceh.[26]

On the ground, local police arrested GAM members Usman Lampoh Awe, Nashruddin Ahmad, Teuku Kamaruzazaman, Sofyan Ibrahim Tiba, Ammni, and Ahmad Marzuki. They also detained Acehnese members of the International Monitoring Mission. According to HDC, "International and local staff were harassed and threatened by police."[27] University rectors and local legislators were assassinated. The government launched its largest military operation in Aceh since 1975. The HDC initiative unraveled, and personnel with the International Monitoring Mission were withdrawn.

· · · · ·

Aceh was devastated by a tsunami on December 26, 2004. With its epicenter off the west coast of northern Sumatra, the earthquake measured 9.1 on the Richter scale and caused a huge surge of water that swept across Aceh. An estimated 200,000 people perished, and much of the city was under water, leaving tens of thousands homeless.

Both the GAM and TNI were affected. The TNI base on the Aceh coast was completely wiped away. GAM facilities were mostly inland in the jungle at higher altitudes, but the coastal capital of Banda Aceh was destroyed. Its streets were lined with debris—mangled vehicles, buildings, and boats piled high.[28] Hundreds of international aid organizations rushed to Aceh in the tsunami's aftermath. The government had previously prevented international agencies from working in Aceh. However, President Bambang's new, democratically elected government, which had just taken office in October 2004, was more open to international cooperation. Internationalizing humanitarian assistance and reconstruction in Aceh had a profound effect on the psychology of combatants from both sides.

After the tsunami, GAM declared a unilateral ceasefire. It abandoned demands for independence and accepted autonomy as a starting point for negotiations. A series of meetings ensued, coordinated by Conflict Management Initiative, an NGO based in Helsinki and led by former President Martti Ahtisaari. The GOI and the GAM signed a peace agreement on August 15, 2005. The agreement ended the Acehnese rebellion after twenty-nine years. Decades of violent conflict had devastated livelihoods and taken 15,000 lives.[29]

My association with Aceh endured over the years. Zaini Abdullah became Governor in 2012 and served until 2017, with Muzakir Manaf, a former GAM commander serving as Vice Governor. Zaini and I met several times in the ornate Governor's Place that was spared damage by the tsunami. Malik stayed on as Wali Nangro until his recent retirement

The 2014 ISIS crisis threatened to radicalize the Acehnese. Although hundreds of Indonesians went to join ISIS in Syria and Iraq, few foreign fighters hailed from Aceh. With backing from the Ford Foundation, Suraiya and I sponsored a series of workshops beginning in the fall of 2014 called "Social Harmony Teachings in the Qur'an and Sunnah: Islam, Dialogue and Modernity". The workshops highlighted the peace-loving side of Islam. Scholars from Islamic state universities across Indonesia came together at the Islamic State University of Aceh (UIN ar-Raniry) to discuss Islamic teachings on democracy, human rights, and conflict resolution. Papers by Professor Yusni Sabii and others were co-published by Columbia University and the Institute for Islamic Studies and Interreligious Dialogue, headed by Suraiya at the University of Banda Aceh. After a meal hosted by the Governor and President of UIN ar-Raniry, the publication was presented at a packed forum in the University's elegant Theater Room and Gedung Museum on November 13, 2015. Men were stylishly attired in their traditional black hats and batik, while the women wore colorful batik dresses.

Bonnie Miller, Columbia's senior education adviser, traveled to Banda Aceh to conduct two weeklong trainings on conflict transformation, communication techniques, creative problem-solving, and cultivating empathy. The first group of Acehnese who were trained included professors from seven universities, who then used the training and materials for their classes. The second workshop was comprised of GAM ex-combatants. Scholars joined this training, demonstrating a high level of cooperation between GAM and civil society. This workshop would not have happened without the support of Muzakir Manaf, GAM's former commander. Miller performed heroically when the training assistant from Columbia fell ill with food poisoning. She worked on her own until my arrival in Sabang, an island off the coast of Aceh.

We discussed follow-up activities using the materials and techniques they had learned from Miller. Bonds of friendship were established with many Acehnese including Juwanda, Renaldi, Iskandar, and Ima, who worked with Suraiya to organize the seminars. When we adjourned, the group headed to the seaside for snorkeling and water sports. Modest Muslim women entered the ocean fully clad in burqas.

In 2015, Columbia initiated a 10-Year Implementation Review Conference of the Aceh Peace Agreement. Indonesians involved in the peace process attended, as did many of the international mediators. The event was hosted by Governor Zaini Abdullah and Professor Farid Wajidi, Rector of Ar-Raniry State Islamic University. Unfortunately, I did not make it to Banda Aceh for the celebration. When my Malaysian Air flight from Kennedy Airport was canceled, there was no way to arrive in time for the festivities.

To help boost the Acehnese economy, I tried to market Sumatran coffee to retail outlets in the United States, with a percentage of the proceeds directed towards Aceh's reconstruction. However, the cost of buying and transporting coffee beans was too great and outside my expertise. I have stayed in close contact with Suraiya and Izwandy, her husband, who works for the state coffee cooperative. Memories of my work in Aceh span many years.

Notes

1   Aubrey Belford, "Hasan di Tiro, Who Led Indonesia Rebels, Dies at 84," *New York Times*, June 3, 2010, https://www.nytimes.com/2010/06/04/world/asia/04tiro.html.

2   *Harper's Magazine*, August 1905.

3   Salim Said, "The Political Role of the Indonesian Military: Past, Present, and Future," *Southeast Asian Journal of Social Science* (1987). www.jstor.org/stable/24491631.

4   "Too High a Price: The Human Rights Cost of Indonesian Military Activity,"

Human Rights Watch, June 20, 2006, https://www.hrw.org/report/2006/06/ 20/too-high-price/human-rights-cost-indonesian-militarys-economic-acti vities.

5   Encyclopedia Britannica, https://www.britannica.com/topic/Pancasila (ac-cessed April 23, 2020).

6   Vincent Bevins, "What the United States did in Indonesia," *The Atlantic,* Octo-ber 20, 2017, https://www.theatlantic.com/international/archive/2017/10/ the-indonesia-documents-and-the-us-agenda/543534/.

7   Lung-chu Chen, *An Introduction to Contemporary International Law, A Policy-Oriented Perspective* (Oxford University Press).

8   James Summer, *Peoples and International Law: How Nationalism and Self-Deter-mination Shape a Contemporary Law of Nations* (Martinus Nijhoff Publishers, 2007).

9   See generally, Geoff Gilbert, "Autonomy and Minority Groups: A Right in In-ternational Law," *Cornell International Law Journal* 35, no. 307 (2002); Phil-ip Alston, "Peoples' Rights: Their Rise and Fall," in *Peoples' Rights,* ed. Philip Alston (2001).

10 CCPR, Article 2(1), 26; CESCR, Article 2; Declaration on Minority Rights, Article 2.1: Universal Declaration of Human Rights, Article 2.

11 European Framework Article 9.

12 CCPR, Article 1; CESCR, Article 1; Draft Declaration on Indigenous Rights, Article 3.

13 CCPR, Declaration on Minority Rights Article 4.5.

14 CCPR, Declaration on Minority Rights Article 2.3; WG Commentary para 71; ILO, CCPR 27, GC 23#7, ILO Convention No. 169, Article 1(1).

15 Ernest Z. Bower, "The Legacy of Abdurrahman Wahid, Gus Dur, Fourth Presi-dent of the Republic of Indonesia," *Center for Strategic and International Studies,* December 30, 2009.

16 *Asia Society Policy Institute,* https://asiasociety.org/policy-institute/marty-na talegawa (accessed May 5, 2020).

17 *US Department of State,* https://1997-2001.state.gov/about_state/biogra phy/gelbard_r_indonesia.html (accessed May 5, 2020).

18 *Columbia University,* http://weai.columbia.edu/ann-marie-murphy/(accessed May 5, 2020).

19 *Council on Foreign Relations,* https://www.cfr.org/expert/karen-b-brooks (accessed May 5, 2020).

20 *Centre for Humanitarian Dialogue,* https://www.hdcentre.org/activities/aceh-indonesia/ (accessed May 5, 2020).

21 "Joint Understanding for Humanitarian Pause of Aceh," *The Center for Humanitarian Dialogue,* https://www.hdcentre.org/wp-content/uploads/2016/10/Joint-Understanding-for-a-Humanitarian-Pause-12-May-2000.pdf (accessed May 05, 2020).

22 Wayne Arnold, "Exxon Mobil, in Fear, Exits Indonesian Gas Fields," *New York Times,* March 24, 2001, https://www.nytimes.com/2001/03/24/business/exxon-mobil-in-fear-exits-indonesian-gas-fields.html.

23 Konrad Huber, "The HDC in Aceh: Promises and Pitfalls of NGO Mediation and Implementation," *East-West Center,* https://www.eastwestcenter.org/system/tdf/private/PS009.pdf?file=1&type=node&id=32016 (accessed May 05, 2020).

24 Delphine Alles, "Transnational Islamic Actors and Indonesia's Foreign Policy: Transcending the State," 2016.

25 "Cessation of Hostilities Framework Between Government of the Republic of Indonesia and the Free Aceh Movement," *The Center for Humanitarian Dialogue,* https://www.hdcentre.org/wp-content/uploads/2016/10/Cessation-of-Hostilities-Agreement-9-December-2002.pdf (accessed May 05, 2020).

26 "Aceh Initiative," The Center for Humanitarian Dialogue, November 2003, https://www.hdcentre.org/wp-content/uploads/2016/10/Aceh-internal-review-HD-Centre.pdf.

27 Ibid.

28 "Boxing Day 2004 Tsunami: Banda Aceh—Then and Now," *The Guardian,* December 10, 2014, https://www.theguardian.com/global-development/ng-interactive/2014/dec/10/boxing-day-2004-tsunami-banda-aceh-then-and-now.

29 "Aceh Initiative."

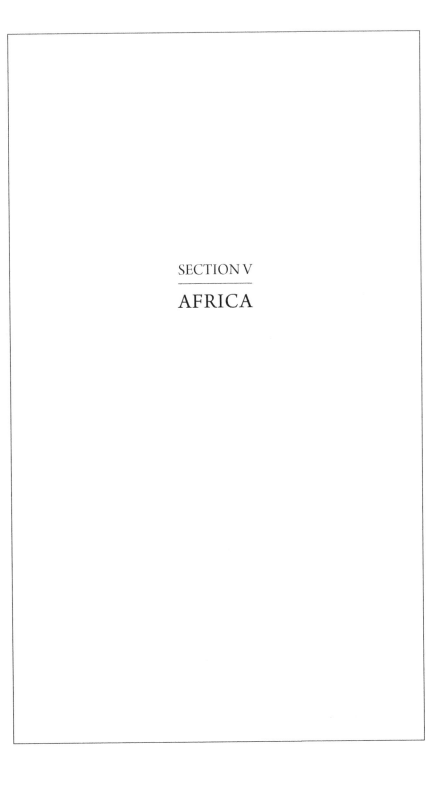

SECTION V

AFRICA

CHAPTER 14

ENDING APARTHEID

Nelson *Mandela* came to Washington to address a Joint Meeting of the US Congress on June 26, 1990. He had recently been released from prison, having served twenty-seven years of a life sentence with hard labor for his role fighting South Africa's apartheid system of white supremacy and institutionalized racial segregation. The final years of his prison term were spent on Robben Island, a maximum-security prison off the coast of Western Cape Province.

Gaining entry to the US Capitol for Mandela's speech was the hottest ticket in town; I was fortunate that Congressman Tom Lantos (Democrat, California) had an extra pass and gave it to me.

. . . . .

Mandela and the African National Congress (ANC) initially practiced non-violent resistance. However, Mandela and other younger members were radicalized by the government's increasing repression and deadly reprisals and they ultimately turned to armed struggle. After the 1960 Sharpsville Massacre, Mandela founded Spear of the Nation (*Umkhonto we Sizwe*), the ANC's military wing. In 1980, he smuggled a letter from prison: "United! Fight on! Between the anvil of united mass action and the hammer of the armed struggle we shall crush apartheid."[1]

Mandela was freed from prison in February 1990 by South Africa's President F.W. de Klerk. His release was a big step towards dismantling apartheid, a policy of separate development adopted by the National Party after coming to power in 1948. Apartheid means "apartness" in Afrikaans.

The Afrikaner government was led by the descendants of predominantly Dutch settlers who arriving at the Cape of Good Hope in the seventeenth and eighteenth centuries. By the twentieth century, the National Party was systematically oppressing Blacks and minorities. It established ten Bantu homelands, known as Bantustans, to segregate whites from Blacks. The government forcibly moved 3.5 million Black South Africans from cities and rural areas, which were designated for whites only. Black-owned farms were seized and sold to white farmers at a discount. The Bantustans also served the government's security agenda. By isolating Blacks from one another, it sought to prevent them from unifying in opposition to apartheid.[2] Bantustans were also an instrument of economic oppression.

De Klerk was a pragmatic man, not a reform ideologue. South Africa's isolation, which resulted from international monetary sanctions and cultural and sports boycotts—all called for by the ANC—were taking a heavy financial and psychological toll on the white population. He started releasing political prisoners, in addition to Mandela. He lifted the ban on the ANC and other liberation movements, and suspended capital punishment. Mandela's "long march to freedom" from Robben Island to Capitol Hill was a remarkable political odyssey for the world's most celebrated political prisoner.

The Congressional chamber was buzzing with excitement on the historic occasion of Mandela's address. Mandela was the first Black man to speak before a joint meeting of the US Senate and House of Representatives. Members of the Cabinet, including Colin Powell, were in the front row. I was seated in the gallery far from the podium alongside other enthusiastic guests.

Mandela entered the chamber to a standing ovation. He had been a boxer in his youth, a large imposing man. However, after being incarcerated for decades, he was thinner yet still regal in his bearing. As he stood in the Speaker's well, I watched him looking around the chamber, nodding his head and taking in the moment. He finally succeeded in silencing the audience, then delivered a compelling address:

> We must contend still with the reality that South Africa is a country in the grip of the apartheid crime against humanity. We still have a struggle on our hands .... It must surely be that there will be born a country on the southern tip of Africa, which you will be proud to call a friend and an ally. Let that day come now. Let us keep our arms locked together so that we form a solid phalanx against racism to ensure that that day comes now. Peace will not come to our country and region until the apartheid system is ended.

Mandela thanked Congress for imposing sanctions in 1986, which included trade and travel restrictions. He called on US legislators to keep up the pressure until South Africa's system of institutionalized racism was fully dismantled and Black South Africans had the right to vote. His appearance before Congress was a celebratory moment. It was also a call to action; more work was needed to end apartheid in South Africa.

. . . . .

I was inspired by Mandela and became active in the anti-apartheid movement. Sharon Gelman, an activist from Los Angeles who headed Artists for a New South Africa, then called Artists for a Free South Africa, introduced me to Donald Woods, the former editor in chief of *The Daily Dispatch*, who had been banned by the apartheid government for his political activities and fled into exile. Woods was a liberal journalist who, like other whites, was a beneficiary of the apartheid system that he opposed. His deeper awareness about racial injustice was awakened by Steven Biko, a leader of the Black Consciousness Movement. Biko explained that Black consciousness was about developing a sense of humanity. He warned that South Africa would change either in partnership between whites and Blacks—or in bloodshed.

Biko was one of many Blacks who refused to submit to the racist apartheid system. He inspired others to resist. Schoolchildren in the Soweto township rejected a system that was established to make them inferior. They protested a new law forcing them to study in Afrikaans, "the language of the oppressor." Asserting their cultural rights, they demanded to study Black history and Black culture. On June 16, 1976, police opened fire on peaceful student protesters in Soweto, killing seven hundred and wounding more than four thousand. The atrocity galvanized the movement in South Africa and brought worldwide condemnation.

Woods and Biko met soon after the Soweto massacre. During a series of interviews, Woods was impressed by Biko's intelligence, moderation, and integrity. Through his interactions with Biko, Woods realized the injustice of white privilege and vowed to use his platform as an editor to tell Biko's story. Then Biko was assassinated on September 12, 1977. The official cause of death was a "hunger strike." It was a blatant lie; Biko had been tortured and badly beaten.

By spotlighting Biko's murder in *The Daily Dispatch*, Woods was banned for his complicity with the Black Consciousness Movement. Banning was an administrative measure in accordance with the Internal Security Act used to suppress opponents of apartheid. A banned person was placed under severe restrictions with limitations on their freedom of travel and association. At forty-one years old, Woods was denied contact with any other banned person and forbidden to participate in political activity. He and his family were harassed and their lives threatened. His days in South Africa were numbered.

Woods had written a manuscript about Biko, which he wanted to publish. Doing so would have landed him in jail with a lengthy sentence, so he plotted his escape from South Africa. After a perilous clandestine journey, Woods made it to Lesotho. There he met his wife Wendy and their five young children. They were given UN passports and, with a Lesotho official, flew together to Zimbabwe. From there, they went to the United Kingdom, where he connected with the British anti-apartheid community and film producer Sir Richard Attenborough. The film, "Cry Freedom," a major motion picture starring Denzel Washington as Steve Biko and Kevin Kline as Woods, tells the story of their friendship and Woods's personal transformation and harrowing escape from South Africa.

Some ANC members criticized Woods because Attenborough focused the film on him, not Biko. Woods, however, used his celebrity to advance the cause. He also funded scholarships for Biko's children and a number of other promising young Black South Africans, some of whom went on to hold prominent political positions and leadership roles in the new South Africa. Woods was an extremely likeable personality, jocular yet serious with a sardonic sense of humor. He drank margaritas like water. We would spend a lot of time together over the coming years.

Gelman arranged a forum for Woods in Los Angeles; the Woods anti-apartheid tour then went to Washington. In addition to arranging a forum with the Congressional Human Rights Caucus, Gelman and I set up meetings with prominent figures in the US Congress so that Woods could lobby for the continuation of sanctions. I reached out to Nancy Soderberg, legislative assistant to Senator Ted Kennedy (D-MA). Woods and Kennedy had a stimulating discussion about the situation in South Africa. Just being in the room and listening to them was a great learning experience.

The Minnesota Lawyers Committee for Human Rights hosted Woods at a standing room only event for lawyers and activists in the Twin Cities. The conference was chaired by Senator Walter Mondale (D-MN). Woods focused his remarks on the value of sanctions in pressuring the Pretoria regime. He heralded the Anti-Apartheid Act of 1986. House Resolution 1580 was known as the Dellums Amendment after its primary sponsor, Congressman Ronald Dellums (D-CA0, who introduced it a decade before it finally passed into law. The bill called for trade restrictions against South Africa and immediate divestment by American corporations. It enumerated specific conditions for lifting the sanctions, including the release of all political prisoners and the repeal of laws that buttressed the apartheid system.

President Ronald Reagan preferred constructive engagement with the Pretoria regime. He vetoed the bill, but Congress eventually overrode the veto. Woods expressed his respect for Congressman Dellums and appreciation for the legislation. Support from the US Congress was a turning point in the campaign to end apartheid. He called for more stringent enforcement of the Anti-Apartheid Act, intensifying South Africa's ostracism and isolation.

From Minneapolis, we headed to Los Angeles where the World Affairs Council of Southern California hosted a lunch for Woods at a fancy hotel in Beverly Hills. Woods described the economic and political impact of sanctions but suggested that the greatest impact of sanctions was psychological. White South Africans have a special relationship with their national rugby squad, the Springboks. The International Rugby Federation barred the Springboks in 1974 because the club was not racially integrated. Consequently, the Springboks were prevented from joining matches in Britain, Ireland, France, or Australia. The Springboks were, however, invited to a tournament in New Zealand in 1981. People protesting apartheid followed the Springboks wherever they went, which was a huge embarrassment to fans traveling with the team. Making matters worse, the Springboks were excluded from the Rugby World Cups in 1987 and 1991. Woods was a huge rugby fan but endorsed restrictions on sport and culture.

Gelman arranged for us to meet the Hollywood Women's Political Committee, which included high-powered figures in the entertainment industry, and produced a fundraising event at the home of Stanley Sheinbaum on Rockinghorse Lane. Sheinbaum was a progressive icon who gained widespread attention for going to Stockholm and meeting Yasser Arafat to encourage peace in the Middle East. I thought that Woods might be uneasy about the event with Sheinbaum, but he did not hesitate; Palestinians and the ANC have a shared sense of solidarity based on their common struggle against oppressive regimes.

Woods, Gelman, and I were due in San Francisco for a VIP reception and dinner. Given the tight schedule, I contacted my friend Michael Sautman, a Tibetan human rights activist and currency speculator, to ask for a ride in his private plane. We met at the Santa Monica airport and flew to the Bay Area, arriving just in time for events that evening. The anti-apartheid movement was a collective effort. People pitched in however they could to help.

Dinner was hosted at the luxurious Fairmont Hotel by its owner, Steven Swig. Guests included Senator Dianne Feinstein and her husband, Richard C. Blum, an investment banker and founder of the American Himalayan Society. While imbibing many margaritas, Woods was lucid and compelling. He was a brilliant policy analyst and a charming rogue. The evening ended with a roomful of admirers who were eager to join the struggle against apartheid.

Organizing the Woods tour required constant multitasking. There was a comical moment before dinner when Gelman and I were working the phones to finalize arrangements. At a phone bank in the lobby of the Fairmont, I was on two calls simultaneously with a phone on each ear. I glanced over at Gelman; she also had two calls going at the same time. She was just as manic as me. We looked at each other and burst out laughing. Traveling with Woods was purposeful and rewarding. It was also a lot of fun.

· · · · ·

The anti-apartheid movement consisted of social justice activists from around the world. Black South Africans were its core, but whites and Asians were also involved.

Woods helped me understand nuances of the movement. The Congressional Human Rights Foundation focused on advocacy in Washington.

We hosted ANC figures such as Walter Sisulu, who was the ANC's Secretary-General and Deputy President. He had recruited Mandela into
the ANC and they were dear friends, serving time together on Robben
Island and in Pollsmoor, where Sisulu was imprisoned for more than
twenty-five years. Regimes often think they can incarcerate the leaders of
a movement and undermine their efforts by isolating them. On the con-
trary, jailing leaders at the same prison creates a fraternity and strength-
ens bonds of cooperation. Prison also served as an incubator for other
movements, such as Palestinians and the Kurds in Turkey. It is possible
to lock up the leaders, but revolutionary ideas are not bound by the bars
of a prison cell.

Why was the South African apartheid regime so hostile to Sisulu and others? Grey-haired and mild-mannered, Sisulu was a gentleman and principled advocate.[3] The regime should have worked cooperatively with Sisulu
and Mandela to make them partners in political transition. Viewing them
as national security threats and putting them in jail merely enhanced their
stature, giving rise to a younger generation of revolutionaries. Killing Steven Biko made him larger than life. He became a martyr who inspired
generations of other youth activists.

The multi-racial nature of the anti-apartheid movement was a unique feature that enhanced its effectiveness. South Asians were also an oppressed
group who had marginally more freedoms than Blacks in South Africa,
but far less than whites. Many played an important role in the ANC and
partner organizations.

Gelman introduced me to Ahmed Kathrada, Mandela's longtime friend
and fellow prisoner on Robben Island and Pollsmoor. Kathrada, affectionately called "Kathy," was born to Indian immigrant parents in the
Transvaal. He was involved in the Passive Resistance Movement against
the Asiatic Land Tenure and Indian Representation Act. Also known as
"The Ghetto Act," it restricted where South Asians could live, own land,
and do business.[4] Kathy was a leading figure of the South African Indian
Congress, which collaborated with Mandela and Sisulu.[5] He gained no-
toriety by helping to organize the "Campaign of Defiance against Unjust
Laws," targeting the most egregious and unjust restrictions—Pass Laws,
the Group Areas Act, the Suppression of Communism Act, and the Bantu
Authorities Act.[6]

Although apartheid was intended to advance the interests of white South Africans, whites were also harmed by the unjust system. An increasing number of whites resented the authorities for committing crimes in their name. Blacks, Asians, and whites were all part of a coalition that opposed the regime. The movement was inclusive from the beginning. The 1955 Freedom Charter asserted, "South Africa belongs to all who live in it, black or white."[7]

I had the honor of meeting a number of other distinguished South Africans: Richard Goldstone was a former South African Supreme Court Justice who gained international recognition for prosecuting war crimes in Yugoslavia and Rwanda. He also led the UN Fact Finding Mission on the Gaza Conflict. Albert "Albie" Sachs was an activist and a former judge on the Constitutional Court of South Africa. Helen Suzman was an outspoken critic of apartheid and human rights defender as a Member of Parliament, for many years the lone woman and the lone member who opposed apartheid. Nadine Gordimer received the 1991 Nobel Prize in Literature.

Mandela had ample time for reading books during his years on Robben Island. In addition to Gordimer, he read Jewish philosophers, such as Leo Baeck and Martin Buber. Many of South Africa's white progressives were Jews with a profound commitment to social justice based on their Jewish values and experience with the Holocaust. Jews played a prominent role in the anti-apartheid movement. Joe Slovo, Ruth First, Ronnie Kasrils, and Sam Kahn joined the Communist Party to fight apartheid. The involvement of Jews fueled anti-Semitism among Afrikaner nationalists who were the backbone of South Africa's racist regime.

Israel sought to cultivate friendly relations with African states, establishing commercial relations with South Africa and engaging in weapons transfers. However, some Israeli political figures opposed cooperation with Pretoria. Ben-Gurion and Golda Meir evoked the Holocaust experience in condemning apartheid and opposing arms sales from Israel to South Africa.[8]

· · · · ·

Woods's escape and the release of "Cry Freedom" came at a strategic moment in South Africa's evolution from dictatorship to democracy. Under pressure from the international community, the National Party government of Pieter Botha sought to institute some reforms, including abolition of the pass laws and the ban on interracial sex and marriage. The reforms were too few and too late. In 1989, Botha stepped aside in favor of F.W. de Klerk, who tried to manage political change by repealing the Population Registration Act and other legislation that formed the legal basis for apartheid.

De Klerk freed Mandela on February 11, 1990. In the aftermath of Mandela's release, de Klerk and Mandela entered into discreet and then formal negotiations between their parties and others on a new constitution, which would enfranchise Blacks and other racial groups. A dramatic outcome to the freedom struggle was at hand. However, South Africa's transition was threatened by hardline Afrikaners and smaller regional parties that vied for influence. Civil society's experience was shallow. Without a tradition of compromise, Afrikaner nationalists fomented and supported Black-on-Black violence in order to derail progress.

The Congressional Human Rights Foundation hosted Mangosuthu Buthelezi, leader of the KwaZulu Inkatha Freedom Party, in November 1993. His visit to Washington was an important opportunity to try to dissuade Buthelezi from continued collaboration with the National Party. A formal deal between the National Party and KwaZulu Inkatha would marginalize the ANC, making the realization of democracy more difficult and potentially more violent. After his DC trip, Buthelezi and the leaders of twenty other small opposition parties came together in a coalition, pledging cooperation with the ANC and a government of national unity.[9]

In December 1993, Mandela and de Klerk were jointly awarded the Nobel Peace Prize. The award was an endorsement of South Africa's peaceful transition. Some anti-apartheid activists criticized the Nobel Committee's decision to include de Klerk, since his National Party had been the instrument of oppression for decades. The decision to give the award jointly was an investment in South Africa's peaceful transition and pluralist future. De Klerk's participation was needed to fully dismantle apartheid without additional bloodshed.

South Africa's interim constitution took effect in 1994, followed by elections between April 26 and 29. More than 22 million South Africans waited in long lines to cast ballots in the country's first multiracial election. It was a joyous moment. People wore their finest clothes. Children accompanied their parents, who danced in the streets. The Interim Constitution was the fundamental law of South Africa from the first non-racial general election on April 27, 1994 until it was superseded by the final new constitution, which was approved by the Constitutional Court on December 4, 1996 and took effect on February 4 of the following year.

The new coalition government led by Mandela and the ANC also included de Klerk's National Party and Buthelezi's Inkatha Freedom Party. Elections occur on a specific date, whereas reform is an ongoing process. The ANC adopted an aspirational platform that endorsed a nonracial, non-sexist society based on democratic principles and human rights. It pledged to uphold workers' rights, eliminate rural poverty, and address inequities in education, housing, and health.[10] In May 1994, Mandela was inaugurated as president, becoming South Africa's first Black head of state.

Addressing the legacy of human rights abuses was a huge challenge for the new government. South Africa established a Truth and Reconciliation Commission (TRC) in 1995. The TRC was mandated to uncover crimes and foster reconciliation in society. Bringing the perpetrators and victims together required an agreement on accountability. Under the principled and able leadership of Anglican Archbishop Desmond Tutu, the 1984 Nobel Peace Prize recipient, the TRC focused on gathering testimony and evidence and exposing crimes. To avoid recriminations that could further divide society and derail the progress of democracy, the TRC emphasized truth, remorse, and forgiveness rather than prosecuting individuals for past crimes. "The Arch," as Tutu was affectionately called, explored the difficult balance between accountability and forgiveness. Without Tutu's moral authority and political support from Mandela, a witch-hunt could have occurred, opening wounds and undermining healing.

Mandela was an extraordinary human being who guided South Africa's transition and democratization. However, Mandela's immediate successors lacked his charisma and character, setting back progress. Corruption and incompetence undermined economic advancement.

I met Thabo Mbeki at a forum convened by the Carnegie Endowment for International Peace in early 1990. Dr. Pauline Baker chaired the meeting, which occurred while the ANC and the National Party were secretly negotiating the details of transition. Mbeki may have been tired from his flight, but he was listless and did not impress. Mandela was a leader, while

Mbeki seemed more like a bureaucrat. He served as South Africa's second post-apartheid president from 1999 until 2008. South Africa's economy suffered during these years.[11] Faced with a rapidly burgeoning AIDS pandemic, Mbeki also denied that HIV caused AIDS and rejected scientific research and medical treatments, compounding a major public health crisis and preventing necessary programs to address the deadly epidemic, resulting in an estimated 330,000 unnecessary deaths.

He was succeeded as president by Jacob Zuma, who served from 2009 until 2018 and further tarnished the ANC's sterling reputation. Zuma was acquitted of rape in 2005, but allegations of racketeering and corruption dogged his years in office. He spent state funds to upgrade his rural estate in Nklanda, resulting in condemnation by the Constitutional Court and a failed impeachment attempt in 2016.

Winnie Mandela, Nelson's second wife, often accompanied him after his release in 1990. She was called "the Queen of Africa" and, in South Africa, "Mother of the Nation." She was a positive force for change, especially during the years that her husband was imprisoned. She was, however, disgraced by accusations of murder and fraud,[12] as well as infidelity. She and Nelson separated in 1992 and divorced in 1996.

Today's President Cyril Ramaphosa is a businessman who made his fortune in the mining industries. He is a big improvement over his immediate predecessor, but lacks the leadership qualities that made Mandela so special.

. . . . .

I took the train to visit Donald Woods and his family in 1996. The Woods family lived in a modest middle class home in Surrey about one hour from London. Wendy was an active member of the Black Sash, a non-violent liberal white women's resistance organization. She worked with various charities and set up the Donald Woods Foundation after her husband's death. One son was an aspiring rock musician.

Over margaritas (of course), Woods confided in me his disappointment. He abandoned his home and property in South Africa in order to become an international anti-apartheid advocate. With Mandela's ascendance to the presidency in 1994, Woods dreamed of being appointed South Africa's ambassador to the UK. Despite his close coordination with the ANC, the London diplomatic post was a plum assignment that the ANC reserved for one of its own. Despite close cooperation between Woods and the ANC, he never joined the party. Until his death on August 19, 2001, Woods was a prominent public intellectual, writing and lecturing about South Africa and social justice issues.

The multiracial nature of the anti-apartheid movement was a distinguishing feature. After coming to power, however, the ANC became less inclusive. Although the ANC included prominent white, "coloured," and Indian members, loyalty and patronage were pervasive. South Africa suffered, and the movement shifted from its initial goals that had garnered so much international support.

Notes

1 Letter dated June 10, 1980, https://www.history.com/topics/africa/apartheid.

2 https://www.history.com/topics/africa/apartheid (accessed July 2, 2020).

3 https://www.sahistory.org.za/people/walter-ulyate-sisulu (accessed July 2, 2020).

4 https://www.kathradafoundation.org/2017/02/09/passive-resistance-shaped-our-democracy-it-still-can/ (accessed July 7, 2020).

5 https://www.sahistory.org.za/people/ahmed-mohamed-kathy-kathrada (accessed July 2, 2020).

6 Ibid.

7 https://www.history.com/topics/africa/apartheid (accessed July 2, 2020).

8 https://www.thejc.com/news/news-features/mandela-and-the-jews-1.46 7000 (accessed July 2, 2020).

9 https://books.google.com/books?id=J-SrdFtSuDUC&pg=PA26&lp g=PA26&dq=buthelezi+visit+dc+in+1993&source=bl&ots=gqzY he72JV&sig=ACfU3U1XEBkK53EdEIqyTHJ4q_Fupq2J8A&hl=en&sa=X &ved=2ahUKEwix1uCAtrHqAhWQoHIEHavDCW0Q6AEwAHoECAo QAQ#v=onepage&q=buthelezi%20visit%20dc%20in%201993&f=false (accessed July 3, 2020).

10 https://www.sahistory.org.za/article/south-african-general-elections-1994 (accessed July 3, 2020).

11 http://aodl.org/PaulineBakerCollection/about (accessed July 3, 2020).

12 https://www.theguardian.com/world/2018/apr/02/winnie-madikizela-mandela-obituary (accessed July 3, 2020).

CHAPTER 15

NIGERIA AND THE NOBEL LAUREATES

Elie Wiesel received the Nobel Prize for Peace in 1986. Wiesel inspired through both his actions and words:

> "I swore never to be silent whenever and wherever human beings endure suffering and humiliation. We must always take sides. Neutrality helps the oppressor, never the victim. Silence encourages the tormentor, never the tormented."[1]

He wrote his internationally acclaimed memoir, *"Night" ("La Nuit")*, describing the horrors of the concentration camps during the Holocaust. *"Night"* became Wiesel's lesson for humanity—silence is complicity. Having personally experienced suffering so vast and the world's problems so profound, Wiesel came to appreciate the value of collective action. During my term as Executive Director of the Elie Wiesel Foundation for Humanity (EWF) from 2004 to 2007, he launched the Nobel Laureates Initiative as a vehicle to foster cooperation among laureates. Their combined voices amplified Wiesel's lifelong struggle against indifference, intolerance, and injustice.

In 2004, we organized the first annual Nobel Laureates Summit in Petra hosted by Jordan's King Abdullah. Few Nobel Peace Laureates attended; they were uneasy about Wiesel's unflinching support for Israel. Of course, there were exceptions. Wiesel and the Dalai Lama had a close relationship; human rights abuses against Palestinians did not deter the Dalai Lama from attending. Nigeria's Wole Soyinka, recipient of the 1986 Nobel Prize for Literature, was another stalwart. They shared a belief that every person can make a difference, both individually and through collective action. At Petra I, Wiesel issued an impassioned call to action:

> "We must harness our rich human potential in service of peace, progress and prosperity. To these ends, peoples must realize that no one is superior to another. No nation is worthier than another. No religion is holier than another. Racism, ethnic discrimination and religious fa-

naticism lead to antagonism, not salvation. I fear that humankind is on a train hurtling towards an abyss. Unless we pull the alarm, it may be too late. It is time to show the world that we can restore humankind's dignity, its hope and future."[2]

Wiesel loved Israel, whose safety and sustenance was his top priority. In addition, he was genuinely concerned about other victims the world over. He was a staunch supporter of the Kurds, visited the refugee camps of Cambodia, defied apartheid in South Africa, and opposed ethnic cleansing in the former Yugoslavia. He also helped the Miskito Indians of Nicaragua during the Miskito-Sandinista conflict and supported the Desaparecidos of Argentina. Wiesel believed that saving one life had the potential to save thousands more.[3]

I first met Wiesel when I was in my mid-thirties at an event for the American-Jewish World Service. I wrote him a personal note of appreciation, to which he responded: "Thank you for giving voice to the voiceless." I framed the letter and hung it in my office. It was a great honor to know him and to work with other Nobel Laureates, including fellow faculty members at Columbia University, Erik Kandel and Richard Axel, recognized for their scientific achievements.

. . . . .

Wole Soyinka is a Nigerian playwright, poet and essayist, and the first African to be honored with the Nobel Prize for Literature. He is a compelling figure, tall and strapping with a head of abundant white hair. Wole and I became friendly during the Petra process; I learned from him about the sectarian fissures in Nigerian society between Muslims in the North and Christians in the South, between tribes such as the Yoruba and Hausa, and the clashes between the Itsekiri and the Ijaw in Delta, Bayesla, and Rivers states, oil-rich lands on Nigeria's Atlantic coast.

The Biafra region of Nigeria declared independence in 1967 after a massacre of Igbo the previous year. Up to three million people perished, most of them from starvation, during the ensuing civil war.[4]

I gained an awareness of suffering in my youth and was moved to action. When I was growing up, the Phillips family had a morning ritual. I would sit at the breakfast table with my father, who read out loud an article in the world news section of *The New York Times*. As an eight-year-old, I was ignorant of the complex ethnic issues that gave rise to conflict in Nigeria and could not even find Nigeria on a map. Yet I was horrified by reports of mass starvation.

I taped an appeal in the elevator of my home at 885 Park Avenue, asking neighbors to send food donations to our apartment. Many boxes of food were delivered to our doorstep. We provided canned goods and other non-perishable items to an aid agency, which sent the supplies to Biafra. It was my first humanitarian project. I had no way to foresee that conflict prevention in Nigeria would become a passion later in life.

At the Petra Conference of Nobel Laureates in May 2005, Wole gave a speech to his fellow Laureates on conditions in Nigeria and its environmental, economic, and political crises and conflicts. Wiesel asked Wole to prepare a report, summarizing the situation and suggesting possible actions for the Nobel Laureates. To fully assess the situation on the ground, EWF sponsored a fact-finding trip for Wole and I to visit the oil-rich Niger Delta region.

We met at the airport in Lagos and flew together to Bayesla State. Strangers greeted him as "Prof" (for Professor), addressing him in reverential tones. He was respected by all. On the plane, Wole gave me a tutorial on the resource-related conflict in Bayelsa.

The Niger Delta region includes nine states, including Delta, Rivers, and Bayelsa, which adjoin Gulf of Guinea on the Atlantic Ocean. It includes forty ethnic groups, constituting over twenty million people who speak distinct languages and dialects. At least seven million Ijaw, Ogoni, Itsekiri, Andoni, Ibibio, and a host of other peoples speaking different languages live in Bayelsa, Rivers, and Delta states alone.

The world reacted with horror when Ken Saro-Wiwa was executed, along with eight other members of the Ogoni people, by the Nigerian State on November 10, 1995. Ken was the leader of a campaign against oil pollution by Royal Dutch Shell in the Niger Delta and was convicted for his activism on environmental justice.[5]

The Niger Delta region was known for its extensive lowland tropical and fresh water forests, aquatic ecosystems, and biodiversity. Residents cultivated rice, sugarcane, plantain, palm oil, yams, cassava, and timber.

However, the discovery of oil by Royal Dutch Shell in 1956 transformed the Delta Region. Nigeria's forty billion barrels of proven "sweet crude" reserves are prized by refineries in the United States, which purchase about 40 percent of the country's production, 10 percent of total US oil imports. Nigeria is also home to the world's ninth largest supply of natural gas and the largest in Africa.

The discovery of oil was a windfall for Nigeria. It earned over $400 billion from Niger Delta oil between 1970 and 2010. Earnings represented two-fifths of government revenues and roughly 95 percent of export earnings. Yet energy exploitation did not result in socioeconomic development for the people of Nigeria. Most Nigerians live in poverty on less than $2/day and with some of the worst social indicators in the world. Hospitals and schools were built by oil companies, but lack staff and equipment. Bayelsa state has only one multi-lane, paved road.

Nigeria suffers from the "oil curse." Many countries with oil as their primary source of income, including Nigeria, develop corrupt and ineffective governance. The Niger Delta was impoverished by a series of measures that benefited the government at the people's expense. The 1969 Oil Revenue Act transferred all energy earnings to the federal government. The 1978 Land Use Act made the federal government the owner of all land in the country. Furthermore, the 1999 Constitution, which vests predominant powers in the executive branch, placed the president in charge of all major Nigerian political and economic issues.

In the process, the Niger Delta region was turned into an environmental wasteland. Oil spills killed fish populations and polluted drinking water. The Nigerian National Oil Spill Detection and Response Agency estimates that around 2,400 oils spills occurred between 2006 and 2010 alone,[6] leaking 260,000 barrels/year. Oil slicks cover the region. Blowouts and leaks affect creeks, streams, and related traditional sources of livelihood, destroying mangrove forests, eroding soil plots, and killing aqua life. Hundreds of well sites have flares that come from the burning of associated gas. The flares release five million tons of carbon dioxide and twelve million tons of methane annually. The resulting sulfuric acid mists damage plants and forests. Flares pollute rainwater, cause acid rain, and exacerbate climate change. Many local residents suffer from oil poisoning.

Shell, ExxonMobil, Chevron, Total, Eni/Agip, Elf, and Texaco are some of the major partners with the Nigerian National Petroleum Company, which retains up to 60 percent of earnings from joint ventures and heavily taxes profits of the oil companies. The Nigerian constitution requires that 13 percent of oil revenues go to the oil-producing states in addition to their portion of federal revenues that are shared with all thirty-six states. In fact, only a fraction of revenues benefits oil-producing communities. Revenue that is returned to the state is controlled by corrupt governors who use it for patronage and personal enrichment.

Nigeria has a democracy deficit, exacerbated by a series of corrupt and authoritarian leaders. Rigged elections in 1999, 2003, and 2007 rendered the people of the Niger Delta voiceless at all levels of the Nigerian government. The region is heavily militarized; powerful politicians and their clients sponsor armed groups to protect their theft of oil wealth. Militias have positioned themselves as alternatives for political influence and economic sustenance. Hostage taking and the kidnappings of Nigerian and foreign oil workers are widespread. The Nigerian military gets paid to guard energy producing facilities from rebel groups such as the Movement for Emancipation of the Niger Delta (MEND).

. . . . .

I did not know what to expect upon arrival in Bayelsa. Wole told me that we would be guests of Governor Goodluck Jonathan. He also contacted MEND and proposed a meeting at one their remote encampments in the Delta.

We were met at the airport by a convoy of SUVs and whisked away to the residence of Governor Goodluck Jonathan. A prominent Christian figure, Jonathan would serve as Nigeria's President from 2010 to 2015. The governor met us in his reception hall that was packed with visitors, including many women brightly clad in traditional dress. People formed a long queue to speak with the governor. We waited for the crowd to thin before approaching him.

After a good meal and stimulating conversation, we retired to the governor's quarters for a much-needed rest after my trans-Atlantic flight. The following day, Wole made arrangements for our visit with MEND. We boarded the governor's vehicles, escorted by a heavily armed security

team. When we got to the end of the road, there was another set of vehicles waiting for us. The State's official security warmly greeted armed
MEND representatives. They embraced and smoked cigarettes, listening
to Nigerian popular music called Jùjú, derived from traditional Yoruba
percussion. In addition to smoking and music, they shared an evident respect for Wole. The official escort departed, leaving us in the hands of
MEND.

We were driven to a jetty and boarded a hydrofoil boat for our journey
upriver. The region is a maze of creeks, streams, and swamps formed by
the Niger River as it divides into six main tidal channels before spilling
out into the Atlantic Ocean. We stopped at an Ijaw community and interviewed the elders and other civil society representatives. MEND representatives appeared, and we sat outside in ubiquitous white plastic chairs
discussing the situation.

They presented a summary of the situation along with policy recommendations. MEND would be willing to disarm as part of a comprehensive package of amnesty, weapons buyouts, job programs, and sensible
law enforcement initiatives. In return, they wanted the government to
publish a detailed report on the oil industry and fully comply with the
Extractive Industries Transparency Initiative (EITI). The reform pact,
promulgated by President Olusegun Obasanjo in 2003, intended to improve Nigeria's macroeconomic environment, pursue structural reforms,
strengthen public expenditure management, and implement institutional
and governance reforms. EITI's overall goal was transparent and prudent
management of oil revenues to reduce poverty and ensure sustainable
development. MEND proposed coercive measures to guarantee that oil
companies join EITI, and fulfill their obligations. It also proposed international observers to ensure compliance.

In addition, MEND sought confidence-building measures (CBMs) to
reduce tensions. CBMs emphasize comprehensive and sustainable development in the region. To mitigate corruption, it proposed that the
government demonstrate its credibility by arresting the national political
kingpins who benefitted from oil bunkering. Rank-and-file members of
MEND and other militias sought educational opportunities, job training
programs, and employment-generating projects. Militia leaders wanted
to be included on the federal payroll through buyout packages and via

government appointments. MEND also endorsed electoral reform and monitoring to strengthen grassroots democracy.

We headed back towards Yenagoa, Bayelsa's capital, stopping to inspect an oil facility. Crude was seeping out of the ground, compounding the effects of a recent oil spill. The oil field reeked of methane, an especially potent greenhouse gas. The noxious methane by-product can be treated either by flaring, whereby the gas is burned off emitting large quantities of carbon dioxide into the atmosphere, or by venting, simply releasing it directly into air. It felt like an inferno; the area was scalding hot from methane flaring.

Wole arranged a town hall meeting so we could hear from directly affected populations at a nearby village. The meeting was interminable, as one person after another described in graphic detail their symptoms of oil poisoning and the impact of methane discharge. Elders and women shared their personal tragedies. Evangelical representatives also proposed a regular forum for dialogue about the concerns of the evangelical community.

Our meetings in Bayelsa were not a mere exercise in storytelling. MEND and civil society asked that we share our impressions with Governor Goodluck Jonathan, who could act at the state and local levels. They also wanted us to brief Wole's fellow Nobel Laureates. They hoped that we would mobilize the moral authority and political influence of the Nobel Laureates Initiative to promote greater peace and prosperity in the Niger Delta region.

· · · · ·

Back in New York, I submitted my trip report to EWF. Neither Wiesel nor his wife, Marion, was particularly interested in Nigeria; however, they wanted someone of Wole's stature to be involved in EWF activities to demonstrate its broad base of support. Wole's ideology and ethnicity made him a particularly valuable partner for EWF.

In September 2006, EWF chose to institutionalize its work in Nigeria by establishing a "Commission of Nobel Laureates on Peace, Equity, and Development in the Niger Delta Region of Nigeria." Using the Commission as a vehicle for engaging Nobel Laureates, EWF organized a joint appeal endorsed by sixty-five Laureates on December 2, 2006. The statement focused on the development and environmental crisis in the country while offering specific policy recommendations. Nobel Laureates:

- Proposed that oil companies in the Niger Delta states audit and publish their revenues;

- Called upon oil companies to establish a "Community Investment Fund," earmarking a percentage of revenues directly to local community organizations working in the fields of health, education, micro-credit, and infrastructure development;

- Asked oil companies to clean up oil spills, eliminate gas flares, and provide special compensation to communities devastated by environmental degradation; and

- Recommended that oil companies hire and train residents from affected populations in the Delta region.[7]

Environmental issues were a symptom of Nigeria's broader governance problems. Vote rigging and electoral fraud marred general elections for president and the national assembly, which were held on April 21, 2007. Umaru Yar'Adua of Obasanjo's ruling People's Democratic Party won handily; however, international observers questioned the election results. Observers from the European Union described the elections as "the worst they had ever seen anywhere in the world," noting "rampant vote rigging, violence, theft of ballot boxes and intimidation."[8]

In a statement I prepared for Wiesel, he warned, "Bogus elections raise serious questions about the new government's legitimacy. The best way to prevent violent conflict is through electoral reform and a new ballot." These concerns were echoed in a statement endorsed by forty-eight Nobel Laureates, criticizing electoral fraud in Nigeria:

> International and domestic monitors have determined that Nigeria's recent elections fell far short of acceptable standards, having failed the test of a free and fair ballot. We, the undersigned Nobel Laureates, are concerned that the new government's lack of legitimacy increases prospects for violent conflict with serious consequences for Nigeria and the region. Therefore, we recommend a conference of national unity involving government officials, civil society, religious and business leaders to dis-

cuss the current crisis and set a date within 18 months for early elections, along with electoral reform. Our recommendation is offered in all responsibility, to help consolidate Nigeria's transition to democracy after decades of military dictatorship. It is made without prejudice to potential legal recourse by aggrieved candidates. Nor does our recommendation obviate the need for a credible enquiry into the electoral process that has undermined confidence of Nigerians in constitutionalism and the rule of law.[9]

The statement garnered considerable attention in Nigeria's media and elite political circles. On June 3, 2007, I published a piece in *The New York Times* highlighting Nigeria's flawed election. "For sure, the end of brutal military rule represents progress. But Nigerians deserve better than rigged elections that preserve the power and patronage of an entrenched elite. Bogus elections do not a democracy make."[10]

. . . . .

I served as EWF's Executive Director for less than three years. Frankly, it was not a very good fit. I was used to acting in my own name, not as someone's representative. The Petra conferences were a cornerstone of our work.

At Petra III in 2006, we planned a follow-up to Wiesel's meeting with Israeli Prime Minister Ehud Olmert and the Palestinian Authority's Abu Mazen. To do so, I arranged a bus to bring Nobel Laureates from Petra to Ramallah in the West Bank. The logistics were complicated but not impossible. I could not, however, get Wiesel's commitment. He finally confided his concern: to transit through the West Bank to Ramallah, we would have to pass through several checkpoints of the Israeli Defense Forces. Wiesel worried that the Laureates might witness an incident that could diminish their support for Israel.

To plan the bus trip, I needed to coordinate with the Palestinian Authority. During a trip to Israel for EWF, I faced a fork in the road. I could go to Ramallah for meetings that were potentially important to the peace talks. Or I could visit the Beit Tzipora educational centers in Ashkelon and Kiryat Malachi, where more than one thousand Jewish boys and girls from Ethiopia were enrolled in after-school programs. "Named in memory of Elie Wiesel's younger sister who died in Auschwitz, these centers have become a major part of the Foundation's work and remain a passion of the Wiesels."[11] I chose Ramallah.

Going to Ramallah was the wrong choice for Wiesel and his wife. Marion in particular was furious with me for failing to visit her schools. That fallout was the catalyst for me to accept Columbia's offer to direct the Program on Peace-building and Human Rights. I left EWF with my love and respect for Wiesel undiminished.

Elie Wiesel passed away on July 2, 2016. The *Daily News* asked me to write an obituary:

> From his personal experience as a survivor of the Holocaust, Elie Wiesel derived a deep affinity for oppressed peoples. "Never again" applied not only to the Jewish people, but to everyone who suffered deprivation and violations of their human rights.
>
> Despite his celebrity, he was a humble man who balanced a common touch with profound empathy and steely resolve. When we visited members of the Nobel Committee for Peace in Oslo, Elie Wiesel was unabashed sharing his views. He envisioned the Nobel Prize for Peace as a tool for conflict prevention, not only awarded to recognize past actions but as an investment in what could be done.
>
> He understood that the world's most pressing problems were too big for one person to solve. Elie Wiesel launched the Nobel Laureates Initiative in 2001. Bringing Nobel Laureates together harnessed their skills and influence in common purpose.
>
> Elie Wiesel championed justice the world over. Elie Wiesel organized a petition signed by 52 Nobel Laureates, urging Turkey to recognize the Armenian genocide.
>
> He highlighted environmental abuses of the oil and gas industry in the Niger River Delta of Nigeria. When there

were reports of electoral fraud, Elie Wiesel raised his voice in support of free and fair elections.

He did more than talk about the victims of genocide in Darfur. He wanted to go there, bear witness, and report back to the international community.

In 2002, Elie Wiesel brought Israel's Prime Minister Ehud Olmert and the Chairman of the Palestinian Authority, Mahmoud Abbas, together in Petra. He hoped the meeting would revitalize the peace process.

Elie Wiesel had big ideas, but was a man of simple tastes. At the buffet at the Grand Hotel in Norway, he was content with bread and butter. He delighted in a bowl of cherries, telling me that he never thought he'd ever see cherries again while in the concentration camp.[12]

Wiesel was a force for good in the world. After his death, I was asked to give the Elie Wiesel Memorial Lecture at colleges in New York and Boston. Remembering him and speaking about him was a heart-wrenching experience. Wiesel had an uncanny ability to touch people. Speaking about him, I shed tears of remembrance and loss.

He spoke truth to power, whether addressing school children from Ethiopia or kings, queens, and heads of government. "Indifference is the epitome of evil," he said. "Neutrality helps the oppressor, never the victim."

He wrote the foreword to my book on the Armenian Genocide, titled "Unsilencing the Past." He taught me a writing technique that I still use. Instead of declarative statements, he suggested I frame assertions as a question.

Reflecting on his experiences as a survivor of Auschwitz and Buchenwald, he asked: "Where is God in this place? Why must evil triumph at all while the good and the righteous are abandoned to ruin and forfeiture?"[13]

Elie Wiesel was always questioning. He inspired many, myself included, with his probing queries. He also inspired many with his humanitarian heart.

Notes

1 Katie Reilly, "Read Elie Wiesel's Nobel Peace Prize Acceptance Speech," *Time*, July 2, 2016, https://time.com/4392267/elie-wiesel-dead-nobel-peace-prize-speech/.

2 "Petra Conferences," *The Elie Wiesel Foundation for Humanity*, https://eliewie selfoundation.org/conferences/petra-conferences/ (accessed April 27, 2020).

3 Michael Dunnings, "Visiting Scholar Lectures Mercy about the Importance of Elie Wiesel's Work," *The Impact News*, October 11, 2018, https://theimpact news.com/news/2018/10/11/elie-weisel-finding-humanity-after-silence/.

4 M. Norman and P. Ueda, "Biafran Famine," In *Handbook of Famine, Starvation, and Nutrient Deprivation*, eds. V. Preedy and V. Patel (Cham: Springer, 2017), https://link.springer.com/referenceworkentry/10.1007%2F978-3-31 9-40007-5_8-1.

5 "Nigeria: Advocates Remember Ken Saro-Wiwa, Convicted of Murder & Executed after He Protested Oil Pollution by Shell," *Business and Human Rights Resource Center*, November 10, 2015, https://www.business-humanrights. org/en/nigeria-advocates-remember-ken-saro-wiwa-convicted-of-murder-ex ecuted-after-he-protested-oil-pollution-by-shell.

6 "Nigeria," *Energy Information Administration Country Analysis Brief*, August 2011, http://www.eia.gov/EMEU/cabs/Nigeria/pdf.pdf.

7 Jide Ajani and Vanguard [Nigeria], "Way out of N-Delta Crises, by 65 Nobel Laureates," *Odili*, December 2, 2006, https://odili.net/news/source/2006/dec/2/398.html.

8 "Nigerian Election Pushed back a Week," *CNN Wire Staff*, April 4, 2011.

9 Sahara Reporters, "48 Nobel Laureates Criticizes Electoral Fraud in Nigeria—Calls for New Elections in 18 Months," May 21, 2007, http://saharareporters. com/2007/05/21/48-nobel-laureates-criticizes-electoral-fraud-nigeria-calls-new-elections-18-months.

10 https://www.nytimes.com/2007/06/03/opinion/l03nigeria.html (accessed April 29, 2020).

11 "Biet Tzipora Centers," *The Elie Wiesel Foundation for Humanity*, https://eliew ieselfoundation.org/biet-tzipora-centers/.

12 David L. Phillips, "Elie Wiesel's legacy remains a passionate peace, human rights advocate among defenseless victims," *NY Daily News*, July 3, 2016, https://www.nydailynews.com/new-york/eli-wiesel-remains-passionate-hu man-rights-advocate-article-1.2697350.

13 Uthman Shodipe, "Elie Wiesel and the unfathomable God," *The Guardian*, July 14, 2016, https://guardian.ng/opinion/elie-wiesel-and-the-unfathomable-god/.

CHAPTER 16

SAVE DARFUR

Janjaweed terrorized Darfur beginning in February 2003. The term "janjaweed" is derived from the Arabic *jinnī* (spirit) and *jawad* (horse). It means spirit horse and mounted men with guns. Cooperation between the Janjaweed and the Government of Sudan (GOS) dates back to the 1980s when Sudan's President Omar al-Bashir armed Arabic-speaking Abbala nomads as a deterrent against incursions from neighboring Chad. The militias raided villages along the Chad-Sudan border throughout the 1990s, escalating conflict between farmers and pastoralists over land and water rights.

Darfuri rebel groups protested against discrimination and marginalization in Darfur, a huge territory in Sudan's western region roughly equivalent to the size of mainland Spain. When the Justice Equality Movement (JEM) and the Sudan Liberation Army (SLA) raided the El-Fasher Air Base in April 2003, Bashir reactivated the Janjaweed as a counterinsurgency force.[1] Sudan's Antonov warplanes and helicopter gunships targeted villages, followed by Janjaweed fighters on horseback and camels. In spasms of ethnic cleansing, they slaughtered male villagers, raped women, and killed or kidnapped children. They also burned agricultural fields and thatched roof homes, poisoned water wells, and stole livestock of the Fur, Masalit, and Zaghawa peoples.[2]

Over a five-year period, from 2003 to 2008, hundreds of thousands of Darfuris were murdered and millions were displaced. US Secretary of State Colin Powell testified before the Senate Foreign Relations Committee on September 9, 2004, citing a "consistent and widespread" pattern of atrocities and insisting, "genocide has been committed." According to Powell, "This was a coordinated effort, not just random violence."[3]

The 1948 United Nations (UN) Convention on the Prevention and Punishment of the Crime of Genocide imposes obligations on its signatories. Powell was clear that "[t]he government of Sudan and the Janjaweed bear responsibility." Events in Darfur met the UN definition of genocide because the GOS targeted a "national, ethnic, racial or religious group" in order to bring about their destruction "in whole or in part."[4]

UN Security Council (UNSC) Resolution 1556, which passed on July 30, 2004, affirmed that "[t]he situation in Sudan constitutes a threat to international peace and security and to stability in the region."[5] The resolution called for restrictions on arms transfers to all "non-governmental entities, including the Janjaweed." It demanded that the GOS disarm the Janjaweed and restore security within thirty days. It set the stage for intervention under Chapter 7 of the UN Charter.

Powell urged the GOS to reflect on the UNSC resolution and stop its slaughter. "We are not after Sudan," he maintained. "We are not trying to punish the people or the Sudanese government. We are trying to save lives." UNSC Resolution 1564, adopted on September 18, 2004, threatened sanctions on Khartoum and authorized the establishment of an international Commission of Inquiry "to investigate reports of violations of international humanitarian law and human rights law in Darfur by all parties, to determine also whether or not acts of genocide have occurred, and to identify the perpetrators of such violations with a view to ensuring that those responsible are held accountable." The resolution also pressed the GOS to accept the African Union's (AU) monitoring force.[6]

The resolution was a shot across the bow. Diplomacy backed by a credible threat of force is most effective to address a fast-moving humanitarian emergency and security crisis.

· · · · ·

The Save Darfur Coalition consisted of 160 organizations that demanded more robust international action to prevent genocide in Darfur.[7] Jewish organizations, including the American Jewish World Service, founded by my father and financially supported by my family, were among the most outspoken. On April 30, 2006, the Save Darfur Coalition organized the "Save Darfur: Rally to Stop Genocide" on the National Mall in Washington, DC. It was one of twenty events held simultaneously around the country. The Darfur crisis was unfolding on the tenth anniversary of the Rwandan genocide, which energized genocide prevention activists.[8]

I was Executive Director of the Elie Wiesel Foundation for Humanity (EWF) at the time. Wiesel and I flew to DC and headed to the National Mall, which was flooded with 15,000 people demanding action by the administration of President George W. Bush. Backstage was crowded with luminaries: the actor George Clooney, Sen. Barack Obama (D-IL), House Democratic Leader Nancy Pelosi (D-CA), and the Reverend Al Sharpton.

We mingled backstage with other guests. Clooney, clad in a black T-shirt and khaki pants, was joined by his father, Nick, a journalist and TV anchor who was dedicated to the Darfur cause. They had just returned from Darfuri refugee camps in Chad. Clooney was the big draw, yet he was a man of conspicuous modesty, approachable and down to earth, especially at an event to stop genocide.

It was a warm day and I was concerned that Wiesel, an older man, would get sunstroke, so I arranged with the organizers for him to speak first. Wiesel stepped to the microphone with the crowd chanting, "Not on our watch!" He endorsed more intensive international humanitarian action, proclaiming, "Darfur deserves to live. We are its only hope." Drawing on his personal experience as a Holocaust survivor, he declared: "As a Jew, I'm here because when we needed people to help us, nobody came." The crowd was full of banners, some in Hebrew, identifying synagogues across the country. Wiesel is an unmatched orator.

> In Darfur, humankind's center of suffering today, men, women and children are uprooted, starved, tortured, mutilated, humiliated and massacred and the whole civilized world knows it. And little or nothing significant is being done to stop these massive violations of human rights. Who is guilty? Those who commit these crimes. But to the question, 'Who is responsible?' We are compelled to say: 'Aren't we all?' From the last century, the bloodiest in human history, we must take at least one lesson. Those who commit genocide cannot hide behind national borders and claims of sovereignty. There is no choice but to act in defense of defenseless people."[9]

He was also a man of action, not just words. Wiesel announced the creation of a Noble Laureates Commission on Darfur to advocate policies to prevent genocide. He implored, "For the sake of humanity, save Darfur."[10]

Other speakers were equally as impassioned in their appeals to the audience. Obama addressed the crowd: "If we care, the world will care. If we act, then the world will follow." Clooney emphasized that US and UN policies were failing, and citizens must demand change. He called on the Bush administration to back a multinational peacekeeping force.[11]

The Save Darfur Coalition was at the peak of its influence. As a result of its efforts, the US government agreed to pay hundreds of millions of dollars in peacekeeping costs and a billion dollars more in humanitarian aid. The Bush administration endorsed economic sanctions on Sudan. Bush declared, "Not on my watch," and supported an investigation by the International Criminal Court (ICC) despite his deep-seated philosophical opposition to the ICC. According to Bush, "There have to be consequences for murder and rape, which means you have to have a presence on the ground that can use force."

Darfur became a bipartisan cause. Congressional advocates for Darfur – Democrats like Donald Payne, head of the Congressional Black Caucus, and Republicans like Sam Brownback, a leading proponent for religious freedom – had been engaged in Sudan since the 1990s. They were drawn to the country because of its bloody civil war in the 1980s and 1990s and the persecution of Christians in Southern Sudan. A civil war between North and South Sudan started in 1983 and claimed two million lives before it ended in 2011.

However, not everyone was on board. In 2005, Columbia University's Institute for the Study of Human Rights (ISHR) hosted a Conference on Economic Development in Darfur where I jousted with Mahmood Mamdani, head of the African Studies Department at Columbia, who called the Save Darfur Coalition a Zionist conspiracy to defame Bashir. Mamdani served on ISHR's advisory board. However, he was an anti-Semite in addition to lacking seriousness as a policy analyst. Events on the ground bore witness to Bashir's crimes.

·   ·   ·   ·

Diplomacy was intermittent and ineffective. Susan Rice was at the Brookings Institution before joining the Obama administration. During an interview on November 17, 2006, Rice issued an ultimatum to the GOS: either accept UN peacekeepers or face military force. She advocated air strikes against Sudanese military assets and a blockade of Port Sudan from which most of Sudan's oil is exported. Her threats were aimed at pressuring the GOS to accept a consensual deployment of UN forces to protect civilians.

The UN General Assembly (UNGA) adopted the Responsibility to Protect in 2005, as a global political commitment to prevent genocide, war crimes, ethnic cleansing, and crimes against humanity. Russia opposed intervention in Sudan in the wake of the America's invasion of Iraq under false pretenses in 2003. China, another permanent member of the UNSC with veto power, also opposed military action in Sudan because of its extensive oil trade with Sudan and other economic interests.[12]

The US government supported the mediation efforts of Salim Salim, Secretary General of the AU. Witnessed by the US, UN, European Union, Norway, Canada, and the Arab League among others, the GOS signed the Darfur Peace Agreement (DPA) with a faction of the Sudan Liberation Army led by Minni Minawi on May 5, 2006. The DPA addressed issues of power sharing between Khartoum and the regions. It called for demilitarization of the Janjaweed and integration of Darfuri rebels into the police and Sudanese armed forces. It also included measures to expand humanitarian assistance to Darfuri civilians in order to stabilize the region and incentivize the peace process. To advance the demilitarization, disarmament, and reintegration of former combatants, the DPA called for education and training programs to benefit three thousand people. A new body was established, the Transitional Darfur Regional Authority, to ensure implementation and supervise a referendum on establishing Darfur as a unitary region with a single government.[13]

The agreement looked good on paper with benchmarks and a timetable for implementing key components. However, it lacked monitoring capacity and enforcement by the international community. Moreover, it also lacked consensus among Darfuri groups. JEM and the SLA leadership headed by Abdul Wahid refused to sign the agreement, casting doubt on its viability. Civil society did not participate meaningfully in the negotiations. Without the participation of conflict-affected communities and internally displaced persons (IDPs), the DPA had little chance of success.

. . . . .

Darfur was desperate for action by the international community. I worked with David Pressman, a Clooney adviser, to arrange for Wiesel and Clooney to address the UNSC under the Arria Formula, an informal arrangement that allows private persons to brief the Council on international peace and security issues when invited by a UNSC member. I had met US Ambassador to the UN John Bolton when he was the Assistant Secretary of State for International Organizations. Bolton is hard as nails. For sure, I differed with Bolton on many issues, but we were of one mind on Darfur. Without hesitation, Bolton agreed to the Arria Formula on September 4, 2006.

Wiesel, a UN Messenger of Peace, and Clooney met at the Lotos Club before the event. I accompanied Wiesel while Clooney was accompanied by his father, Nick, and a team of advisers, which included Pressman and Samantha Power, who received the 2003 Pulitzer Prize for her book, "A Problem from Hell." Samantha would go on to become Obama's UN ambassador. John Prendergast, who had served as Africa Director at the National Security Council under President Clinton, also joined the meeting. He founded the Enough Project to prevent genocide and co-founded "The Sentry" with Clooney, whose board of directors includes Clooney, Don Cheadle, Matt Damon, and Brad Pitt. Prendergast has the demeanor of a movie star, a celebrity in his own right.

Wiesel was typically disheveled with a mop of grey hair casually pushed to the side. In contrast, Clooney was perfectly coiffed and immaculately attired in a blue suit, white shirt, and navy pattern tie. We entered the UN building to adulation from the staff, about 80 percent of whom were young women. Wiesel turned to me and said, "I can't believe all these people have come to hear my speech."[14] It never occurred to him that the ladies were there for Clooney.

We met NBC's anchorwoman, Ann Curry, in a conference room before the Arria Formula. All fifteen Member States on the UNSC were represented; Bolton chaired the meeting. The Arria Formula was well timed. Just weeks before, the Security Council dedicated a 22,000-man peacekeeping force to Darfur without the consent of the Sudanese government. The UN force was supposed to take over from seven thousand African Union troops that were scheduled to withdraw on September 30.

Clooney predicted mass slaughter if UN peacekeepers failed to deploy. "All aid workers would leave and the 2.5 million refugees who depend on them would die. So after September 30th, you won't need the UN.

You'll simply need men with shovels and bleached white linen and head-stones. In many ways it's unfair, but it is nevertheless true that this genocide will be on your watch. How you deal with it will be your legacy, your Rwanda, your Cambodia, your Auschwitz."[15] Clooney warned that Darfur represents "the first genocide of the 21st century and, if it continues unchecked, it will not be the last. My job is to come here today and to beg you on behalf of the millions of people who will die—and, make no mistake, they will die—for you to take real and effective measures to put an end to this."[16]

Wiesel called Darfur: "the world capital of human suffering, humiliation and despair .... You know that the tragedy there seems endless as well as senseless. It has all the components of the worst and ugliest crimes of the last century: tribal hatred, vicious brutality, and scandalous behavior of raping women [and] killing children." He added, "The victim is always doubly cursed, and doubly punished. First, by being a victim, and then, by being alone. Miserably alone and forgotten by the so-called decent people and their reputable spokesmen and leaders."[17]

Both men were powerful advocates. However, Wiesel was overshadowed by Clooney's celebrity. The Chinese delegation was represented by a junior second secretary. When we adjourned, he approached Clooney and asked for his autograph.

· · · · ·

The Arab League launched a new peace process on Darfur with the State of Qatar as mediator in September 2008. Qatar was a well-qualified for its role. Wealth from its natural gas fields gave it the means to host meetings in Doha, where delegations encamped at the Sheraton Hotel for weeks on end. Qatar held forth the promise of a peace dividend should the parties reach an agreement. Qatar was also an acceptable mediator to the United States, which based 10,000 US troops at the Al Udeid Air Base southwest of Doha.

In July 2008, the ICC declared that Bashir bore criminal responsibility for the crisis in Darfur and accused him of genocide, war crimes, and crimes against humanity. On March 4, 2009, the ICC issued an arrest warrant for Bashir, a sitting head of state, on charges of war crimes and crimes against humanity. A subsequent warrant was issued for Bashir on the charge of genocide.

The GOS was obsessed with clearing Bashir's name and removing sanctions. The US listed Sudan as a state sponsor of terrorism (SST) in 1993. It imposed sanctions in 1997, after attacks against US embassies in Kenya and Tanzania, which were tightened in 2000 when Sudan was accused of colluding with Al Qaeda's attack on the USS Cole while the ship refueled in Aden, Yemen. The attack killed seventeen US sailors and injured scores. The US imposed further sanctions in 2007 in response to events in Darfur.

I met Hamid Ali, a Darfuri in 2008, at a seminar in Washington on transitional issues led by Paul Williams of the Public International Law & Policy Group, a nonprofit organization that advised armed combatants on legal issues that impacted peace negotiations. Hamid also attended Columbia's Conference on Economic Development in Darfur in his capacity as Associate Professor of Public Policy at the American University of Cairo (AUC). We discussed the important role of civil society in supporting negotiations. I secured financing from the State Department via General Scott Gration, Special Envoy for Sudan, whom I knew through the board of the International Rescue Committee. Working with Hamid Ali, Columbia University invited several dozen Darfuri personalities to meet at AUC in Cairo, followed by a series of meetings in Cairo, Khartoum, and Istanbul between 2010 and 2012.

Hamid arranged our use of AUC's Orient Hall adjacent to Tahrir Square. AUC's President Lisa Anderson, formerly the Dean of Columbia's School of International and Public Affairs, was gracious and flexible about arrangements. Orient Hall is an ornate facility with traditional Arab décor and an outdoor shade garden where tea was served. My Columbia team included Professors Elazar Barkan and Dirk Salomons, as well as Danielle Goldberg, my program coordinator and most trusted colleague.

The meeting started with some political posturing. The Darfuris did a lot of venting about Bashir and failings of the international community. On the afternoon of our first day, we transitioned to an in-depth discussion about the role of civil society. The Darfuris suggested we focus on social and economic issues to build support from the broader Darfuri community. I presented the Darfur Development Dossier, a summary of relief and development projects compiled form secondary sources. The Dossier served as a starting point for team building among Darfuris.

We agreed to meet again and institutionalize our cooperation through creation of the Darfur Development Advisory Group (DDAG). Hamid played a supervisory role from his perch in Cairo. Dr. Mohammed Ali Dousa, a pediatrician and neonatologist from El-Fasher in North Darfur, took the lead to organize in-country activities. Former officials, tribal leaders, academics, and women's organizations joined DDAG and participated on its executive committee.

Dirk Salomons, Director of the Humanitarian Affairs Program at Columbia's School of International and Public Affairs, prepared a curriculum for Darfuri community based organizations (CBOs). Salomons worked at the intersection between theory and practice, focusing on the interaction between policy and management in humanitarian operations. He presented the curriculum at Orient Hall on July 17, 2010. "The Curriculum Conference: Enhancing Project and Organizational Development for Darfuri NGOs" lasted a week. Salomons expertly facilitated in-depth discussions about the project cycle, stakeholder analysis, grant writing, human resources management, staff security, and project monitoring and evaluation.

DDAG required a proper registration to operate in Sudan. Our Darfuri partners discussed the registration process with the Humanitarian Affairs Commission (HAC), a branch of state security. When the GOS stonewalled DDAG's application, I went to Khartoum to meet with HAC representatives. Dousa's relative had become head of HAC; he assured Dousa that the application was in order and would be approved. Without registration, DDAG could not open a bank account or function outside of the shadows.

By this point, Columbia had received funding from the US Agency for International Development (USAID) and the Canadian International Development Agency. In 2011, I went to Khartoum for a meeting with DDAG's board, which was hosted at the Canadian Embassy by Ambassador Laurent Charette. I was also invited by Canada's Sudan Coordinator, Ambassador Scott Proudfoot, to brief Canadian officials in Ottawa about Columbia's work in Darfur. Keeping donors informed is critical to funding, especially multi-year funding in complex working environments such as Sudan. Donors also viewed DDAG as a source of information, given their limited access to remote regions in Darfur.

To complement the CBO curriculum, Columbia University invited Darfuris to Istanbul for training on communications and the development of a website. We were hosted by Sweden's Ambassador Torkel Stiernlof at the Swedish Palace on Istiklal Caddesi, a commercial area in the heart of Istanbul. DDAG's website was envisioned as an outreach tool profiling DDAG, its board, member organizations, and specific projects. Developed by Alexander Barlow, a communications strategy sought to maintain public awareness with specific focus on early recovery and development activities. Equipped with an Arabic-language version of the curriculum and a web-based communications plan, DDAG organized dozens of workshops across Darfur's states. Several hundred CBOs received training and showed keen interest in expanding cooperation with DDAG.

Columbia was fortunate to have US and Canadian funding to initiate DDAG and expand its reach. We launched DDAG when interest in Darfur was high. Ambassador Proudfoot and US Special Envoy Ambassador Princeton Lyman were instrumental in arranging seed money. However, funds were limited. In February 2011, Ambassador Charette hosted a presentation by DDAG to the envoys of donor countries in Khartoum. Ironically, the prominent role of the US and Canada was a disincentive to other countries coming on board.

DDAG urgently needed to diversify its revenues, so I reached out to the State of Qatar and arranged to meet its deputy foreign minister on the margins of the UNGA in September 2011. I told him about the extensive CBO network and proposed a multimillion-dollar umbrella grant for redistribution by DDAG to support local projects. I updated DDAG on my contact with Qatari officials: "I've had a series of meetings/discussions with Qatari officials. They want to develop a reconstruction plan, and I've proposed that DDAG draw on its network to identify early recovery projects and participate in reconstruction planning. Qatar is evaluating the proposal. We could learn tomorrow (or any time)." The Qataris showed interest but never finalized a decision on financing. I found the Qatari authorities were "all talk and no walk." DDAG sought funds from the Sheikh Thani Bin Abdullah Foundation, but without success.

Darfur had been the focus of international concern since 2004. However, the international community shifted focus to South Sudan when a referendum on independence was held in January 2011. The results were published on February 7, 2011, with a landslide majority of 98.83 percent voting in favor of severing ties with Sudan. The referendum ended years of violent conflict, but festering issues remained. Negotiations on the status of the disputed Abyei region had broken down in October 2010. Violent conflict also flared in the Nuba Mountains, Blue Nile, and South Kordofan. Much of this was due to the significant oil resources on the border of Sudan and South Sudan—most of which went to the South. The US, Canada, and other governments focused on stabilizing South Sudan. Funds for Darfur disappeared, leaving DDAG without support. Dousa used his savings to sustain DDAG. It became a shell operation without the means to work with Darfur communities.

President Bashir was quick to declare an end to the conflict when the GOS and JEM signed a ceasefire framework agreement in February 2010. Ensuing negotiations led to the 2011 Doha Document for Peace in Darfur (DDPA), which Bashir heralded as a major breakthrough between the parties. However, the DDPA was flawed in several important ways. The SLA, led by Abdel Wahid based in Paris, and Minni Minawi's SLA faction refused to sign. In addition, sustainable peace was elusive without the support of civil society.

· · · · ·

Hamid Ali asked me for a favor. He proposed that Columbia appoint Ahmed Adem as a Visiting Scholar. As JEM's spokesman, Ahmed was controversial because of his ties to the militia group. I submitted the proposal for Columbia's review, and the appointment was approved.

Before Ahmed could come to Columbia, however, he needed to meet the requirements of the University's International Student Services Organization. He had to document enough money in a US bank to cover his costs for the year. He also needed a visa to the United States. When the US government delayed a decision on his visa application, I approached Ambassador Lyman to ask for his help. The visa was finally approved after almost a year. Ahmed had to provide a home address. As the spokesman, he was constantly on the move. When I asked him about his residence,

Ahmed told me that he lived under a tree in Jebal Mara, a remote mountainous region in West Darfur.

Ahmed and I co-chaired the "Two Sudans Project." We regularly published op-eds in *The Sudan Times* and also hosted discussions with US special envoys and other prominent figures. Zach Iscol, a former US Marine who fought in Falluja, Iraq, hosted a reception for Ahmed at his mother's elegant apartment on New York's Fifth Avenue; we held a forum on campus with Francis Deng, formerly the Special Adviser of the UN Secretary General for the Prevention of Genocide and Mass Atrocities, who served as South Sudan's first ambassador to the UN, beginning in 2012. I met Hassan Eltigani and his thirteen-year old son Sami at the meeting with Francis.

Hassan Eltigani had come to the US as a student in February 1982 to study at the International Career Institute. He established a transportation company, Highland International, based in Brooklyn where there is a concentration of Sudanese-Americans. Most of Highland's drivers were Sudanese who fled the country during the civil war in the 1980s. Hassan is an honorable self-made man who was chair of the Sudanese-American community. Despite his business success in the US, Hassan never forgot where he came from—Al-Jazeera Aba, a Darfuri enclave about three hours north of Khartoum in White Nile State.

Unbeknownst to me, Ahmed approached Hassan to request financing for his fellowship. Hassan deposited $12,000 on Ahmed's behalf, clearing one of the criteria for his appointment. Hassan and I became friendly and we worked closely together over the coming years.

I wanted to visit Sudan, but my high-profile activism with Save Darfur was an obstacle. Sudan's Consulate had rejected my visa application, so I asked Hassan if he could intervene with Ambassador Omer Dahab, Sudan's Permanent Representative to the UN. Although Hassan was a Darfuri activist, he also maintained good relations with the GOS. He arranged for me to meet Dahab and a representative of Sudan's intelligence agency (*Mukhabarat*).

Dahab was keen to discuss US sanctions on Sudan and sought my advice about having them removed. I told Dahab that the US would respond to what Sudan does, not what it says, and gave him a roadmap of specific steps that would improve US-Sudan relations. The GOS had launched a charm offensive to recruit advocates for normalizing relations with the United States. I was targeted because of my contacts in Washington and visibility in media circles. Dahab said he would check with the "concerned authorities" about my travel.

The visa was approved, and I traveled to Sudan, accompanied by Hassan in late 2016. The GOS rolled out the red carpet for our visit. An official from the Ministry of Foreign Affairs met us at the airport in Khartoum and coordinated meetings over the coming days. The handler, probably an intelligence agent, spoke English and was helpful. He seemed pleased to make arrangements for an American.

In Khartoum, we met with senior officials including Ahmed Mohammed Haroun, who was wanted by the ICC for war crimes and crimes against humanity in Darfur. He was a hardliner who blamed the Darfuri rebels for starting the conflict and seeking to splinter Sudan. We met Dr. Hassan Omer Amin, who was senior negotiator in the peace process in Sudan. We discussed development issues with Eltigani Sisi, a member of the Fur tribe and a former UN official who was appointed by the GOS to head the Transitional Darfur Regional Authority. His home was a mansion with elegant gardens and water fountains, opulent for an international civil servant.

GOS officials wanted to discuss the criteria, steps and timing for lifting US sanctions. I explained that sanctions relief would depend on Sudan's cooperation on counter-terrorism, efforts to resolve internal conflicts, and humanitarian access to Darfur and other border areas. I was not travelling as a US official but wanted to underscore Washington's message. The US also demanded that Sudan stop its missile sales to North Korea and distance itself from Iran. If Sudan took sustained positive actions, I believed that the US would lift its trade embargo and other penalties that had cut Sudan off from the global financial system. I warned that UN sanctions on Sudanese officials implicated in atrocities in Darfur would remain and that Sudan would be kept on the US list of state sponsors of terrorism, which bans weapons sales and foreign aid.[18]

Dousa hosted me for dinner with DDAG members in the garden of the Lebanese-owned Assaha Hotel. Guests luxuriated under palm trees in the courtyard, smoking hookah. I was offered a puff, but the tobacco was too strong for me. Dousa and his male colleagues were attired in all-white costume and headdress called "Imma." Mona Tazor, a DDAG leader, wore colorful clothing, and her hands were covered with henna ink, a traditional decoration for Sudanese women. I wanted to hear from Dousa and our civil society friends their perspective on normalizing US-Sudan relations.

To my surprise, all DDAG members supported sanctions relief. They stipulated, however, that lifting sanctions should be tied to strict criteria and monitoring to ensure compliance. The threat of sanctions can be far more useful to change a regime's behavior than actually imposing sanctions. Lifting sanctions once benchmarks were addressed would be an inducement to reform. They proposed criteria for sanctions relief, which I promised to share with policymakers and opinion leaders in the US.

· · · · ·

A friend at the UN Department of Peace-keeping Operations arranged a briefing by the Deputy Director of the UN Country Team. Rather than meet at UN headquarters, which had tight security, he came to the Rotana Hotel in Khartoum. He was accompanied by heads of UN agencies such as the World Food Program (WFP), the UN Development Program, and UNESCO. They presented information on operations of the UN country team, and explained that the UN Assistance Mission in Darfur would be scaling back and handing over greater responsibility to GOS agencies.

There were no commercial flights between Khartoum and Darfur's regions, so the GOS arranged our travel to El-Fasher on a UN charter. We arrived at the airport the next morning, but our names were not on the manifest. Airport security told us to check at headquarters and come back another day. I would not take no for an answer and insisted that our handler with the Ministry of Foreign Affairs (MFA) sort it out. Our travel was approved after animated discussion and phone calls to the Ministry. We walked out on the tarmac to our propeller plane with WFP markings.

Vehicles were waiting for us at the airport in El-Fasher and transported us to the heavily fortified compound of Mohammed Haroun, Governor of North Darfur. Sudanese officials were focused on Washington's sanction review. I emphasized the importance of reining in the Janjaweed, which the governor insisted had been disbanded. Upon leaving his office, the streets were shut down and we could not cross. About fifty Toyota trucks came roaring down the road, each with a heavy automatic weapon bolted to the truck bed. I took photos with my cell phone until government agents stopped me. They assured us that the Rapid Reaction Forces were regular army, not Janjaweed. I doubted their claim. None wore regular issue army uniforms. They were smoking, honking their horns, and acting like irregular troops. Janjaweed, I surmised.

Hassan and I went to IDP camps, ZamZam and Abu Shokh. ZamZam's population had exploded. It was a center of human misery in Sudan. Our government handlers arranged interviews with handpicked IDPs. I told our driver to pull over, and Hassan and I walked through the camp. We came across a health center where dozens of brightly clad women were simply sitting in the dust holding their crying children. They explained that supplies of food, water, and shelter were promised, but they had been waiting for days. We stopped at a school funded by USAID. The classroom had no desks or blackboards. The children were sitting on the floor with their teacher; they stood up and started singing when we approached.

The Abu Shouk camp was also a miserable place. It contained 80,000 persons from the Fur, Tunjur, Berti, Zaghawa, Gimer, Fellata, and Hawara ethnic groups in Darfur. Families were listless from the heat and poor nutrition.

Upon return to Khartoum, I met US Special Envoy Donald Booth and members of the embassy team for breakfast. I shared impressions and we discussed sanctions. Booth was cautious about moving too fast to lift sanctions. In Myanmar, precipitous steps to lift sanctions led to backsliding.

Hassan arranged for a group of his Darfuri friends to present on their Gum Arabica product. Sudan's acacia trees are an abundant source of Gum Arabica, used by western companies as a food stabilizer in sodas and yogurt and as a cosmetic supplement. It could be a windfall for Darfuri women's cooperatives, but sanctions on Sudan increase the cost and uncertainty of doing business.

Hassan hosted a reception in my honor that evening attended by dignified and well-dressed guests: UN and GOS officials, Dousa, and some of our DDAG friends. I woke up before dawn for my long onward journey.

. . . . .

Sudan's UN Ambassador Omar Dahab invited me to Sudan's Mission to discuss the trip. At a Sudanese community event in Brooklyn, I went on record calling for the lifting of sanctions. Per DDAG's suggestion, I stipulated that sanctions relief should be based on specific criteria with strict compliance monitoring. Most members of the community were pleased to learn about our trip, but some were upset that we were photographed with the governor. His public relations people released the images as an endorsement of GOS policies in West Darfur.

Dahab asked me to come again for a discussion about removing Sudan from the US list of State Sponsors of Terrorism. We chatted in his office before he invited me into the conference room. It was a set-up. Dozens of Sudanese officials affiliated with the Mission and from Khartoum were waiting. I gave a presentation on criteria for being removed from the SST, emphasizing that progress would require specific actions, not simply spin.

President Bashir was deeply entrenched in power. However, a tipping point is hard to predict and can come suddenly. In December 2018, Bashir's government reduced subsidies for fuel and bread. Protests in eastern Sudan spread to Khartoum. In less than a week, the Transitional Military Council, led by Lt. Gen. Abdel Fattah Abdelrahman Burhan, arrested Bashir. Burhan assumed power on April 11, 2019.[19]

Columbia hosted Dr. Mohamed Nagy al-Asam, head of the Sudanese Professionals Association, on October 10, 2019. Arrangements were made by Mufadal Mufadal, a Columbia colleague. Nagy explained how a network of doctors, lawyers, and young professionals had pushed Bashir from power; youth and women also played a pivotal role. The role of women was dramatized by a Sudanese woman standing on top of a car in Khartoum while she addressed protesters. She was clad in an all-white traditional Sudanese dress and classic Nubia-style gold hoop earrings. People came together as the "Forces of Freedom and Change" to demand a complete overhaul of the system.

Although Bashir was in jail, military and intelligence agents refused to relinquish their power. Peaceful protesters demanding more dramatic change were attacked by the armed forces on June 3, 2019, killing an estimated 280 people. Many bodies were thrown into the Nile. General Mohamed Hamdan Dagalo, referred to as Hemetti, is a Janjaweed from the Rizeigat tribe. As head of the Rapid Reaction Forces, he deployed his troops to protect the protesters.[20] Ambassador Booth played an important role mediating talks on power sharing, which resulted in the formation of a Sovereign Council with eleven members, five civilian, five military, and one member agreed by consensus. The pro-democracy movement nominated the prime minister, and the military chose the ministers of defense and interior. The transition period would last thirty-nine months, followed by elections.

I visited Sudan from February 2–5, 2020, accompanied by Hassan Eltigani and Mufadal. My itinerary was arranged by Sadig Hassan of the Darfur Bar Association. We met GOS officials, including members of the Transitional Council, General Hemetti, and Ahmed Mufadal, the new head of the Mukhabarat. Columbia explored collaboration with Mohammed Babiker, Chairman of the Law Department at the University of Khartoum, on transitional justice.

The visit started with my presentation to a dozen foreign envoys, which was hosted by Sweden's Embassy in Khartoum. The Transitional Military Council and Freedom and Justice Forces adopted a "transitional document" on August 20, 2019. The document called for the creation of a Transitional Justice Commission (TJC) and interim governing structures to guide Sudan from dictatorship to more democratic and accountable government. The slow pace of finalizing a bill to establish the TJC caused concern that Bashir loyalists were biding their time, waiting for an opportunity to regain their power and privileges. Many Sudanese were impatient with the lack of progress establishing a transitional justice mechanism many months after overthrowing Bashir.

The Office of the Prime Minister requested a memo on transitional justice strategies and institutions. My paper identified principles of transitional justice and precedents in other countries. It explained that transitional justice is a term used to describe how a society comes to terms with a legacy of human rights abuses and violations of international humanitarian law. It is critical to sustainable peace, the rule of law, and state building in countries emerging from violent conflict and authoritarian rule. Transitional justice is also a tool for conflict resolution and peace building. It establishes a foundation to address the underlying causes of conflict by enshrining the rule of law and institutionalizing political, civil, cultural, and economic rights. Transitional justice emphasizes accountability, reconciliation, or a combination of the two. The memo described complementary pillars of transitional justice:

- Accountability (investigating and prosecuting those responsible for mass crimes);

- Truth-seeking (uncovering and making public the truth about the violations, including the root causes);

- Repairing the lives of victims (providing redress and reparations); and

- Undertaking reforms (to consolidate democratic developments and prevent recurrence or backsliding).[21]

Sudan was at a fork in the road. Many pro-democracy advocates in Sudan and the international community demand trials for Bashir and his inner circle. They insisted on accountability for crimes they committed in Darfur, Blue Nile, South Kordofan, and the East. If Sudan lacks the will and capacity to try Bashir in a domestic court, he could be sent to the ICC in The Hague. Alternatively, a hybrid court made up of Sudanese and international jurists could also be established.

On February 12, 2020, less than a week after our return to the United States, Sudan's new leaders announced they would cooperate with the ICC. We went to Brooklyn and briefed the Sudanese-American community. Many thought we had gone to Sudan to negotiate Bashir's arrest. They were disappointed, however, to learn that Bashir might not be tried in The Hague. Columbia University was given funds by the National Endowment for Democracy to stay involved and work with Sudanese partners seeking redress and justice after many years of Bashir's dictatorship. Sudan had come a long way since my first involvement. However, transitional justice is a process—not an event. More work remains.

Notes

1   Jonathan Erasmus, "Sudan Orders Airstrikes on Darfur before Arrival of UN Peacekeepers," *Telegraph*, January 7, 2007, https://www.telegraph.co.uk/news /worldnews/1538821/Sudan-orders-air-strikes-on-Darfur-before-arrival-of-UN-peacekeepers.html.

2   Michael Ray, "Janjaweed, Sudanese Militia," *Britannica*, https://www.britanni ca.com/topic/Janjaweed (accessed April 29, 2020).

3 "Powell Calls Sudan Killings Genocide," *CNN*, September 9, 2004, https://www.cnn.com/2004/WORLD/africa/09/09/sudan.powell/.

4 Ibid.

5 The United Nations, https://www.un.org/press/en/2004/sc8160.doc.htm (accessed May 10, 2020).

6 Human Rights Watch, "Sudan-Events of 2004," in *World Report 2005*, https://www.hrw.org/world-report/2005/country-chapters/sudan (accessed April 29, 2020).

7 "Organizations: Save Darfur Coalition", *PBS*, https://www.pbs.org/wnet/worse-than-war/get-involved/organizations-save-darfur-coalition/77/ (accessed May 11, 2020).

8 Holli Chmela, "Thousands Rally in Support of American Aid to Darfur," *New York Times*, May 1, 2006, https://www.nytimes.com/2006/05/01/us/01rally.html

9 David L. Phillips, "Letter to the Editor," *New York Times*, April 6, 2006.

10 Brian Fitzgerald, "Elie Wiesel Urges U.S. Action on Darfur," *BU Today*, May 2, 2006. http://www.bu.edu/articles/2006/elie-wiesel-urges-u-s-action-on-darfur/.

11 Associated Press, "Celebrities, Activists Rally for Darfur in D.C. National Mall Protest Meant to Urge White House to Act on Crisis in Sudan," *NBC News*, April 30, 2006, http://www.nbcnews.com/id/12531663/ns/world_news-africa/t/celebrities-activists-rally-darfur-dc/#.XqnPQpl7lPY.

12 "Will the International Community Act in Darfur?" *NPR*, October 23, 2006, https://www.npr.org/transcripts/6368478.

13 Darfur Peace Agreement, The United States Department of State, May 8, 2006, https://2001-2009.state.gov/r/pa/prs/ps/2006/65972.htm.

14 Conversation with Elie Wiesel, September 4, 2006.

15 "George Clooney, Elie Wiesel Plead for UN Intervention in Darfur," *VOA*, October 31, 2009, https://www.voanews.com/archive/george-clooney-elie-wiesel-plead-un-intervention-darfur.

16 Nikki Finke, "George Clooney Spoke to UN Security Council About Darfur," *Deadline*, September 12, 2006, https://deadline.com/2006/09/george-clooney-will-speak-to-united-nations-security-council-about-darfur-571.

17 "Nobel Laureate Elie Wiesel and Actor George Clooney Urge UN Action on Darfur," *UN News*, September 14, 2006, https://news.un.org/en/story/

2006/09/192142-nobel-laureate-elie-wiesel-and-actor-george-clooney-urge-un-action-darfur.

18 Matt Spetalnick, "U.S. Lifts Sudan Sanctions, Wins Commitment against Arms Deals with North Korea," *Reuters,* October 6, 2017, https://www.reuters.com/article/us-sudan-usa-sanctions/u-s-lifts-sudan-sanctions-wins-commitment-against-arms-deals-with-north-korea-idUSKBN1CB26Q.

19 "Sudan Coup: Why Omar al-Bashir was Overthrown," *BBC,* April 15, 2019, https://www.bbc.com/news/world-africa-47852496 (accessed May 11, 2020).

20 "Sudan Crisis: What You Need to Know," *BBC,* August 16, 2019, https://www.bbc.com/news/world-africa-48511226.

21 AJAR Handbook.

EPILOGUE

*Foreign policy is not architecture. In architecture, you make
a plan down to the last nut, the last bolt, the last stress beam,
and then you build the thing. Foreign policy, in my view, is
more like jazz; it's an improvisation on a theme, and you
change as you go along.*

—*Richard C. Holbrooke*

Holbrooke arranged for the State Department to hire me as a Special
Government Employee. He said that being formally affiliated with
the US government would enhance my credibility. I was also useful to
Holbrooke's mediation in Cyprus. Absent real progress in the negotiations, civil society dialogue created the appearance of motion.

I had the foresight to negotiate a loophole in my employment contract
with the State Department that allowed me to speak and write about my
work with the US government. Even that was not enough. I chafed at the
short leash. Frankly, I am not cut out to be deeply embedded in the US
bureaucratic system. Both in temperament and training, I come from civil
society.

I resigned from the Near Eastern Affairs Bureau when the Bush White
House ignored our recommendations on stabilizing Iraq. I wanted to publish an op-ed in *The New York Times* titled "Talking to the Wrong Iraqi."
Ahmed Chalabi sold the Bush administration a bill of goods, promising
that the US would be welcomed with flowers. We know from the postwar
fiasco that the occupation of Iraq was a mess.

Even with flexibility in my contract, I'd be crossing a red line by directly
contradicting US government policy. A colleague in the Office of the Vice
President with whom I worked on The Future of Iraq Project told me she
was deeply disappointed that I exposed problems with the Bush administration's approach in Iraq. "I thought you were one of us." She believed I
too was a neo-con.

My dissatisfaction with US policy was non-partisan. I attended a briefing
on country situations with officials in the Bureau for South and Central

Asian Affairs and did mot agree with any of the conclusions at the meeting. When the term of my contract expired, I simply allowed the agreement to lapse. Although I liked the people I worked with, being a part of the Obama administration didn't add much to my portfolio of international projects.

When Donald J. Trump became President, a friend on his transition team invited me to submit my resume. Trump badly needed qualified professionals, and she thought I would fit the bill. However, I didn't even return her call. Under no circumstances would I ever join the Trump administration, whose values I do not condone. Besides, since Trump ignored everybody's advice, what could I possibly contribute?

Moreover, the Trump administration didn't countenance dissent. When Special Envoy Richard Grenell gave tacit support to dividing Kosovo and giving territories north of the Ibar River to Serbia, I objected to the deal, writing in the Albanian media:

> The United States and Kosovo have enjoyed a special relationship. Liberating and state-building was a bipartisan endeavor. The Clinton administration went to war to prevent ethnic cleansing of Kosovo Albanians by Serbia and Bush led Kosovo's coordinated declaration of independence. Today, US-Kosovo relations are at their lowest point in years. President Donald J. Trump has betrayed Kosovo's trust in the US, rolling back decades of progress. Trump and his team have forgotten that Kosovo is our ally—not Serbia. Kosovo Albanians were victims of genocide, not Serbs. There is no place for moral equivalency when it comes to Kosovo and Serbia. Washington's moral compass is broken."[1]

The dissent channel provides a forum for State Department employees to differ with administration policy. Nonetheless, the Trump Administration has zero tolerance for contrarian views. I felt like the skunk at the garden party. Better to be principled than to subordinate to an unforgiving system and officials with demonstrable hubris and lack of principle.

Tom Miller, a three-time ambassador and former Special Envoy for Cyprus, admonished me not to challenge the Trump administration's policy on Kosovo. He warned that there is a risk to gratuitously aggravating mean-spirited officials. Of course, Tom was right, but I ignored his advice. I didn't spend thirty-three years of my life working to liberate Kosovo and support its state-building to acquiesce during Kosovo's crucial moment of need.

In fact, throughout my career, I have demonstrated a pattern of behavior that some might call reckless. Telling Radovan Karadžić that he should be tried for war crimes by the International Criminal Court may have satisfied my need for retribution, but it was gratuitous and unnecessary. Exposing Erdoğan's war crimes against the Kurds didn't stop Turkey's aggression. I did succeed, however, in being declared *persona non grata* and banned from visiting the country: a dubious honor.

Channeling Elie Wiesel, I asked myself, "If not me, then who will raise their voice against injustice? Who will give voice to the voiceless if I'm cowed and intimidated? The greater good is a lost cause if good people lack the courage to act and be heard."

. . . . .

The world in 2020 faces extraordinary challenges. The COVID-19 pandemic affects the health and financial situation of every country and every person. Everyone feels vulnerable. Beyond social distancing and wearing masks, people don't know what to do. They are caught between the prerequisites of public health and opening up the country. Addressing the COVID crisis, as well as transnational problems, requires versatility. The US faces a perfect storm of problems: the coronavirus, the economy, outside threats to our national security and election process, and social unrest in response to police brutality. Like jazz, there's no script for addressing today's problems.

Other major global issues include climate change and the environment, globalization and supply chains, and the consolidation of power by authoritarian leaders. So many people are displaced by war, terrorism, poverty, and desertification, which have caused a huge increase in refugees and populations flows. Instead of taking a break during the COVID crisis, many antagonists sought to exploit the crisis as an opportunity to press their advantage. Bilateral and regional conflicts are still raging, and traditional diplomacy is ill-equipped to address them, especially with the current hollowing out of the State Department and the Trump administration's disrespect and disdain toward diplomats and the important role they can play. Innovation is needed now more than ever.

I have been fortunate to have had a career that enabled me to work in hotspots around the world and meet inspirational leaders. Nobody ever told me what to do. There was no road map. I simply took the initiative when I saw the need. This book recounts my efforts over more than three decades. More often than not, I failed to make things better, but I have learned some important lessons.

Patience is necessary. There are some issues I've worked on for many years, taken a break, and then re-engaged. Ripeness is a theory in conflict resolution in which adversaries make peace when they've exhausted the fight and can see a better future. However, waiting for ripeness is not an excuse for inaction. Active measures can ripen a conflict and pave the way for a solution. Nobel Prize-winning diplomat and negotiator, Martti Ahtisaari, told me there is no such thing as an intractable conflict. According to Ahtisaari, it is important to be creative and persevere even when the situation is dire and progress appears remote.

Partnerships are essential to advancing the greater good. When I was younger, I thought that problems could be solved if one simply cared deeply and worked diligently. I learned the hard way that peacebuilding cannot be achieved on my own. The term "stakeholders" is ubiquitous. Partners can include those directly affected by a conflict and concerned international parties. Democracy and human rights are a moveable feast. Their realization is bedeviled by false horizons. Democratization is a work in progress.

What is the situation in 2020 where I have worked over the past three decades? The 1995 Dayton Accords ended the war in Bosnia and Herzegovina, but it remains a divided country. The Republika Srpska is a constant threat to peace through its threats to secede as an independent country or to join Serbia.

The Sudanese are optimistic about their future with new leadership in power and Bashir in jail awaiting trial. Despite progress, the psychological, social, economic, and political consequences of decades of civil war will be challenging to heal in Darfur and other marginalized, conflict-affected areas.

Hopes were high for Myanmar when Suu Kyi won the Nobel Prize and took a greater role in government. However, the military still maintains power. The genocide and displacement of Rohingya and widespread discrimination against other minorities remain major human rights issues for tens of thousands in Myanmar and refugee camps in Bangladesh.

In Sri Lanka, after twenty-six years of devastating civil war, democracy's progress was upended by the return to power of the Rajapaksa clan. Fear has returned for Sri Lankans who face retribution for opposing the government.

Iraqi Kurds voted for independence, but their hopes were dashed. The US adamantly supported a "one Iraq" policy that was impractical and morally bankrupt. The Trump administration's decision to abandon the Syrian Kurds in the autumn of 2019 opened the door for Turkish aggression, which killed hundreds of Kurdish civilians, Armenians and other Christians, while displacing hundreds of thousands in northeast Syria.

For sure, the United States contributed to many conflicts during the Cold War as a result of its ideological confrontation with the Soviet Union. Notwithstanding its previous mistakes, I've always viewed the US as a force for good in the world. Until Donald J. Trump was elected president.

During the Trump administration, the US exacerbated many conflicts through its "America First" policy, disdain for allies, and hostility towards multilateralism. Institutions that emerged after World War II served as a network that advanced shared interests. Tragically, almost all of them have been ravaged by the Trump administration. The real carnage is Trump's doing.

Some countries chose peace over violent conflict. I take some small satisfaction in the belief that my track two activities may have helped to ripen conditions for progress. They may have also served to consolidate agreements and prevent back-sliding. I know, however, that progress is ephemeral. Spoilers are lurking in the shadows.

Oppressed peoples who yearn for freedom must not lose hope, despair, or give up. When facing difficulties, they should persevere. I often recall the Dalia Lama's message—"Go, go, go."

Note

1   By the author, "Trump Betrays Kosovo," *Illyria*, May 4, 2020.

ACRONYMS

ABRI – Indonesian Armed Forces

AKP – Justice and Development Party (Turkey)

AU – African Union

ANC – African National Congress

ARSA – Arakan Rohingya Salvation Army

AWAW – Association of War-Affected Women (Sri Lanka)

BIN – State Intelligence Agency (Indonesia)

BSF – Border Security Force (Syria)

BSPP – Burma Socialist Programme Party

CBMs – Confidence Building Measures

CBOs – Community Based Organizations

CFR – Council on Foreign Relations

CIA – Central Intelligence Agency

COHA – Cessation of Hostilities Agreement

CPA – Coalition Provisional Authority

CPC – Chinese Communist Party

CW – Chemical Weapons

DDAG – Darfur Development Advisory Group

DDR – Disarmament, Demilitarization, and Reintegration

DPA – Darfur Peace Agreement

EITI – Extractive Industries Transparency Initiative

EC – European Commission

ENAC – Ethnic Nationalities Affairs Council

EP – European Parliament

EU – European Union

EWF – Elie Wiesel Foundation

FSA – Freedom Support Act

FTO – Foreign Terrorist Organization

GAM – Free Aceh Movement

GEN – Gender Equality Network (Burma)

GOS – Government of Sudan

GSL – Government of Srti Lanka

HDC – Centre for Humanitarian Dialogue

HDP – Peoples Democratic Party (Turkey)

ELIAMEP – Hellenic Foundation for European and Foreign Policy

ICC – International Criminal Court

ICJ – International Court of Justice

IDPs – Internally Displaced Persons

GOI – Government of Indonesia

HAC – Humanitarian Affairs Commission (Sudan)

ICRC – International Committee of the Red Cross

FRY – Federal Republic of Yugoslavia

FYROM – Former Yugoslav Republic of Macedonia

IMF – International Monetary Fund

INTERFET – International Force for East Timor

ISAF – International Security Assistance Force

ISHR – Institute for the Study of Human Rights (Columbia University)

ISIS – Islamic State of Iraq and Syria

JEM – Justice and Equality Movement (Darfur)

JNA – Yugoslav National Army

KODAM – Regional Military Command Structure (Indonesia)

KOPASSUS – Special Forces (Indonesia)

KOSTRAD – Strategic Reserve Battalions (Indonesia)

KIA – Kachin Independence Army

KIO – Kachin Independence Organization

KLA – Kosovo Liberation Army

KRG – Kurdistan Regional Government

KRI – Kurdistan Region of Iraq

KVM – Kosovo Verification Mission

LDK – Democratic League of Kosovo

LLRC – Lessons Learnt and Reconciliation Commission (Sri Lanka)

LTTE – Liberation Tigers of Tamil Eelam

MCA – Macedonian Chambers of Commerce

MEND – Movement for the Emancipation of the Niger Delta

MFN – Most-Favored Nation (trading Status)

MOH – Ministry of Health

MOU – Memorandum of Understanding

MIT – National Intelligence Agency (Turkey)

NAM – Non-Aligned Movement

NATO – North Atlantic Treaty Organization

NCA – Nationwide Ceasefire Agreement

NEA – Near Eastern Affairs

NES – North and East Syria

NGO – Non-Governmental Organization

NLD – National League for Democracy

NORAD – Norwegian Agency for Development Coordination

NYPD – New York Police Department

OCHA – Office for the Coordination of Humanitarian Affairs

OFA – Ohrid Framework Agreement (North Macedonia)

PASOK – Panhellenic Socialist Movement

PKK – Kurdistan Worker's Party

PLA – People's Liberation Army

POLRI – National Police (Indonesia)

P-TOMS – Post-Tsunami Operational Management System

PUK – Patriotic Union of Kurdistan

PYD – Democratic People's Party

RI – Republic of Indonesia

SAA – Stabilization and Association Agreement

SDF – Syrian Democratic Forces

SDSM – Social Democratic Union of Macedonia

SEVE – Chambers of Commerce of Northern Greece

SFRC – Senate Foreign Relations Committee

SGE – Special Government Employee

SLMM – Sri Lanka Monitoring Mission

SOMO – State Organization for Marketing Oil

SST – State Sponsor of Terrorism

TAL – Transitional Administrative Law

TARC – Turkish Armenian Reconciliation Commission

TGTE – Transitional Government of Tamil Eelam

TNI – Indonesian Armed Forces

TRC – Truth and Reconciliation Commission

TRNC – Turkish Republic of Northern Cyprus

WFP – World Food Program

WRC – Women's Refugee Commission

UIN Raniry – Islamic State University of Aceh

UN – United Nations

UNAMET – United Nations Mission in East Timor

UNESCO – United Nations Educational, Scientific and Cultural Organization

UNFC – United Nationalities Federal Council

UNGA – United Nations General Assembly

UNHRC – United National High Commissioner for Refugees

UNPREDEP – United Nations Preventive Deployment Force

UNPROFOR – UN Protection Force

UNSC – United Nations Security Council

USIA – United States Information Agency

VMRO – International Macedonian Revolutionary Organization

VJ – Yugoslav Armed Forces

WMD – Weapons of Mass Destruction

YPG – Peoples Protection Units

YPJ – Women's Defense Units

ZELS – Association of Unites of Local Self-Government